I0666170

Copyright © 2025 by William J. Striker
All rights reserved.
\*\*\*\*
Revised 2026

First published in the United States by
The Lighthouse Academy Press
Printed by Kindle Direct Publishing, USA
Additional copies for sale at Amazon Books

ISBN: 979-8-9995192-0-7

This work was developed through a human–AI collaboration. Draft materials were produced with the assistance of generative tools, after which the author revised, restructured, and refined all text for clarity, coherence, and fidelity of voice. See *Author's Note*.

The quote from the back cover — "I do not believe in God and I am not an atheist." — is from *Notebooks 1942–1951* by Albert Camus, translated by Justin O'Brien, Vintage International, 2008.

The
Lighthouse
Academy
Press

# Beneath an Indifferent Sky

*Imagined dialogues on the life and thought of Albert Camus*

by

## William J. Striker

# Contents

# Contents

# Contents

*"La lutte elle-même vers les hauteurs suffit à remplir le cœur d'un homme."*
    —   Albert Camus, *Le myth de Sisyphe*

*"The struggle itself toward the heights is enough to fill a man's heart."*
    — Albert Camus. *The Myth of Sisyphus.* Translated by
    Justin O'Brien, Vintage International, 1991

# Preface

Albert Camus once wrote of the "benign indifference of the universe," a phrase that captures the vast, impersonal backdrop against which each human life is lived. *Beneath an Indifferent Sky* is an attempt to illuminate one such life — the life of Camus — in a way that is both imaginative and true to the spirit of the man.

This book unfolds through a series of fictional dialogues across Camus' lifetime. These scenes, grounded in history but shaped by literary invention, explore the philosophical, moral, and emotional evolution of a writer who refused to surrender to life's indifference. In these imagined conversations, Camus speaks with friends, rivals, mentors, and strangers at pivotal moments — not as an icon, but as a man in motion. The result is a speculative biography rendered in dialogue form: scenes composed not to reconstruct events, but to reflect the kind of clarity, conflict, and conscience that marked Camus' inner and outer life.

While inspired by real people and events, the conversations in these pages are inventions. The words are not Camus' — but they are built on his voice. What he says here is not always what he said, but it is what he might have said, consistent with his works, letters, and actions. This is not a chronicle; it is a portrait. And like any portrait, it contains a blend of fidelity and interpretation — a way of seeing through, not just at, the subject. The goal has been to reach a kind of inner truth, even if it required imagined form.

Dialogue was chosen as the structure not simply for style, but for substance. Camus' world was shaped by dialogue: with teachers, comrades, and critics — and with the contradictions of his time. Dialogue allows thought to breathe. It invites tension and counterpoint, hesitation and breakthrough. In casting Camus' life this way, the book joins a long tradition: from Plato's dialogues to the theatrical cadence of Shakespeare, ideas have often come alive through the rhythm of exchange. For Camus, who rejected rigid systems and ideological catechisms, dialogue was not merely a method — it was a mode of existence.

What emerges is a figure not easily categorized. Camus resisted the labels assigned to him in his lifetime — existentialist, absurdist, philosopher — and insisted instead on remaining a writer, an artist. His was a rebellion of clarity, not chaos. He challenged both nihilism and revolution, both quietism and fanaticism. He believed in the dignity of moderation and the courage of honesty. He paid for this position with criticism, misunderstanding, and isolation. But he did not yield.

The man revealed in these dialogues is often conflicted, sometimes uncertain, but always striving to remain faithful to his sense of decency and justice. The goal of this book is not to explain Camus but to let him walk again — to hear him speak and be spoken to, to feel the gravity of his questions and the temper of his refusals. Not every scene will align with documented reality. But the intention throughout has been to remain consistent with Camus' character and with the moral arc of his journey.

To write a book like this is to engage in an act of listening. Not just to sources, but to tone. The sources include Camus' essays, notebooks, interviews, letters, and fictional works — as well as the writings of those who knew him. The tone is more difficult to capture. It resides in restraint, in doubt expressed with conviction, in rebellion carried out without hatred. The hope is that readers will recognize this tone in the pages that follow — not only as Camus', but perhaps also as their own.

If there is one message to carry forward, it is that Camus was not offering conclusions. He was offering presence. He did not provide answers to the absurd, but he lived a response to it. That response — lucid, loyal, and unbowed — still speaks. These dialogues invite the reader to enter into that response, to accompany Camus not as a student might follow a teacher, but as one human being walks beside another — down a quiet road, under a vast sky, toward the next village of meaning.

May these scenes serve not as a monument, but as a meeting — and may what begins as fiction end as something remembered.

# Author's Note

This book began with a simple question: how does one approach a man like Albert Camus without reducing him to a system, a label, or a conclusion?

Camus resisted explanation. He resisted enclosure. He wrote not to resolve existence, but to remain honest within it. Any attempt to write about him must therefore proceed with care — not to define him, but to follow him.

*Beneath an Indifferent Sky* was written in that spirit. It does not attempt to reconstruct events as they occurred, nor to speak in Camus' voice as authority. It is an imaginative work grounded in his life, his writing, and the trajectory of his thought. The dialogues presented here are not records. They are acts of interpretation — efforts to remain faithful to tone, to character, and to the movement of a mind that never settled into doctrine.

This approach carries risk. To imagine is to step beyond what can be verified. But it also offers something that strict analysis cannot: the possibility of seeing a figure not as an object of study, but as a presence encountered. The aim has not been to explain Camus, but to let him appear — within the limits of language and form.

The work was developed using contemporary tools that assisted in the drafting and exploration of dialogue. These tools contributed language and variation, but not judgment. The direction of the work, its structure, tone, and final form, remained the responsibility of the author.

This distinction matters. Language can be generated. Meaning cannot. What is chosen, what is refused, and what is allowed to stand — these define authorship. Every line of this work has passed through that filter.

In the end, what matters is not the method, but the result. If the book succeeds, it will do so by remaining faithful to the spirit of Camus — his clarity, his restraint, and his refusal to say more than what can be honestly sustained.

If it fails, it fails on those same terms.

Nothing more is claimed.

# Beneath an Indifferent Sky

# Prologue:
# The Empty Bench

Good evening. I hope you don't mind — this bench was empty a moment ago, and something about an empty bench at twilight always encourages a man to speak. Have you noticed that curious effect? The hush of dusk can draw out confessions that midday would silence, especially between strangers.

For my part, I've spent many evenings here with only my thoughts. Sometimes the quiet becomes too loud, and the simple act of sharing a few words feels like a small rescue. There is a certain freedom in speaking to someone you've just met, don't you think? A stranger has no expectations, no entanglements — just presence. You can say anything, or nothing at all, and no judgment will follow you home.

I wasn't always drawn to park benches and gentle conversations under a dimming sky. There was a time when I moved through life with great urgency and confidence. I believed everything I did was important, that the world was watching and waiting for my next step. It's almost amusing to recall it now — the vanity of that certainty. Life has a subtle way of evening out such conceit: a quiet evening like this eventually comes for all of us, and with it, questions we never thought to ask.

For a long while I told myself comforting stories. We all do, to some extent — little narratives about why we are right, or how we're doing our best, or how the fault lies elsewhere. I was no different; I constructed a life I could justify to myself at every turn. But after enough lonely sunsets, you start to see the cracks in your own story.

I remember one evening, years ago, when I first noticed one of those cracks. Someone dear to me was in pain, and I... I did nothing. I sat still and silent, telling myself it was not my responsibility, that it was not my place to interfere. By the time

I found the courage to act, it was too late. She was gone — drifted out of my life like a boat unmoored, while I watched from the shore and pretended the tide would bring her back.

For a long time I refused to face what that loss truly meant. It was easier to blame circumstance or bad luck or any excuse at hand. But late at night, when even lies grow tired, the truth would show its face: I had been a coward. I betrayed not only her trust, but my own better nature. Realizing that was like finding a mirror I had kept covered — suddenly, there I was, without disguise, stark and humbled.

Forgive me, I think I'm making this rather grave. We all have our shadows, don't we? Perhaps you understand — I suspect you do. Everyone has a memory that pricks them like a thorn when the night grows quiet. It's nothing to be ashamed of. In fact, I'm convinced that these aches we carry can shape us, teaching us compassion if we let them.

So what does one do after seeing oneself so honestly? At first, I admit, I despaired. It's a strange thing — to suddenly doubt everything you were once sure of. The world seemed off-kilter then, emptied of the meaning I'd painted onto it. I felt as if I were stranded on that silent shore where I'd watched my old certainties sail away.

But after a time, something quietly rebelled in me. I did not want my life to be defined solely by what I had failed to do. Perhaps it was pride, or perhaps a love for the small things still left to me. One morning I remember noticing the sunrise as if for the first time in ages — realizing that even if there was no grand design in the sky, the dawn was reason enough to begin again. The sun still rose every day, after all; why shouldn't I?

So I carried on, but with new humility. I began to cherish questions more than answers, knowing any answer would always be incomplete, and I valued compassion more than pride. I found that sharing even a little of one's truth — just as I'm doing now — can feel like a release, like a lantern gently set afloat in the dark. Even these solitary evenings on this bench felt different; the silence around me no longer unnerved me as it once had.

Forgive me if I'm rambling. Old habits die hard. When someone finally listens — even the quiet presence of a stranger — years of thoughts can tumble out at once. But I should not keep you much longer.

I mention all this not to burden you, but because I sense that you, too, carry questions, perhaps even a bit of that quiet ache I've been describing. Maybe that's what led you to sit here tonight. And perhaps — just perhaps — you're seeking something, as I was.

I won't pretend to have answers for you. I'm done with pretending. But I can tell you this: you are not alone. The questions and longings you feel — others have them too. Others have sat where we sit now, their hearts heavy with unspoken thoughts.

In fact, there are others along this very path, farther down the night, with their own stories and confessions. If you listen, you may hear their voices rising softly out of the darkness. Each voice speaks in good faith — from the heart — rather than from any pulpit of theory. They won't offer you dry lectures or rigid doctrines. What they offer are glimpses of life, fragments of understanding distilled from experience — the kind of truths you can only glimpse at the edge of silence.

Let's sit a while longer in the soft quiet, you and I. There's no need to rush. After all, it's at the edge of silence that the clearest truths appear.

# Part I:
# Youth & First Fire

# Chapter 1
## Under the Algerian Sun

*It is late 1923 in Algiers. The last rays of afternoon pour through high windows in a primary school classroom in Belcourt, Algiers. The city hums faintly beyond the shutters. A young Albert Camus, who had just turned ten, sits alone at his desk as the other boys have gone home. Across from him, Louis Germain — his gentle-eyed teacher — lingers with chalk on his hands and patient wisdom in his voice. The moment is quiet, sunlit, full of beginnings.*

**Albert:** *(sitting at his desk after the other pupils have left)* Monsieur Germain, may I ask you something? The classroom feels so different now, with everyone gone. The sun is coming in low… it makes the dust in the air look like tiny stars.

**Germain:** *(smiles and leans against the desk)* Yes, the afternoon light in Algiers has a way of turning even dust into gold. What's on your mind, Albert?

**Albert:** I was just thinking… *(pauses, choosing his words carefully)* Why do you stay with me after class to help me so often? You've been so kind. I know I'm just one student out of many.

**Germain:** *(gently)* I stay because you have a spark, Albert. You're curious, and you work hard. It gives me joy to help you learn. You ask questions even after the bell rings — like now. *(chuckles softly)* Not every pupil does that.

**Albert:** I *do* have a lot of questions. Every book you lend me shows me something new. I can't help it. I want to understand… well, everything, I suppose. *(hesitant)* Is it foolish

7

that I dream of things beyond our neighborhood? Beyond Belcourt?

**Germain:** No, that isn't foolish at all. In fact, it's wonderful. *(He glances out the window at the bright street beyond.)* You come from a humble part of the city, Albert, but the world is much larger. With study and curiosity, you can travel that world in mind, even if you stay here in Algiers. Education will open doors for you — doors out of poverty.

**Albert:** *(earnestly)* I want that, Monsieur. Not just for me. If I could do something for Maman and even Grandmother… to give them a better life someday. They both work so hard. I want to make them proud.

**Germain:** They are proud, I'm sure. Your mother can't read the way you do, but she understands the value of what you're doing. *(pauses, speaking more solemnly)* Still, I know your family needs you to earn money before long. Your grandmother expects you'll leave school soon to start working, like your brother did.

**Albert:** *(looking down)* Yes. She talks about it often. She thinks studying isn't "real work." Sometimes I feel guilty sitting with books when I know there's so little money at home.

**Germain:** *(reaches out and pats Albert's shoulder encouragingly)* You have nothing to be guilty about. Learning is also work — work of the mind — and it can change your future. In fact, I've spoken with Headmaster about a scholarship for you to attend the Lycée next year.

**Albert:** *(eyes widening in astonishment)* A scholarship… for me? To go to high school?

**Germain:** Yes. You have the talent, Albert. With a scholarship, the costs will be covered — tuition, books, even a meal in the morning before class. I'm tutoring a small group of pupils for the scholarship exams, and I want you to be part of it. If you're willing to put in the effort, we can get you there.

**Albert:** *(voice quiet with emotion)* I am willing. I'll do whatever it takes. Getting up early, extra studies… anything. Thank you, Monsieur Germain. Truly. *(his voice trembles slightly on the last word)*

**Germain:** *(warmly)* You've earned it with your dedication. I merely pointed the way. *(He tilts his head, studying the boy's face.)* Tell me, what do you love so much about learning? I see your eyes light up in class — like when we discuss history or read a new story. What drives you?

**Albert:** *(thoughtful)* I… I think it's that everything I learn feels like another piece of a puzzle. Like I'm slowly seeing a bigger picture. In our neighborhood, everything is always the same — people just trying to get by. But in books, in ideas, I discover a larger world where things *mean* something. Where even poor kids like me can think about justice, or beauty, or why things are the way they are. It makes me feel like life isn't just whatever is handed to us. It can be understood, maybe even improved.

**Germain:** *(nods approvingly)* That's a very lucid way to put it, especially for someone your age. You're right: knowledge lets us question the world. And once we question, we can strive to improve things. Tell me, when you say "justice," what does that mean to you, Albert?

**Albert:** *(frowns in concentration, as if searching within himself)* I'm not completely sure… But I know how I feel when I see something unfair. Like when I saw one of my classmates take another boy's sandwich at lunch because he had none — just snatched it from him. It wasn't right. I felt angry inside, even though it wasn't happening to me. Or how some of us can't afford shoes for school while others can buy new ones every term. It... it bothers me, Monsieur. Not because I envy them, but because it seems unjust that chance decides so much — who is born rich or poor, who has a father and who loses him in a war... *(he trails off, suddenly self-conscious)*

**Germain:** *(softly, with empathy)* Your father — yes. You never knew him, but you feel that loss every day.

**Albert:** *(quiet)* Maman doesn't speak of him much. I know he died in the war when I was a baby. I sometimes wonder what he was like... if he would have taught me things, or been proud of me.

**Germain:** He was named Lucien, wasn't he? Like your brother. I did not know him personally, but I remember hearing of him. He was called up to fight in 1914 and fell at the Battle of the Marne, one of the first from our town to give his life. That is an honorable legacy, Albert, though a tragic one. He died a young man, but bravely, by all accounts.

**Albert:** *(in a small voice)* It is strange. I didn't even get to know him, yet because of him I've grown up without a father, and Maman without a husband. It doesn't feel entirely honorable — it feels... empty. Unjust.

**Germain:** War is the harshest kind of injustice, I think. It takes good men away from their families for reasons those families can hardly understand. *(sighs)* But your father's sacrifice is part of why you value justice. You've seen what losing him cost your family. It's made you sensitive to unfairness.

**Albert:** Maybe. I just know I want to make things a little fairer if I can. At least in my own life. I want to show that even a poor boy, a boy with no father and a mother who can't even hear well or read, can still hold his head high. *(he looks up at*

*Germain earnestly)* You taught me that, sir — that we all deserve dignity. That poverty doesn't make a person less worthy.

**Germain:** *(his eyes shine with pride, voice gentle)* And you must never forget it. Money or no money, you have dignity. Every human being does. Don't let anyone treat you otherwise. If someone laughs at your patched clothes or humble home, remember that a kind heart and an honest mind count for more than a full purse.

**Albert:** I will remember. Sometimes I worry, though… If I go to the Lycée, there will be many wealthy students from different backgrounds. What if they look down on me?

**Germain:** They might, some of them. It can happen. At high school you'll meet sons of businessmen, officials… boys who've never had to worry about a meal. You may even feel embarrassed about your family's situation. But listen: **never** be ashamed of where you come from. *Everyone* has to come from somewhere. Your pride should come from how you carry yourself and how hard you work, not from how much money your family has.

**Albert:** *(slowly nodding)* I understand. I think I might feel hurt if someone makes fun of my mother being a cleaning woman… but I'd feel even more ashamed of myself if I denied her or looked down on her work. She is the kindest person I know.

**Germain:** Exactly. Be honest about who you are. There is nothing in your life to hide. In fact, I suspect your background will give you a perspective that those other boys lack. You know what hardship is. You know the value of kindness and fairness firsthand.

**Albert:** *(smiles a little, encouraged)* When you talk about it that way, I feel less afraid. More… excited, even. Monsieur

Germain, do you really believe I can do well at the Lycée? Sometimes I doubt myself.

**Germain:** *(laughs kindly)* Believe me, you can. You have a sharp mind, Albert. And a hunger to learn — that matters more than anything. The Lycée will challenge you, but you'll flourish. You might even go further, to university one day. *(grinning)* Who knows? Perhaps you'll become a teacher or a writer or a great thinker, and you'll tell others about these days in Belcourt.

**Albert:** A teacher, a writer… *(he smiles at the idea, then ducks his head bashfully)* I don't know if I could ever be *great* at anything like that. But I would like to continue studying as far as I can. There's so much to read and so many ideas to discover. Even just reading the novels you lent me — I loved them. Especially the one by Monsieur Gide.

**Germain:** Ah, André Gide. You enjoyed *Les Nourritures terrestres* (Fruits of the Earth)?

**Albert:** Very much. It felt alive, all that talk of living fully and embracing the beauty of the world. It made me look at the sea and the sky differently, as if they were calling me to enjoy them.

**Germain:** Gide is a passionate writer. I'm happy you liked it. Loving literature will serve you well — books can be loyal friends in hard times, and wise guides too. *(he straightens up from the desk)* Speaking of hard times, I know things at home aren't easy. But if you ever need extra help — books, supplies, even a word with your grandmother — please tell me. I want to make sure nothing stands in your way.

**Albert:** You've already done so much… more than I ever expected anyone would. You believed in me when no one else even thought there was anything to believe in. I — I won't disappoint you, Monsieur. *(his voice fervent with feeling)* I promise to work as hard as I can, and to remain honest, like you taught me.

**Germain:** *(quietly, moved)* I have no doubt you will, Albert. And remember, you're not doing it for me. You're doing it for yourself — your future — and for those you love. *(He picks up a piece of chalk and absentmindedly draws a small sun on the corner of the blackboard as he talks.)* The world can be unjust, yes, but that is why we must bring justice to it ourselves. Through our actions, our words, our lives. You have that desire in you — hold on to it.

**Albert:** I will hold on to it. *(He watches the chalk sun on the board, its rays extending like the real sun outside.)*

**Germain:** You see this sun I've drawn? The Algerian sun outside is bright, almost blinding at times. But it illuminates everything clearly. I think of truth and knowledge as a kind of sunlight, too — chasing away shadows of ignorance. Keep that image with you. Always seek clarity, like a sunlit day, especially when life feels confusing or unjust.

**Albert:** *(looking from the chalk sun to the golden light streaming through the window)* Clarity… like the afternoon light right now. I'll remember, Monsieur Germain. When things seem dark or unfair, I'll try to recall this light, and what you've said.

**Germain:** Good. *(He dusts chalk from his hands and glances at the clock on the wall.)* We should probably head out. It's getting late, and I don't want your grandmother worrying I kept you too long.

**Albert:** *(hurriedly gathering his thin books and worn notebook)* Yes, of course. She'll be calling me for supper soon.

**Germain:** Albert, one more thing. *(He waits until the boy meets his eyes.)* Never lose that curiosity and sense of wonder I see in you.

Even as you grow older, even when life is difficult — hold on to it. It will keep you young in spirit and strong in purpose.

**Albert:** I'll try, sir. Sometimes I feel like my questions are endless. But I don't want to lose that, ever. It's like there's a small fire inside me that wants to know, to understand.

**Germain:** *(smiling fondly)* That fire is a precious thing. It will light your way.

**Albert:** *(softly)* Thank you. For everything. I won't forget what you've done for me, Monsieur Germain. *(He pauses, then adds with youthful sincerity)* I hope one day I can do something that makes it all worth it.

**Germain:** *(opens the classroom door as they exit together into the fading sunlight)* It's already worth it, my boy. Seeing you grow is the reward. Now go home, enjoy your evening. Tomorrow we'll tackle those scholarship exercises with the others.

**Albert:** *(standing at the doorway, books clutched to his chest, the sunlight on his face)* I will. Good evening, Monsieur Germain.

**Germain:** Good evening, Albert. And remember — no matter how dark the world can be, there is always a light to be found. Keep your eyes and your heart open.

---

*They part ways, the young student stepping out into the amber Algerian sun, full of hope, as his teacher watches proudly from the schoolhouse door.*

---

# Chapter 2
## A Sudden Chill

*It is 1930 at his Uncle Gustave's flat. The winter light slants through a cracked window in a backroom apartment above the port. Albert Camus, seventeen and gaunt from his first encounter with tuberculosis, lies propped on thin pillows, his breath shallow but steady. His older brother Lucien, still in his work clothes, sits beside the bed. Outside, Algiers lives on — but inside, the stillness carries the weight of a young man asking whether life, so fragile and unjust, is worth holding onto.*

**Lucien:** *(whispering as he enters the dim bedroom)* Albert? You awake?

**Albert:** *(lying in bed, turns his head slowly)* Lucien… You came. *(His voice is soft and a little raspy.)* You didn't have to whisper. I'm not sleeping — just resting.

**Lucien:** I didn't want to wake you if you were. *(He steps closer and sits carefully on a chair beside the bed.)* How are you feeling today?

**Albert:** Better than yesterday, I think. The fever's down. I can breathe a bit easier. *(He offers a faint smile.)* And the afternoon sun is coming through the window — look. It's bright, even if I can't go out in it.

**Lucien:** *(follows his gaze to the slice of light on the wall)* It's a beautiful day out. Warm for winter. I wish you could see the bay right now — blue as ever. When you're stronger, we'll go for a walk by the sea, alright?

**Albert:** *(closes his eyes as if to picture it)* I'd like that. I miss the sea. And the football matches on Sundays... Do you still play with the neighborhood team?

**Lucien:** Sometimes. It's not the same without our star goalkeeper. They all ask after you, you know. Everyone misses you at the field.

**Albert:** *(smiles a little more)* I miss them too. It feels like ages since I kicked a ball. But... *(his smile fades)* at one point I wasn't sure I'd ever play again. I wasn't even sure I'd... *(he trails off, unable to say "survive," but the word hangs in the air)*

**Lucien:** *(quickly, in a reassuring tone)* But you're still here, Albert. You made it through the worst. Doctor Bernard said the crisis passed last week. You just need time and rest now. You'll get your strength back, you'll see.

**Albert:** *(opens his eyes and looks at his brother earnestly)* I believe you. It's just — when I was at my sickest, burning with fever night after night, coughing so much... I really thought I might die, Lucien. And that thought... it was terrifying.

**Lucien:** *(reaches over to adjust the blanket around Albert's shoulders, an awkward gesture of comfort)* I know. We were all so scared. Maman was beside herself with worry, even if she tried not to show it. She prayed by your door every night.

**Albert:** Maman... *(his eyes grow moist)* I heard her once, you know. Late one night when she didn't realize I was awake. I heard her crying quietly in the next room. I'd never heard her cry before, ever.

**Lucien:** Nor had I. When Father died, she was stone-faced, they say — too shocked to weep. And all these years, through every hardship, she's been silent and strong. But when you took ill... It's as if all the sorrow she normally holds inside came to the surface. Just a little, just enough that we saw how much her heart was breaking.

**Albert:** *(voice thick)* I wanted to call out to her that night, to comfort her. But I could barely speak. And part of me felt guilty, like I was the cause of her pain.

**Lucien:** It's not your fault. Illness comes on its own. You're as innocent in this as she is.

**Albert:** I know. *(He coughs lightly, then continues, eyes distant.)* Lying here day after day, I had a lot of time to think — maybe too much time. In the worst moments, when every breath felt like knives in my chest, I wondered if there was any meaning to it. Why should a seventeen-year-old be stuck in bed coughing up blood when others are out playing football or sitting in class? What sense is there in that? I couldn't find any reason.

**Lucien:** Sometimes there isn't a reason, little brother. Sometimes people just get sick. *(He says it plainly, but then adds in a softer tone:)* Or maybe — if you ask the priest — he'd say God has His reasons, even if we don't understand them.

**Albert:** *(turns his head on the pillow to face Lucien, expression skeptical)* Do you believe that? That it's part of some plan?

**Lucien:** *(shrugs uncertainly)* I don't know. Grandmother would say yes, for sure. She'd scold me for doubting. But watching you suffer… I found myself doubting a lot. What kind of plan puts someone through this? If God has reasons, He keeps them to Himself.

**Albert:** *(a faint, wry smile)* That's exactly how I feel. If there is some higher meaning, it's kept secret. From where I lay, there was no grand design — only pain and the will to survive. I kept asking myself, **why?** Why me? Why now? And there was no answer. None. The world was silent as a grave on that question.

**Lucien:** *(looks down at his hands)* When I sat outside your door listening to you cough, I asked "why" a lot too. Why you, and not me? You've always been the frail one, but also the bright one, the one with so much promise. It seemed so cruel that you'd be struck with that cursed illness... *(he swallows hard, not finishing the sentence)*

**Albert:** *(quietly finishes it for him)* ...that I might be taken away? *(He sighs, a mix of resignation and relief.)* I thought about death, Lucien. I truly did. In fever dreams, I saw myself on the edge of a dark abyss. It made no sense to me that I could stop existing while the world went on outside — people laughing on the street, the sun rising each morning over the bay. How could that beautiful sun shine and I not be there to feel it on my face? The thought made me so sad and angry all at once. It felt... *absurd*, in a way.

**Lucien:** *(frowns)* Absurd?

**Albert:** Absurd, yes. That life can be so beautiful — I was remembering the sound of the waves at Tipaza, the color of the sky at dusk, the taste of ripe figs last summer — so beautiful, and yet at any moment it can be cut off. Ended, *just like that*. No matter how good you are, no matter how much you still want to do. *(His voice trembles slightly, with frustration or passion.)* I did nothing wrong, but I got tuberculosis. Father did nothing wrong, but he caught a bullet in a war he likely didn't even understand. Where is the justice in any of it?

**Lucien:** *(sadly)* There isn't any, I guess. Not in sickness or early death.

**Albert:** Right. It's not just or unjust by any higher law — those are human words. The universe just... lets things happen. Good people, bad people, young or old — disease doesn't care. A war shell doesn't care who it blows up. It's all so senseless.

**Lucien:** Hearing you talk like this — *(he musters a teasing smile)* — you sound like an old philosopher, not my kid brother. Since when did you get so serious?

**Albert:** Since I had a lot of time to stare at the ceiling. *(He returns a weak grin.)* Sorry. These thoughts just keep circling in my head.

**Lucien:** Don't apologize. I understand. *(He reaches over and squeezes Albert's hand briefly.)* Honestly, I've been thinking about all that too. How fragile everything is. I go to work each day and it's normal… then I come here and see you pale as a ghost, fighting to breathe, and I realize how quickly normal can shatter. It scared me, Albert. It still does.

**Albert:** It scares me as well. But you know what surprised me even more? Along with the fear, I felt this… this fierce love for life. Even when I was delirious, in those rare calm moments when the pain stopped, I'd think about the simplest things: the orange trees by the road, or playing football barefoot in summer, or Maman's face in the morning light. And I would think, *I don't want to leave this.* Life was suddenly so precious — every little bit of it. Even just lying here feeling the breeze from the window on my face became a gift.

**Lucien:** *(smiles)* You always did find joy in small things. When you were a little boy you'd get excited by, oh, a pretty pebble or the pattern of sunlight on the floor. I used to laugh at you, remember?

**Albert:** *(chuckles softly)* Yes. I was a serious little fool even then, pondering my "pebble of the day." But maybe that's a good thing. Those small joys… they kept me going these past weeks. I'd lie here thinking: if I get better, I'll go watch the sunset from the shore again. I'll swim in the sea, feel salt on my skin. I'll eat a fresh baguette from old Monsieur Antoine's bakery and taste every crumb. It's silly, but those thoughts were like promises I made to myself: *survive, and you can do these simple, wonderful things again.*

**Lucien:** That's not silly at all. That's hope. Clinging to the good bits of life — maybe that's what we all do to get through the worst. I'm glad you had those thoughts. And you *will* do those things again, I'll make sure of it. As soon as you're able, we'll walk down to the bakery, and then straight to the seaside. I'll even let you dunk me in the water if it makes you happy.

**Albert:** *(grins)* I'll hold you to that.

**Lucien:** *(takes a breath, then speaks in a more serious tone)* You know, while you've been in here recuperating at Uncle Gustave's, a lot has happened outside. But nothing mattered to us as much as seeing you get better. Grandmother even allowed Maman to miss some work so she could help Aunt Antoinette care for you. That's how worried she was.

**Albert:** Grandmother did that? *(He sounds surprised; their grandmother is known for her strictness.)*

**Lucien:** She did. And she sends over broth every other day, the way *her* mother used to make for the sick. She doesn't say much when I bring the pot, but you can tell she poured all her care into it.

**Albert:** I'll have to thank her when I see her.

**Lucien:** She'll grumble that it was nothing, but she'll be happy to know you appreciated it. *(Lucien hesitates, then adds quietly:)* We were really afraid, Albert. I even thought, "What if I lose my only brother, just like that?"

**Albert:** *(reaches out and puts a thin hand on Lucien's arm)* But you didn't lose me. I'm still here.

**Lucien:** And so relieved. *(He manages a smile, covering the emotional moment with a touch of humor.)* You're stuck with me, little brother, at least for a while longer.

**Albert:** *(smiling back)* Good. I'd hate to leave you alone to deal with Grandmother's scoldings.

**Lucien:** Oh, that would be cruel indeed. *(Both chuckle softly.)*

**Albert:** *(after a brief coughing fit, he continues more somberly)* This experience — being ill like this — it's changed something in me, Lucien. I can't quite explain it yet.

**Lucien:** Changed you how?

**Albert:** I've always known life was hard; we grew up knowing that. But now I see how fragile it is too, and how *unpredictable*. We have so little control. One day we're laughing, the next day we're in a hospital bed… or a war… *(he closes his eyes a moment)* I think about Father a lot now. He was, what, not even thirty when he went to the front? And then he never came back. I'm seventeen and I've been knocked down by disease. It's as if life is always waiting to pull the rug from under us.

**Lucien:** It can feel that way.

**Albert:** So I ask myself: if life is so unpredictable and unfair, how should I live? What should I do with the time I have, however long or short it is? *(He grips the bedsheet lightly, as if anchoring himself.)* I don't have the full answer. But I know I don't want to waste a moment. I want to live, truly *live*, and help those I love to live, too.

**Lucien:** You will live. You'll recover, and you have a long life ahead. You'll finish school, maybe go to university — imagine that! You could become a professor or a writer like you always talk about. You'll make a difference, I'm sure of it. And we'll both take good care of Maman as she gets older.

**Albert:** *(smiles wistfully)* I hope you're right. There are moments, even now, when I feel so alive, so ready to take on the world. Like when the fever breaks and I can think clearly for a while — I get ideas, even dreams of what I might do. Then other times I'm just tired and nothing has shape or purpose. It's like… like being caught between two states: one where everything matters intensely, and one where nothing means anything at all.

**Lucien:** That's the illness talking. It saps your strength and your spirits. Don't trust those empty feelings, Albert. They'll pass as you heal.

**Albert:** Perhaps. Yet part of me thinks those thoughts — both the hopeful and the hollow — will stay with me long after I'm well. I've seen something true about life: it *is* beautiful, and it *is* unjust, both at once. That won't change even when I'm up and walking. The question is, how to carry that truth?

**Lucien:** How do you mean?

**Albert:** *(searching for words)* I mean… knowing what I know now — feeling how close everything is to being lost — how do I not despair? And also, how do I not take life for granted? There must be a way to live with this awareness. To still find joy, and to do good, without shutting my eyes to how cruel fate can be.

**Lucien:** You've wrestled more with these thoughts in a few weeks than many do in a lifetime, brother. Honestly, I don't have the answers. I fix machines at the workshop; I'm not a thinker like you. But I do know this: we just have to keep going. For Maman, for each other, for ourselves. Keep going and make the best of whatever comes.

**Albert:** *(softly repeats)* Make the best of whatever comes... *Yes.* I think that's as good a answer as any. Perhaps the only one. *(He looks over at the sunlight creeping along the wall as afternoon wanes.)* We carry on, even without any promise that things will make sense. We just live, and love what we can love, and try to be decent to each other along the way.

**Lucien:** That sounds right to me. And we don't do it alone — we've got each other. Our family may be quiet and small, but we stick together.

**Albert:** *(smiling at Lucien)* I'm lucky to have you all. Many facing what I did might be alone, or give up. I had Maman's prayers, you sneaking in to see me, Uncle's odd remedies and books... Everyone gave me strength. I want to be worthy of that kindness.

**Lucien:** You are, Albert. And when you're better, you'll return that kindness in your own way, I'm sure. Maybe to us, maybe to others. You have a good heart.

**Albert:** *(teasing lightly)* Careful, you'll make me blush.

**Lucien:** *(laughs)* Well, can't have that, the patient turning red — doctor might think it's a rash.

**Albert:** *(joins the laughter softly, then grows thoughtful once more)* Lucien... do you ever think about Father?

**Lucien:** Sometimes. I have a couple of blurry memories — him lifting me up in the air once, playing with me. I was only three when he left for the war, but I remember his face a little from a photograph Aunt told me about. Why?

**Albert:** When I was at my worst, I wondered if I was going to meet him — wherever people go when they die. It's a childish thought, perhaps. But I felt close to him suddenly. As if, in facing the possibility of death, I understood him more. He was so young when he went to war. He must have been scared too, like I was.

**Lucien:** I'm sure he was. But he went anyway.

**Albert:** Yes. He went, likely because he had no choice — duty called. And he died far away, probably afraid and suffering in his last moments. Just as I was afraid here in bed. It's strange... across time, I felt a kinship with him. A man I never knew, yet I felt we were both shouting into the dark, asking "Why must it end like this?"

**Lucien:** *(listening quietly, taken in by Albert's train of thought)*

**Albert:** Of course, I didn't die. I have been spared — for now. Father wasn't. That makes me feel... *(he struggles for the word)* responsible, somehow.

**Lucien:** Responsible? For what?

**Albert:** To live. To live *well.* To not waste the chance that he, and so many others, never got. I survived this bout — by luck or fate or whatever you call it. I must do something with that survival. Otherwise, what was the point?

**Lucien:** There you go again, trying to find the point in things. *(he says it gently)* Maybe there isn't one given to us, Albert. Maybe we just... carry on, like we said, and make our own point.

**Albert:** *(a light comes into his tired eyes)* Exactly. That's exactly it. If there is no grand meaning handed down, then we have to make our own. Fill the void with our own small meanings — love, work, understanding, whatever we choose. That's the only way to beat the emptiness and unfairness, I think.

**Lucien:** That's a lot for one person to take on — creating meaning. But you're not alone in it. We all try, in our humble ways.

**Albert:** *(reaches for his brother's hand and grasps it weakly yet firmly)* Thank you for hearing me out. I know I sound like I swallowed a philosophy book.

**Lucien:** *(smiles and squeezes Albert's hand)* It's alright. You've been alone with your thoughts too long; you needed to share them. I'm glad you did. And for what it's worth, little brother, I think you're onto something. Life knocked you down hard, but you're getting back up with more determination than before.

**Albert:** I have to. There's too much I still want to do. Even just ordinary things — finish school, swim in the sea, maybe write a story about all this one day. If I can do those things, then I've made a little meaning, haven't I?

**Lucien:** You have. And you will. One step at a time. For now, your job is to rest and heal. Everything else will come after.

**Albert:** Under orders to rest — yes, doctor. *(He chuckles, which turns into a brief cough.)*

**Lucien:** Easy now. Here, drink some water. *(He helps Albert take a sip from a glass on the bedside table.)*

**Albert:** *(after drinking)* Thank you. You'd make a decent nurse, Lucien.

**Lucien:** Oh, I think one patient is enough for me. Maman and Aunt Antoinette do the hard part — I just sneak in as the comic relief. *(He winks.)*

**Albert:** You've done more than that. You've given me something to look forward to. Promise we'll do those things you said — bakery, seaside — when I'm able?

**Lucien:** I promise. As soon as you're steady on your feet, we'll reclaim all the pleasures you've been dreaming of. And maybe a few new ones for good measure.

**Albert:** New ones?

**Lucien:** Sure. Perhaps a trip up to the hills, or a night at the theater — whatever you like. After facing what you did, you deserve to enjoy life twice as much.

**Albert:** *(smiling, eyes shining with gratitude)* I'd like that. To feel alive in every sense. You know, lying here I realized how much I love life, even with all its pain. I don't understand how it can be so unfair and yet so beautiful — but I want to experience as much of that beauty as I can, and fight against the unfairness where I see it.

**Lucien:** That sounds like a good plan for a life.

**Albert:** *(quietly, with determination)* It's more than a plan — it's a resolve. I've been given a second chance. I won't waste it. Even if the world ultimately makes no sense, I'll try to live as if my life *does* — as if it can matter that I was here.

**Lucien:** It *does* matter. To us, it does.

**Albert:** *(a single tear slips down his cheek, which he quickly wipes away, embarrassed)* I'm glad.

**Lucien:** And now, little brother, you should rest. You've talked a lot and you need your strength. *(He stands, patting Albert's arm.)* I'll come back in the morning before work, alright?

**Albert:** Alright. Thank you, Lucien.

**Lucien:** Don't thank me — just get better. That's thanks enough for all of us.

**Albert:** I will do my best. Good night, Lucien.

**Lucien:** Good night, Albert. Sleep well. And remember, we all love you.

**Albert:** *(closing his eyes)* I won't forget.

---

*Lucien steps out quietly, leaving the young man in gentle twilight, alive to see another day.*

---

# Chapter 3
## Flames on the Waterfront

*The year is circa 1936, at the Théâtre du Travail. The sun has set behind the cranes of the Algiers harbor. At the Théâtre du Travail a half-lit rehearsal hall buzzes with laughter and the scrape of chairs. Camus, now twenty-three, walks outside with a fellow actor and comrade. The street smells of salt and woodsmoke. They stop at the railing above the sea, still flushed from performance. Below their debate is the question that will follow Camus all his life: can revolution be waged without betraying truth?*

**Yves:** *(hurrying alongside Albert as they exit the makeshift rehearsal space by the Algiers waterfront)* That was an intense rehearsal! The scene where the miners set the docks aflame... I had chills, Albert. This play is really going to stir people up.

**Albert:** *(runs a hand through his hair, still caught in thought)* The cast put real passion into it tonight. Did you see the faces of the dockworkers who watched us practice? Some of them looked ready to join the revolt right then and there.

**Yves:** That's exactly what we want! *(He stops to light a cigarette, the flame briefly illuminating his eager face in the dusk.)* We want them fired up. Art for the people, to wake the people. You should be proud — *Révolte dans les Asturies* is powerful stuff.

**Albert:** *(offers a thin smile)* I am proud of what we've done, Yves. It's just...

**Yves:** *(takes a drag and exhales, eyeing Albert shrewdly)* Just what? I know that tone. Something's on your mind.

**Albert:** *(pauses by the waterfront railing, looking out at the harbor where a few fishing boat lanterns flicker like stars on the water)* Tonight, during the scene where the miners talk of justice, I watched the faces of those workers in the back. They looked so hungry for hope, for change. And I thought: *What if we're giving them false hope?*

**Yves:** False hope? How so?

**Albert:** Our play… we make the revolt seem heroic, inevitable. In reality, the Asturian miners' strike was crushed brutally. Many good people died, and their cause failed in that moment. We don't show that on stage — we end on a rousing note of defiance, a call to arms. It feels honest in the moment, but is it the truth? Or are we manipulating their emotions?

**Yves:** *(frowns)* Albert, it's a call to arms because we want the audience to *act*, not to wallow in defeat. Sure, the historical revolt was put down. But its spirit lives on. We're trying to inspire the workers here not to give up, to keep fighting for justice.

**Albert:** I agree with the intention. I want them inspired too. But I'm grappling with whether we've sacrificed complexity — truth — for the sake of a clear message. Real life isn't as black-and-white as our play. In reality, even some of the strikers did awful things, and some of those soldiers who fired on them were just poor conscripts… It's messy. But we painted it as pure good versus evil.

**Yves:** *(waves his hand dismissively)* That's artistic license for the greater good. People don't need all the messy details; they need a story that clarifies who the enemy is and why it's right to resist. The point isn't to educate them on every nuance — it's to ignite their sense of injustice so they'll stand up and change things.

**Albert:** I know… I know. *(He leans on the railing, the salt breeze brushing his face.)* And yet, I feel uneasy. If we simplify too much, are we really respecting those people, or just using them?

**Yves:** Using them? We *are* them, Albert. You and I are sons of working-class families too. We're not outsiders exploiting anyone — we're part of this fight.

**Albert:** *(turns to face Yves, brow furrowed)* That's true. We are. But I have to be able to look at myself in the mirror. If I rouse someone with lofty ideals, I want those ideals to be grounded in truth, not in a lie or omission I made up just to sway them.

**Yves:** You think we're lying? What lie have we told? That oppression exists? That workers have the right to rebel? None of that's a lie.

**Albert:** Not outright, no. But I keep wondering: are we presenting revolution as something too clean, too noble? When in fact it can be bloody and cruel, even on the side of the oppressed.

**Yves:** *(snaps a bit)* Would you rather we show the miners infighting, or the ugliness of violence, and leave the audience discouraged? We're trying to build morale, Albert! Do you think the bosses and the government worry about "truth" when they spread their propaganda? They twist reality every day to keep people subdued. And you're worried that we sugarcoat the heroism of a few miners?

**Albert:** *(holds up a hand defensively)* I understand the argument. "The other side lies, so why shouldn't we?" But that logic troubles me. If we start justifying lies or half-truths because our cause is righteous, we become more like our enemies than we'd care to admit.

**Yves:** It's a *tactic*, not a moral failing. Look, sometimes you have to exaggerate or simplify to reach people's hearts. We're in a fight. In a fight you do what you must to win.

**Albert:** *(shakes his head slowly)* To me, the means matter as much as the ends. If we win by betraying the truth, is it really a victory? We might free the workers from one form of oppression only to shackle them in another illusion.

**Yves:** You're sounding awfully idealistic. As if truth is some absolute thing that must never be bent. Albert, this is revolution we're talking about, not a philosophy salon. We can't afford such purity. People are suffering now — poverty, injustice, colonial brutality right here in Algeria. Should we not push them to change things because we're afraid of a little propaganda?

**Albert:** *(voice passionate but calm)* I feel that suffering, Yves. You know I do. I report on it in the paper; I talk to those families in the casbah living eight to a room. I'm not blind to their plight. That's *why* I care so much that we do right by them. They've been lied to enough — by colonial officials, by factory owners, by politicians. If we, who claim to stand for justice, start lying to them as well, even for a good cause, then what makes us different?

**Yves:** *(stubs out his cigarette, frustration evident)* What makes us different is that we're on their side! We want to better their lives, not exploit them. Don't be so damned philosophical that you equate us with those who oppress. Our intentions matter.

**Albert:** Intentions do matter, absolutely. But intentions alone can't justify everything. I'm not equating us to the oppressors, but I fear the *methods* could converge if we aren't careful. If the Party line tomorrow said to spread a false rumor because it might spark a rebellion, would you do it?

**Yves:** *(folds his arms)* If it helped liberate people in the end… possibly, yes.

**Albert:** That's what I'm afraid of. That mindset — "the end justifies the means" — it opens the door to all kinds of abuses. Today it's a false rumor, tomorrow it's turning a blind eye to an innocent man punished "for the cause." Where does it stop?

**Yves:** *(squints at Albert through the twilight, trying to read him)* You've changed, Albert. When we started this workers' theatre, you were as fiery as anyone, eager to serve the revolution. Now you sound almost… skeptical. What happened?

**Albert:** *(sighs and rubs the bridge of his nose)* Maybe I've been reading too much and seeing too much. I read the reports coming out of the Soviet Union — some from Gide, some whispers from Russian exiles. Not everything in the "workers' paradise" is as we imagined. Writers silenced or imprisoned for speaking an inconvenient truth, farmers forced into famine… It's made me realize that even revolutions can become unjust, can betray their original hopes.

**Yves:** Gide — bah, he went to the USSR for a few months and came back spouting bourgeois criticisms. He's given ammunition to the enemies of socialism. Of course building a new world isn't pretty — there will be mistakes, even brutality. But think of the greater achievement: a classless society someday.

**Albert:** Someday… *(he looks back out at the dark water, voice quieter)* We always talk about future utopias. But people live and die in the present. I can't console myself that "someday" it will justify what's happening now. If innocent people are being crushed now — in Spain, in Russia, here in Algeria — I can't ignore that just because a theory promises a bright future.

**Yves:** So what, exactly, are you saying? That you'll stop supporting the revolution because it isn't pure? That you prefer to sit on the fence and criticize both sides?

**Albert:** I'm not on the fence at all. I stand firmly for the downtrodden, for freedom and equality. But I also stand for truth and individual human lives. I won't sacrifice one for the other. If that makes me unpopular in the Party, so be it.

**Yves:** It will, you know. Make you unpopular. People are noticing your... let's call it *independent streak*. Some of the Party organizers muttered that you're too "liberal" in your views, too soft on certain "bourgeois" values like free expression.

**Albert:** *(lets out a small laugh)* Free expression is a bourgeois value? Since when is honesty a class privilege? It should be a universal value. If the revolution won't allow free expression, what exactly are we fighting for? Just another form of tyranny?

**Yves:** You and I both know any movement has to maintain discipline. Dissent can weaken the cause. That's what they're concerned about — that your questioning attitude might spread doubt.

**Albert:** If our cause can't survive a little honest questioning, then it's on shaky ground indeed.

**Yves:** *(places a hand on Albert's shoulder, voice earnest now rather than combative)* Listen, Albert. I admire your integrity, I really do. But you must choose your battles. You can't fight for justice *and* insist on absolute truth-telling all the time in the middle of a struggle. There are practical realities.

**Albert:** *(turns to face Yves fully, meeting his gaze)* And I'm telling you, **for me** truth and justice are inseparable. A justice won by deception or by trampling on the innocent isn't justice at all.

Maybe that's an absolute, but it's one I have to hold. Otherwise, I'd lose respect for myself.

**Yves:** *(searches Albert's face, then sighs)* I worry for you, my friend. The world isn't kind to idealists with consciences. The Party can be especially unkind.

**Albert:** Perhaps. They might expel me one day, or I might leave if I find I can't agree with their demands. It would sadden me, but I won't regret keeping my conscience intact.

**Yves:** If it came to that, you know what they'd call you? A traitor. A reactionary. I've seen it happen — good men cast out and labeled because they didn't toe the line exactly.

**Albert:** *(shrugs slightly)* Words. Let them call me what they want. I'd rather be called a traitor for being honest than be hailed as a hero for spreading lies.

**Yves:** *(shakes his head)* You and your principles… You realize most people don't think like this when they're trying to change the world, right? They pick a side and fight. You keep reflecting mid-fight about whether the sword should even be swung.

**Albert:** *(a faint smile)* Perhaps I'd make a poor soldier. Too much thinking. But maybe that's my role — to be the one who asks why we do things a certain way, to challenge us to stay true to our best ideals.

**Yves:** We need soldiers and poets both, I suppose. And you're a bit of each, Albert. *(He offers his hand suddenly.)* I don't want to quarrel with you. We're friends and comrades, even if we disagree.

**Albert:** *(grasps Yves's hand firmly)* Comrades, yes. I'm sorry if I came off as holier-than-thou. I respect your dedication, Yves, more than I can say. You work tirelessly for the cause, and I know your heart is for the people.

**Yves:** I know you care too. You've got a real fire for justice in you — ironically, that's why you're so hard on our methods. Because you care so damned much that it hurts you to compromise even a little.

**Albert:** That's one way to put it. It does hurt, the thought of betraying what I believe is right. I think it would hurt me more than any punishment the Party could inflict.

**Yves:** *(half-joking)* That moral backbone of yours might be the death of you one day, mon ami.

**Albert:** If it is, at least I'll know why I'm dying. *(He smiles, though his eyes are serious.)* I just hope it never comes to that. I'd much prefer to live and see a better world — one that we can build without losing ourselves in the process.

**Yves:** I hope for that too. Truly. *(He glances back toward the city, where a few lights are coming on in the early night.)* Look, it's late. We should head home. Tomorrow's performance will be a big day.

**Albert:** Yes. And despite all my philosophizing, I am excited — and a bit nervous.

**Yves:** *(grins)* That's normal. This is our first major play for the workers. The Party officials will be watching too.

**Albert:** I noticed. Did you see Baptiste in the back, taking notes like a hawk?

**Yves:** *(rolls his eyes)* He's evaluating its ideological purity, no doubt. If we miss a slogan, he'll tell us.

**Albert:** *(wryly)* That's exactly what worries me.

**Yves:** Don't think about him. The piece is strong. Just deliver your lines with conviction. You speak the final monologue so passionately — by the end, when you shout "We will not be slaves forever!" even *I* want to grab a torch and man the barricades.

**Albert:** It is a good line, isn't it? *(he nods, resolved)* Alright, I'll focus on that. On giving these people hope and dignity, as honestly as I can.

**Yves:** And I'll focus on not missing my cue in the second act. *(laughs)*

**Albert:** Please do, or I'll be left alone on stage with a fake rifle and no revolution to start.

**Yves:** Don't worry, I'll be there. *(He puts a friendly arm around Albert as they begin to walk.)* You know, Albert, despite our arguments, I'm glad we talk like this. It keeps me on my toes.

**Albert:** Likewise. You challenge me as well — force me to defend my beliefs and think through them.

**Yves:** That's what comrades are for, hmm? We push each other to be better. Somewhere between your purity and my pragmatism, maybe there's a balance.

**Albert:** I hope so. Because I refuse to give up on either: a just cause and an honest path. *(He gazes one more time at the dark water, where the reflection of a distant harbor flame dances.)* The world can be changed, I believe that. But it must be changed without destroying what is best in ourselves.

**Yves:** Perhaps that is the true revolution — to change the world *and* keep our souls intact.

**Albert:** Amen to that.

**Yves:** Did you just say "amen"? That's not very godless-communist of you.

**Albert:** *(chuckles)* Figure of speech. Don't report me to the Party for piety.

**Yves:** *(laughing)* Your secret's safe with me, mon ami. Now, let's get going. We both need some sleep.

**Albert:** Yes, let's. Tomorrow, the flames we kindle on stage might just spread in the hearts of those watching.

**Yves:** *(with a determined glint)* From the stage to the streets, that's the idea.

**Albert:** Just so long as those flames bring light, and not just heat.

**Yves:** Ever the clarifier… *Bonne nuit*, Albert.

**Albert:** *Bonne nuit*, Yves. See you in the morning.

---

*The two friends depart along the moonlit quay, the evening breeze carrying with it the sound of gentle waves and the faint echo of their ideals, burning brightly against the coming night.*

---

# Chapter 4
## The Schoolhouse

*It is 1937. Late in the day, a young man in his lycée uniform pushes open the door to his old elementary school. The desks are smaller than he remembers, the blackboard still dusted with a day's worth of questions. Louis Germain, his former teacher, looks up from a pile of graded papers. This is a return — not only to a place, but to a thread of gratitude and the moral clarity that first lit Camus' path. Outside, the Algerian sun sets behind the hills, but inside, the conversation is just beginning.*

**Albert:** *(standing at the threshold of the familiar classroom)* Monsieur Germain? May I come in?

**Germain:** *(looking up from a pile of copybooks on his desk, surprised and pleased)* Albert! Mon garçon, of course, come in, come in. *(He rises and extends his hand warmly.)* What a sight to see you back here.

**Albert:** *(entering with a grin, shaking Germain's hand respectfully)* It's so good to see you, sir. I hope I'm not interrupting your work.

**Germain:** Not at all. I was just finishing grading these exercises. Nothing that can't wait a bit. *(He looks Albert up and down appraisingly.)* You've grown taller since I last saw you in person — and a bit thinner too. How are you feeling?

**Albert:** I'm well now, thank you. Much stronger than I was a few months ago. I even walked here from home today.

**Germain:** That's excellent. When I heard you'd fallen ill last year, I was terribly worried. Tuberculosis since seventeen... I remember thinking, "Life can be so unfair." We nearly lost you, didn't we?

**Albert:** *(nods slowly)* Yes. There were a few nights when I thought I wouldn't see another sunrise. It was a close call. But I pulled through.

**Germain:** *(gestures to a chair)* Please, sit down. *(They both sit, sunlight slanting through the tall windows onto the old wooden desks.)* You've returned to classes now, I hope?

**Albert:** I have, part-time. The doctor advised me not to overexert myself, so I'm easing back into my studies at the Lycée. I'll have to repeat the year I missed, but I don't mind. I'm just grateful to be back at all.

**Germain:** And we're all grateful you're back. The schoolmaster told me how you insisted on returning as soon as you were able. That determination doesn't surprise me. *(He smiles.)* Do you remember how you used to come an hour early for the free breakfast, then stay after class for extra lessons? You've always been resolute when you set your mind on something.

**Albert:** I remember. *(Albert glances around the room, as if the memories are fluttering out of the dust motes in the air.)* This room… it feels smaller than I recall, but otherwise just the same. The blackboard, the maps, the way the afternoon sun falls across the first row of desks — nothing's changed, yet everything's changed.

**Germain:** How so?

**Albert:** *(with a gentle laugh)* I suppose *I've* changed most. When I sat here as a little boy, the world was simpler to me. My biggest worry was a spelling test or whether Maman would be angry that I tore my only good shirt. Now… *well,* now I've glimpsed how fragile life can be, how complicated.

**Germain:** You've had to grow up faster than many, Albert. Facing a serious illness, enduring what you did — it forces a kind of wisdom on a person. Though I must say, you were always an old soul, even at ten. *(He points at a spot by the window.)* I recall one day you lingered after class right there, staring at the dust in the sunlight, telling me it looked like stars.

**Albert:** *(smiles)* I remember that. You laughed and said perhaps I'd be an astronomer. I think I just enjoyed how the light made something ordinary seem magical.

**Germain:** There's a lesson in that, isn't there? That even in the mundane, a certain beauty can be found if one has the eyes for it. You always did.

**Albert:** I try to hold on to that way of seeing. Especially after being sick. When I was confined to bed, I started to treasure small things — the pattern of light on the wall, the breeze through a crack in the window, the distant sounds of the city carrying on without me. Those little details were life-affirming when I was too weak for anything else.

**Germain:** It doesn't surprise me that even in illness, you found insight. *(His face grows serious.)* Tell me, if you're comfortable… what did you go through in your thoughts during that time? How did it change you?

**Albert:** *(looks down for a moment, collecting himself)* At first, I felt only physical misery — the fevers, the weakness. But once I realized it could be fatal, a kind of clarity came over me. I began to see all the assumptions I'd lived under fall away. I used to think life naturally had meaning — that if I worked hard and was good, things would turn out well. Getting tuberculosis out of the blue shattered that naive faith. It showed me that bad things happen without rhyme or reason.

**Germain:** Life's unpredictability... yes.

**Albert:** Exactly. Suddenly, nothing was guaranteed. Not tomorrow, not next year, nothing. It was as if I were staring the absurdity of existence right in the face. I asked myself, "If I die at seventeen, what was the point of all this — of school, of dreams, of being a decent person? Does it matter at all?"

**Germain:** A profound question — and a scary one.

**Albert:** It was terrifying. I flirted with despair, truly. But then, something inside pushed back against that void. I thought of Maman and Lucien, of you and my friends. I thought of the books I still wanted to read, the sunsets I wanted to see again. And I realized that **if** there is no inherent meaning, I would have to create my own. However small, however fragile. I decided that if I got another chance — if I lived — I would dedicate myself to things that *do* matter to me: loving my family, seeking truth, fighting injustice where I see it, and savoring every moment of beauty I can.

**Germain:** *(listening with glistening eyes)* That's a remarkable conclusion to reach, Albert. Many go through life never confronting these questions. You wrestled with them and found an answer that rings true. So you found a sense of responsibility in the face of absurdity?

**Albert:** Yes, responsibility is the word. I feel responsible to justify my life, since I've been lucky enough to keep it. Responsible to those who didn't get a chance — like my father, or others who died young. And responsible to the values I care about, because if I don't uphold them, no one else will do it for me.

**Germain:** And what values are those, in your heart?

**Albert:** Honesty, for one. I never want to live by lies, even comforting ones. Compassion — if we all understood each other's suffering, maybe we'd be kinder. And justice, of course. I can't stand by if I see someone treated unfairly. Perhaps that's the strongest one in me.

**Germain:** It always was. I remember you sticking up for that shy boy — what was his name? — Ismail, I think. Some of the other children teased him for his accent. You defended him, almost got into a fistfight over it. You were eleven.

**Albert:** *(nods)* I remember. I just couldn't bear the bullying. Ismail's family was Arab and poor, and the other boys acted like that made him less somehow. It made me furious. I think of him sometimes even now, especially when I see how our society treats the Arab workers. It's not so different, just on a larger scale.

**Germain:** The world has many such injustices, big and small. I'm heartened to hear you haven't lost your resolve to confront them. *(He leans forward, his face earnest.)* But Albert, I must caution you too. You're young, and you carry these grand ideals, which is admirable. Life, however, has a way of testing and tempering ideals. There may be times when the world forces you to compromise or to choose the lesser of two evils. I wouldn't want you to be disillusioned when that happens.

**Albert:** *(smiles faintly)* I understand what you're saying. I've thought about that as well. In fact, I've already felt some of that tension. You know I've been involved with a workers' theatre group and some political activities…

**Germain:** Yes, I'd heard. A leftist theatre, correct? Some even said you joined the Communist Party?

**Albert:** Briefly, yes. I was drawn by their talk of equality and justice for the poor — ideas that resonate with me deeply, as you know. And we did good work, bringing plays to working-class audiences, highlighting social issues. But... *(he sighs)* I've found myself at odds with the party line at times. They can be dogmatic — insisting that art must serve the revolution in a very narrow way. I raised questions, and that wasn't always welcome.

**Germain:** It sounds like you're learning how ideals can collide with reality — particularly political reality.

**Albert:** Exactly. I haven't lost my ideals; I still want freedom and justice. But I'm beginning to realize I cannot give up my honesty or my independent thinking, even for a cause I believe in. If I see something isn't right — whether done by "our side" or not — I feel I must speak. That doesn't make me popular in political circles. *(He chuckles ruefully.)*

**Germain:** It might not, but it shows integrity. And integrity is rare.

**Albert:** Maybe it comes from you, in part. You taught me to think for myself, to never accept injustice as normal. That stays with me.

**Germain:** *(smiling)* I'm glad some of what I taught stuck. Though you've far surpassed the simple lessons of primary school, Albert. You're tackling life's hardest questions now, and I'm very proud of how you're handling them.

**Albert:** *(meeting Germain's eyes earnestly)* I wanted to tell you... you have been in my thoughts so often. When I was ill, I remembered lessons from this very room. Not just facts, but values. Like when you read us the fable about the oak and the reed — how the reed survives by bending. I thought about that: whether to bend with fate or stand firm. It gave me

44

comfort somehow, recalling those old stories and your voice reading them.

**Germain:** I'm touched that you remembered. Though if I recall, at the time you argued that one could be like an olive tree — both strong and flexible. *(laughs)* Even as a child, you debated me.

**Albert:** *(laughs as well)* Guilty. I suppose that was a hint of my future self.

**Germain:** And now, having faced a storm, did you bend or stand firm?

**Albert:** I think I did both. I endured the illness — bending in the sense of accepting what I could not change. But I also stood firm in my will to live and in holding onto my values. I refused to surrender to despair. Perhaps the olive tree was a good analogy after all.

**Germain:** Indeed. Olive trees are native to our land — they belong in harsh sun and poor soil, yet they live long and bear fruit. There's a fitting metaphor for you: from rocky ground, a strong tree grows. You came from a very modest, rocky ground, and look at you now.

**Albert:** *(with warmth)* Whatever I've grown into, you watered the seed, Monsieur Germain. Without the education you gave me, and the confidence you instilled, I might never have risen above any of the hardship.

**Germain:** *(waves a hand modestly)* You give me too much credit. I opened a door, yes, but you walked through it. Many students have had the same door opened; not all step through as boldly as you did.

**Albert:** Still, I want you to know how much it mattered. I remember you convincing Grandmother to let me continue school, promising her I'd get a good job one day because of it. If you hadn't done that... I'd likely be shining shoes or hauling crates on the dock right now, not finishing my studies.

**Germain:** There is great dignity in shining shoes or hauling crates — honest labor is honorable. But I knew that wasn't your path. Your talents were elsewhere. And selfishly, I wanted the world to benefit from them. It would have been a loss for you to stop learning so young.

**Albert:** You believed in me more than I did in myself at times. *(His eyes moisten slightly.)* That kind of belief... it's like a gift not even a lifetime can repay. But I intend to try.

**Germain:** *(quietly, touched)* You owe me nothing, Albert. Seeing you become the man you are is my reward. Teachers live for moments like this — for a student to return and say, "I remember what you taught me, and it helped me."

**Albert:** Then allow me to give you that: everything you taught me **did** help. It wasn't just the history dates or the grammar. It was the ideals, the sense of right and wrong you subtly wove into lessons. The patience you showed, the fairness in how you treated us — that educated my heart as much as school educated my mind.

**Germain:** *(his voice gets a bit unsteady with emotion)* Thank you. I couldn't ask for a more gratifying affirmation.

**Albert:** *(smiles, blinking away a tear)* I actually have a small token for you. *(He reaches into his satchel and pulls out a thin, well-worn book.)* This is a book of essays I've been working on — my own writing. It's not formally published yet, just some pages I bound together. But I wanted you to have the first copy, so to speak.

**Germain:** *(takes the booklet reverently)* Your own writing…
*"L'Envers et l'Endroit"* — "Betwixt and Between." You wrote
this?

**Albert:** Yes. It's a collection of reflections — some on my
childhood, on Algiers, on life and people I've met. The title is
meant to capture that feeling of being caught between two
worlds or two states of being — something I've felt often. It's
not much, but…

**Germain:** It's wonderful. I am honored, truly. I will read it
with great interest — every word. *(He flips through a few pages, then
looks up.)* Already I see a piece titled "Between yes and no."
Intriguing.

**Albert:** That one…I wrote that one when I was convalescing.
It's about oscillating between despair and hope — between
saying yes to life and no to it. A feeling I think many experience
at some point.

**Germain:** I suspect it will resonate with me. Perhaps I'll even
share a selection with the older students if you permit. They
might find inspiration knowing it was written by someone who
sat in these same desks.

**Albert:** Of course, if you think it useful. I only worry it might
be a bit heavy for them — I did pour a lot of serious thought
into those pages.

**Germain:** Children can surprise us with what they grasp,
especially when it's heartfelt. And everything you've ever done
has been heartfelt. *(He sets the book gently on his desk.)*

And what about now? You went on to the lycée, of course —
did you continue to the university?

**Albert:** Yes. In fact, I've already started attending some classes at the University of Algiers, when I feel well enough. I've been drawn to philosophy. I want to understand more systematically these questions of meaning and ethics that life has thrown at me.

**Germain:** Philosophy! I might have guessed. *(laughs)* The boy who questioned the meaning of justice at age ten is now formally pursuing answers. That suits you.

**Albert:** I hope to become a writer or a teacher, maybe both. Though with my health, teaching might be difficult — I've been told the state is hesitant to hire someone with a chronic illness.

**Germain:** *(frowns)* I should hope that's not true. But even if it is, do not be discouraged. If one door closes, another opens. You have a talent with words — perhaps writing will be your true vocation.

**Albert:** Perhaps. I do feel alive when I write, like I'm doing something that matters. And through writing, I can reach people beyond the classroom. I can speak about Algeria, about people like Maman or Uncle Gustave, about the sun and the sea and what they mean to a life. There's so much I want to share with the world.

**Germain:** And the world will be richer for it, I've no doubt. *(He pauses, choosing his words carefully.)* The themes you mentioned — beauty of the sun and sea, simple people, justice — they remind me of something. Do you know, when I read the newspapers and see how dark and violent the times are becoming — Europe is in turmoil, wars and conflicts brewing — I often think voices like yours are needed. Voices that remind us of basic goodness, of clarity and honesty.

**Albert:** The times are troubled, yes. I worry too. It feels as if a great storm is on the horizon. That's partly why I feel urgency to define my values and speak them. We may all be tested in the years to come.

**Germain:** If that happens, hold on to what you believe. I have a feeling you'll be a moral compass for others around you. You always were, in small ways, even here as a child.

**Albert:** I'll try. Though I'm just one man. But perhaps one man's voice can influence another, and that one another, and so on. Like passing a flame.

**Germain:** Exactly. A candle loses nothing by lighting another candle, and the world gets a bit more light. *(He smiles warmly.)*

Before you go, there's something I want to give you as well. *(He opens a drawer and pulls out an old fountain pen.)* This was my pen when I attended the teacher's college. I wrote many an exam with it. I'd like you to have it.

**Albert:** *(surprised and moved)* Your pen? But, Monsieur, that's a keepsake…

**Germain:** And I am keeping it — just in different hands. *(He presses it into Albert's palm.)* I want you to use it for your own writing. Think of it as a small symbol that I have faith in the words you will write and the lessons you will teach, whether in books or in life.

**Albert:** *(closes his fingers around the pen carefully)* I… I don't know what to say. Thank you. I'll cherish it. Every time I write with it, I'll think of what you've taught me.

**Germain:** That is thanks enough.

**Albert:** *(after a quiet moment, filled with emotion)* You know, when I was in that sickbed, I promised myself something if I recovered: I promised to thank the people who have shaped me. You, Monsieur Germain, were top of that list. I even started drafting a letter, but now I get to tell you in person. *(He takes a steadying breath.)* Thank you for giving a poor child a chance. Thank you for showing me what a true educator and a true human being looks like. Without your guidance, I truly believe I wouldn't be alive — at least not living a life of the mind and heart, as I am now.

**Germain:** *(by now visibly moved, his voice husky)* It has been one of the great privileges of my life to see you blossom, Albert. You always had it in you; I just cleared a bit of the path. And hearing this from you… well, it means more than any award or recognition I could ever receive. It's why I became a teacher.

**Albert:** *(smiling with tears in his eyes)* If I ever do become a teacher, I hope I can impact one student's life the way you did mine.

**Germain:** I suspect you'll impact many more than one, whether as a teacher, writer, or simply as the person you are. *(He stands, and Albert follows suit.)*

Look at us — both getting teary in a schoolhouse after hours. *(He chuckles, wiping his eye.)* The new pupils will be arriving in the morning, bright and boisterous, and here we are reminiscing.

**Albert:** Let them come — I think we've earned a few tears of happiness.

**Germain:** Indeed.

**Albert:** I should be going. I don't want to keep you from your evening. Maman will be expecting me too.

**Germain:** Of course. Give your mother my regards, please. She must be very proud of you.

**Albert:** I will. She doesn't say it, but I think she is. She sees me reading or writing late at night and just pats my shoulder with a little smile. That's how she shows it.

**Germain:** Her way may be quiet, but the love is loud if you know how to hear it.

**Albert:** I've learned to hear it. *(He moves toward the door, then turns one last time to his teacher.)* Will I see you again soon?

**Germain:** My door is always open to you, Albert. Come whenever you like — whether to talk about ideas or just to say hello. And I expect updates on your studies and your writing!

**Albert:** *(laughs lightly)* You'll have them. Perhaps I can even sit in the back of class one day and watch you teach — relive a bit of those early days.

**Germain:** You'd be welcome, though I warn you, you might get roped into helping me with a lesson or two. The children would be amazed to meet a big lycée student or an author.

**Albert:** I'd be delighted to, actually.

**Germain:** Very well. We'll arrange it. But for now, go home and get some rest. You still need to take care of your health.

**Albert:** I will. *(He steps out into the doorway. The evening sky outside is painted with the colors of sunset.)* Oh, look at that sky, sir — orange and red. It's going to be a fine night.

**Germain:** *(joining him at the threshold, gazing up)* Beautiful, isn't it? Even the end of day has its grandeur.

**Albert:** *(quietly)* Especially the end of the day, perhaps. It reminds us that something lovely can come after a long, hard daylight.

**Germain:** And the dawn will come again. There's always a new morning.

**Albert:** Always a new morning... yes. *(He holds out his hand again.)* Goodbye, Monsieur Germain. And thank you, once more, for everything.

**Germain:** Goodbye, Albert. And thank **you** — for giving meaning to my efforts. Take care, my boy.

**Albert:** *(with a hopeful smile)* I'll do my best.

---

*They part as the Algerian sun sets, the teacher watching the young man stride away with renewed strength. In the gentle twilight, both feel the glow of gratitude and purpose — the first fire of youth now tempered, but burning ever more steadily as night falls and the future beckons.*

---

# Part II:
# La Résistance

# Chapter 5
## The Knock at the Door

---

*Paris, winter 1943. In a tiny Left Bank apartment, shadows dance in candlelight against peeling wallpaper. Outside, the Occupation's curfew hushes the streets. Inside, Albert Camus sits at a rickety table, the air thick with the smell of damp stone and fear. A sudden knock breaks the silence — urgent, muffled. In this dark hush of wartime, each knock at the door carries the weight of fate.*

---

**Camus:** (standing slowly, whispering to himself) *Who... at this hour?* (He approaches the door, voice low) Who is it?

**Pia:** (hoarse whisper from the other side) It's Pascal. Open up, Albert.

**Camus:** (exhales in relief, unbolting the door) Pascal. (He ushers him in and quickly shuts the door) You gave me a scare.

**Pia:** (eyes alert behind round spectacles) Sorry. There was no other way – I had to come. (He removes a damp coat) The police picked up two of our guys distributing *Combat* last night. They're interrogating... (voice tight) We have to assume they know something.

**Camus:** (jaw clenches) Who was taken?

**Pia:** Jean and Maurice. They knew the risks. But now *we* must be careful. If the Gestapo follows any trail here... (He glances at the tiny flat, the scattered papers) Perhaps you shouldn't stay here much longer.

**Camus:** (quiet resolve) I've already moved twice this year. I won't run again unless it's critical.

**Pia:** (placing a hand on Camus' shoulder) Critical is precisely the word. A single knock at the wrong time – and it's over. We can't court fate.

**Camus:** (nods, then forces a thin smile) You look exhausted. Sit, Pascal. (They both sit at the small table. Camus pours a bit of leftover coffee from a pot on a stove) It's not hot, but it's coffee of a kind.

**Pia:** Merci. (He wraps his hands around the cup) Cold or not, it's a luxury these days.

**Camus:** (studies Pia's face in the candle glow) Did anyone follow you?

**Pia:** I took the long route, doubled back twice. No one, I'm sure.

**Camus:** Good. (He glances towards the single window, which is covered tightly with a blanket to prevent light from escaping) I sometimes feel I'm being suffocated by all this caution and darkness. But then I remind myself — better a suffocating silence than *their* boots at the door.

**Pia:** The silence outside is deadly, yes. (He stirs the coffee absently) You know, earlier tonight I passed a neighbor in the stairwell. I nodded, he said nothing. Just lowered his eyes. Everyone's afraid to speak, to even look at each other.

**Camus:** (bitterly) Fear has stifled this whole city. That's what they want. The danger is that in our silence, we become accomplices to our own oppression. If we say nothing, if we do nothing, we *agree* by default.

**Pia:** (sighs) Many tell themselves staying quiet keeps them safe. But it's a false safety. Safer for whom? Certainly not for those already dragged from their homes. Not for Jean and Maurice now.

**Camus:** Exactly. If everyone stays mute, the injustice becomes normal. I cannot accept that. I won't. (His voice low but fervent) There's a moral peril in silence. Every minute one remains silent in the face of evil, one *feeds* that evil.

**Pia:** You sound like the editorial you wrote last week – the one we printed on page one. *"Your silence will not save you,"* remember?

**Camus:** (manages a small chuckle) Perhaps I do repeat myself. But only because it's true. Silence does not save – it kills. It kills hope, it kills truth… and finally it kills people.

**Pia:** (nodding) That's why you're here with us. Why you came to Occupied Paris when you could have stayed in Algeria, safe.

**Camus:** (fingers drumming on the table) Safe… I have friends who told me I was a fool to come. With my health, especially. (He coughs faintly as if on cue, then smiles wryly) But how could I stay away? To be safe and silent while others fight and die — no, that would be a living death for me.

**Pia:** (gently) Francine worried about you. She wrote me once, asking me to look after you.

**Camus:** (eyes softening at his wife's name) I know. She wanted me to remain in Oran with her. But I convinced her that I had to do this – that writing in *Combat* was my way of fighting. She understands, as much as it pains her.

**Pia:** You're doing more than your share. We all admire it. (He squeezes Camus' arm) Still, we can't let admiration make us reckless. If something happened to you… (he trails off)

**Camus:** (smiles faintly) If something happens to me, it happens. Others will carry on. The cause is bigger than any one of us.

**Pia:** True. But some voices are harder to replace. Your pen, Albert – your voice – gives courage to so many. That's why I risked coming. To warn you to be on guard. And also… (he hesitates)

**Camus:** Also?

**Pia:** There's an opportunity. A meeting tomorrow night. Some workers from an underground press in the north are sending a man. He has news – and perhaps needs help. It will be very dangerous for him to travel, and for us to gather. But if we succeed, we might strengthen our network significantly.

**Camus:** (leans forward) What do you need me to do?

**Pia:** Offer your place as the meeting point. Just for a couple of hours. It's safer than a café or the street. Fewer eyes.

**Camus:** (glances around the cramped room) Here?

**Pia:** Yes. I know it's risky. But I thought of you because you live alone and have… a reputation for level-headedness. Others trust you.

**Camus:** (without hesitation) Of course. If you judge it's needed, we'll do it here.

**Pia:** Thank you. (He releases a breath) It will be tomorrow, after midnight. He's coming from Lille by train under a false identity. We'll need to keep watch.

**Camus:** We can take turns at the window. I'll tie back the blanket a crack to see the street. (He stands, peeking through the heavy cloth) If the police come instead of our friend… (He doesn't finish the sentence)

**Pia:** (grimly) If they come, we burn any documents and go out the back roof, if possible. But let's hope it doesn't come to that.

**Camus:** (still at the window, gazing at the dark city beyond) Pascal... do you ever feel guilty?

**Pia:** Guilty? For what?

**Camus:** For being alive, when so many others are suffering or gone. Sometimes I lie awake at night and feel this heavy guilt that I'm here, breathing, relatively free – while others rot in camps or die in front of firing squads. (His voice falters) I wonder, why them and not me?

**Pia:** (quietly) Survivor's guilt, they call it. Yes, I feel it too at times. René... (he swallows; Camus turns to look at him) René Leynaud told me once that he felt guilty just for having a warm meal when others starved.

**Camus:** (soft concern) He still carries that guilt. And yet he never hesitates to risk himself.

**Pia:** (nods) René's been taking more and more risks lately. His name's been mentioned by contacts in Lyon. He's walking a narrow edge.

**Camus:** (his voice darkens) A poet with a pistol and a conscience — that's always a dangerous combination.

**Pia:** (softly) Of course. Hope is also a weapon.

(They share a somber silence. The candle flame gutters slightly as a draft sneaks under the door.)

**Camus:** (suddenly, with force) This is why I despise them – the ones who did this to our friends, to our country. They claim to love their nation, but they've buried it in fear and blood. (His eyes blaze) I told a *German friend* once, before the war, that I wanted to love my country *and* still love justice. I said I don't want a greatness for France that comes from blood and lies; I want France to flourish only through justice.

**Pia:** (listening intently) You told a German that?

**Camus:** An old friend from student days – he embraced the Nazi creed early. We argued fiercely five years ago, just before the war. He said to me that nothing mattered except the greatness of Germany, that anything was justified for that. I told him "No." I said *some means are inexcusable* and that I refused to subordinate everything to a single end. That's when I began losing him to the madness.

**Pia:** (shakes his head) And what did he say?

**Camus:** He said I didn't love my country enough. Imagine – because I wouldn't condone murder and falsehood, I didn't love France! (Camus' voice drops, pained) Many of us have heard that accusation. But I think *those* who truly love France are precisely the ones willing to criticize her injustices, to hold her to her highest ideals. The ones now risking their lives to save her soul.

**Pia:** (firmly) Indeed. Those men and women the Nazis shoot as "traitors" – they are the true patriots. The ones stood against a wall and shot – they did more for France than a hundred boastful collaborators ever will.

**Camus:** Yes… I told my friend something like that too. That the people he scorned – who *he* would call traitors to the nation – those are the ones who actually saved our nation's honor. I don't loathe any nation as a whole, Pascal; I loathe only the executioners. The ones who make a mockery of love for country by filling it with graves.

**Pia:** (a sad smile) "I loathe none but executioners" – that's precisely how you phrased it in that piece you wrote last month, isn't it?

**Camus:** (nods) It's become a core truth for me. I'll never be an enemy of an entire people – not even the German people. I refuse the trap of hatred by race or nation. Only those who *choose* to be executioners earn my hatred.

**Pia:** And that's what separates us from our enemies, I suppose. They hate by category, by nation or by faith. We fight individuals – the ones who are guilty.

**Camus:** (softly) We hope we can keep that distinction clear. War can blind people. Even us. The longer this goes on, the more I worry about the hatred seeping into our own hearts.

**Pia:** Perhaps. (He drains the last of the cold coffee) But better to have a heart that aches from resisting than one comfortably numb in silence.

**Camus:** (reaches over and grips Pia's arm) Agreed. Better to ache than to be complicit. (He manages a weary grin) We're a fine pair of philosophers plotting rebellion at midnight, aren't we?

**Pia:** (smiles back) I've been called many things, but never a philosopher. That's more *your* territory, Monsieur Camus. I'm just a journalist with a printing press and a stubborn streak.

**Camus:** (teasing) Don't sell yourself short. You taught me half of what I know about writing and rebellion. You gave me my start in Algiers, remember?

**Pia:** True, but you had the fire in you already. I only recognized it. (He pats a stack of papers on the table – a draft of an essay Camus has been writing) What's this?

**Camus:** Oh… notes for something. Possibly an open letter. When I can't shout openly, I write letters I might never send. It helps clarify my mind.

**Pia:** (glances at a line on the page) "*I love my country too much to be a nationalist… I loathe none but executioners*". That's strong.

**Camus:** (shrugs, a bit shyly) Perhaps too strong for now. But someday I want to publish these thoughts. Maybe as letters addressed to that old German friend – even if he'll never read them. It's a way to speak to the enemy's conscience, or at least to affirm my own.

**Pia:** Save them. The war won't last forever. Those words will matter when the guns are silent, maybe even more than now.

**Camus:** (distantly) If we live to see that day...

**Pia:** We will. (He stands) We must. And on that day, we'll need voices like yours. So promise me you'll be careful, Albert. No unnecessary risks. We fight, but we also must survive to tell the tale.

**Camus:** (stands as well, offering his hand solemnly) I promise to be prudent, Pascal. And you – promise me the same.

**Pia:** (shakes his hand firmly) I promise. Neither of us will do France any good dead in a ditch.

**Camus:** Precisely. (He walks Pia to the door) I'll be ready for tomorrow night's meeting. Midnight, yes?

**Pia:** Midnight. I'll bring the man here. Keep the lights low, as now. And if there's trouble —

**Camus:** (finishes calmly) – if there's trouble, we hide what must be hidden and escape how we can. Understood.

**Pia:** Good. Till tomorrow then, my friend. (He opens the door a crack and peers out, then slips into the darkness)

**Camus:** (softly as he departs) Stay safe.

---

*He closes the door quietly, shooting the bolt. For a long moment Camus stands in the silence, the faint gold of the candle dancing in his eyes. He presses his back to the door, listening to his friend's footsteps fade. This time, the knock at the door had brought an ally. But he knows all too well that one night — it could be the enemy. Camus blows out the candle, plunging the room into darkness. In that darkness, he makes a vow: that as long as he has breath and ink, he will not let fear silence him.*

---

# Chapter 6
# The Press Underground

---

*Paris, spring 1944. Beneath a boulangerie long shuttered by war, an old wine cellar serves as a clandestine newsroom. A single oil lamp casts a trembling glow over the faces of the Resistance journalists gathered around a battered table. The walls are lined with stacks of paper and ink pots; a small foot-pedal printing press lurks in the corner. In this cramped, smoke-tinged cellar, truth itself is being distilled and set to print, under constant threat of discovery.*

---

**Camus:** (leaning over a typeset tray, sleeves rolled) The headline should read *"A Glimmer in the Dark"*. That will give people hope.

**Jacques:** (a younger man operating the small press) Hope, yes… but should we really print the entire story about the prison camp escape? If the facts are wrong or exaggerated, it could backfire.

**Pia:** (peering at the hand-written draft) The facts come from eyewitnesses, Jacques. Two managed to break out near Compiègne and made it to our network. We corroborated what we could.

**Jacques:** (worried) The part about the conditions in the camp – it's horrifying. Starvation, torture… (he swallows) If we print all that, people might despair or think we're making it up as propaganda.

**Camus:** (looks up sharply) *Making it up?* We are *not* propagandists; we're journalists – even if underground. If horror is the truth, we print it. The people have a right to know what the Vichy and German liars hide.

**Pia:** (nods firmly) To write honestly is itself an act of resistance, Jacques. Under a totalitarian regime, telling the truth is counter-propaganda. Every fact we print is a bullet in the heart of their lies.

**Jacques:** I understand. It's just… I want to keep morale up. Sometimes a comforting lie seems kinder than the naked truth.

**Camus:** No. That's the trap tyranny sets – that we should lie for a *good* cause. But lies, even well-intentioned, only serve the powerful in the end. We will not become like the enemy by adopting their methods.

**Pia:** (with a thin smile) Remember what we used to say at the start: *"We will try to make a reasonable newspaper. And as the world is absurd, it will fail."* (He chuckles softly)

**Camus:** (laughs under his breath) You said that, Pascal – on the very first night we set type for *Combat.* I thought, "What a curious motto." A reasonable paper in an absurd world.

**Pia:** And indeed, many times we nearly failed. But we're still here, absurdly, reasonably.

**Jacques:** (grins despite himself) I do recall our first issue's press run – barely a few hundred copies, hand-cranked quietly so the neighbors wouldn't hear the press clatter.

**Camus:** Yes. And now, how many? A few thousand printed and distributed in secret. Passed hand to hand in cafés, slipped under doors at dawn. We've grown, and so has our responsibility.

**Jacques:** Responsibility... (he rubs ink-stained hands on his trousers) That's what weighs on me. People trust *Combat* now. They trust *us*. We can't mislead them.

**Camus:** Exactly why we must hold ourselves to the highest standard of truth. Even in war.

**Pia:** Especially in war. You're right, Albert. War is when truth is needed most – and most endangered. We have to be the mirror held up to reality, however dark, so that our people see and understand.

**Jacques:** (quietly) The BBC broadcasts sometimes embellish news to keep hope alive... exaggerating enemy losses, omitting Allied setbacks. Should we not do the same? To keep hope alive?

**Camus:** I've thought about that. (He rubs his brow, choosing words) It's true, unvarnished truth can be hard to swallow. But consider: if we lie *now*, even for morale, we become what we oppose. We would be arrogantly assuming that people can't handle reality and need pretty tales. No – I believe the French can handle hard truths *and* still hope. In fact, real hope must be built on truth, or it's false hope.

**Pia:** And false hope, once shattered, leads to despair.

**Jacques:** (slowly nodding) You're right. If our readers found out we'd lied... they would feel betrayed, just as we feel by Vichy's lies.

**Camus:** Precisely. Better to tell the bitter truth than sugarcoat it with lies. Our readers, our fellow citizens, they've been lied to enough by Marshal Pétain's propaganda and Nazi broadcasts. We must be different.

**Pia:** (with a twinkle) Albert, you sound ready to pen another editorial on the ethics of journalism.

**Camus:** (smiles lightly) Perhaps I will. Once tonight's edition is done. (He picks up a proof page) Let's see… I also included a short piece here on the ethical danger of silence. The notion that remaining silent now is a form of complicity. We touched on that in Chapter 1's conversation.

**Jacques:** Ah, your essay "Neither Victims nor Executioners" idea in embryo?

**Camus:** (surprised laugh) That's not written yet! But yes, I've been sketching those thoughts in my notebook. The seed of it is here: we can neither accept being passive victims nor turn into ruthless executioners. Neither one. So I argue that choosing silence in the face of fascism is to side with the executioner, by default.

**Jacques:** Strong, but fair. Silence is what they count on – that good people will do nothing.

**Pia:** And many do stay silent, out of fear or fatigue. Our job is to prick their conscience a bit, stir them.

**Camus:** Exactly. Not with condemnation, but with a reminder that everyone has a choice, even under terror. (He looks at the draft) I wrote: *"Yes, we must raise our voices. Up to this point, we have refrained from speaking the whole truth, lulled by false hopes. But every day of silence is a day of consent. The time for measured words is past – now each of us must choose: to speak and so resist, or to be silent and thereby consent."*

**Jacques:** (whistles softly) That will certainly *stir*, Albert.

Pia: It might even anger some readers – those who haven't yet found courage to do more than listen.

**Camus:** Perhaps. But maybe it will also embolden them. In my experience, people feel relief when someone finally says aloud what they secretly know to be true. The truth takes away illusions and replaces them with clarity. And clarity, even if harsh, can inspire action.

**Pia:** Well said. And indeed the truth is our weapon. As someone noted, dictatorships fear honest words like they fear the plague. Our task is to expose what they hide, to let light into their dark chambers of lies.

**Jacques:** You've certainly given me courage tonight. (He sets a fresh sheet onto the press) I'll print every word, then. The ugly truth about the camp, the story of the escape, your editorial – all of it.

**Camus:** Good. And one more thing – Pascal, did you set Sartre's piece into type yet?

**Pia:** (tapping a small stack of papers) Here. Jean-Paul's article arrived by courier this afternoon. It's short but pointed.

**Jacques:** Sartre... the playwright? He's writing for us now?

**Pia:** Occasionally. Under a pseudonym. He's contributed a vivid account of Paris under Occupation – though we have to edit out a few philosophical flourishes to make it fit the column space.

**Camus:** (smiling) Jean-Paul can never resist a little philosophizing. Even in a war report.

**Jacques:** It's good to have him on board. People respect his name – even if they don't see it printed, word will get around that minds like Sartre's stand with the Resistance.

**Camus:** Yes. And after the liberation, such voices will shape the intellectual climate of France. We'll need honest debate in the open then. But for now, we all toil in the dark, unnamed.

**Pia:** (rubbing ink on his fingers) Speaking of toiling — let's finish in time for distribution at dawn. Paper rationing means we have to be sparing. Jacques, how many pages can we do?

**Jacques:** Four pages at most, given our paper stack and ink.

**Camus:** (checking his list) That covers the camp story, a piece on last week's rail sabotage success, the usual notices from Free France in London, Pascal's editorial cartoon —

**Jacques:** (grins) Ah yes, the little drawing of Hitler being strangled by Marianne. It's bold.

**Pia:** (with a mischievous smile) Sometimes a cartoon says what an essay cannot. And the enemy doesn't read our underground paper to be offended. The readers will enjoy a bit of satirical vengeance.

**Camus:** As long as it's clear our real vengeance is *justice*, not cruelty. (He stretches his back; the lamp light flickers over his tired face) I often wonder, how to balance the tone — between rallying people's anger and guiding their conscience. We have to inspire outrage at evil without unleashing blind hatred that could turn into new evils.

**Pia:** That *is* a fine line. We want people angry enough to resist, but not to become mobs of revenge. Perhaps that's something to address when the time comes — if we win.

**Jacques:** When we win. (He smiles hopefully) I like to say *when*. Even if it's far off.

**Camus:** *When* we win, indeed. (He returns Jacques's smile) And when that day comes, I hope our newspaper can come into the sunlight and still speak the truth, even to our own side.

**Pia:** That will be crucial. A free France will still need the truth — perhaps even more, since power will tempt even the liberators.

**Camus:** (remembering) There's a line I recall from earlier in the war: be wary of those who shout loudest about democracy and liberty, while using fear to silence others. We must hold even our allies to account.

**Pia:** You wrote that down from de Gaulle's broadcast, didn't you?

**Camus:** Actually, I believe it was something I read that resonated… (he flips through a small notebook, then quotes) *"Be suspicious of those who speak the loudest in defense of noble ideals, but whose goal is to instill fear and silence dissent."* It's a reminder that even after the Nazis, other tyrannies can rise — sometimes in the guise of virtue.

**Jacques:** (frowning) You mean the Communists? Some in the Resistance already talk like they'll settle scores harshly and seize power for their party.

**Pia:** We hear things. Once the Boche are gone, the factions may well quarrel. Camus is right — the fight for truth won't end with liberation.

**Camus:** (with quiet determination) And we'll be here for that fight too, if we survive this one. But one battle at a time. Tonight, we fight by printing the truth. No more, no less.

**Jacques:** (sets the type and locks it in the press) Ready to print, then. Shall I begin?

**Camus:** Yes. Let's bring these words to life.

**Pia:** (moving to dim the lamp slightly) Gently on the press, Jacques. We can't have the noise echoing through the sewer tunnels.

**Jacques:** (nods and begins pedaling, the machine clacking in a muffled rhythm) I know, I know – like a mouse printing a newspaper, not an elephant.

**Camus:** (laughs softly, keeping an ear out) If an elephant printed, the whole neighborhood would know.

(They work in concerted silence for a few minutes, the only sounds the soft *chick-chick-chick* of the press and the rustle of fresh-printed pages being laid out to dry. Camus feeds paper into the machine, Jacques pedals, Pia collects pages.)

**Pia:** (whispers, smiling at the first printed page) Look at that. Black ink on white paper – our ammunition. Still warm.

**Camus:** (quietly proud) And there at the top: *A Glimmer in the Dark*. Let it reach whoever needs a glimmer tonight.

**Jacques:** (holds up a sheet, reading a line) "*To write honestly is to uncover what is hidden.*" I think that's your line, Camus?

**Camus:** (modestly) Perhaps. It's what I believe: that every honest word we print is a little act of rebellion, a little piece of freedom. In a dictatorship of lies, telling the truth is a revolutionary act.

**Pia:** Well, comrade revolutionaries, I'll start bundling these for delivery. (He starts stacking the drying pages carefully)

**Camus:** Pierre will come at dawn for the bundle, as usual?

**Pia:** Yes, he'll bicycle them to the cafés and news-drops. By eight in the morning, Parisians will be quietly sharing these pages, reading them behind drawn curtains, on park benches, even sneaking them into factory floors.

**Jacques:** (a fond smile) I once saw an old man read our *Combat* in public, sitting by the Seine as if it were *Le Figaro*. Bold as anything. I nearly ran to him to warn him, but he caught my eye and gave a little nod… He knew the danger, but he read on calmly. That nod said, "Thank you for this."

**Camus:** (eyes shining) Those moments make it worth it, don't they? To know that our clandestine work gives courage to someone, even one solitary reader by the river.

**Pia:** They also remind us to be careful. If a milicien or German had seen him, he'd be jailed or shot for possessing our paper.

**Jacques:** I sometimes forget how much risk the readers take, too. It's not just us.

**Camus:** We're all in this together – writers, couriers, readers. All risking the knock on the door at midnight. (He lowers his voice) That knowledge… it binds us in solidarity, and also in obligation. We owe them nothing short of the truth.

**Pia:** And a bit of hope where we can. But real hope, grounded in reality.

**Camus:** Yes. Hope as strong as our ink and as honest as our word.

**Jacques:** (smiles) That should be our new motto.

**Pia:** (grinning) Perhaps for the masthead of our first legal issue, once we're free: "Honest words, strong hope."

**Camus:** (returns the smile) I'll drink to that when the day comes. In the meantime… (he holds up an freshly printed page, still damp, and reads softly) "*Citizens of France, ten of your brothers escaped the darkness of a camp and brought us the truth of its horror. That truth is their weapon and ours. Do not be afraid of it. Let it strengthen your resolve.*"

**Jacques:** That's powerful.

**Camus:** (lays the page down) If even one person reads that and decides to act – to hide a fugitive, to sabotage a rail line, to simply refuse an order – then we have done our job.

**Pia:** We do our job, and each awakened conscience does theirs. Thus, piece by piece, the wall of silence cracks.

**Jacques:** Until one day, it shatters entirely.

**Camus:** (with conviction) It will. Perhaps sooner than we think. Until then, we'll keep printing in the dark.

**Pia:** In the dark, for the light. (He ties the finished stack of papers into a bundle with twine) There. Tomorrow's edition of *Combat* is born.

**Jacques:** (listening intently) I hear footsteps above... could be Pierre, early?

**Camus:** (blows out the lamp, plunging them into near-darkness lit only by embers of a cigarette) Shh.

(All three freeze, hearts pounding. The footsteps above recede – likely just a passerby or a tenant upstairs. They exhale.)

**Pia:** (relights the lamp halfway) Just someone on the street. (He glances at his watch) Almost 5 AM. Pierre will be here soon. Let's get this upstairs carefully.

**Camus:** I'll help you carry. (He gently lifts the bundle) Jacques, can you manage the lamp and to lock up after?

**Jacques:** Of course.

(They gather their tools, concealing evidence of the night's work. One by one, they ascend the narrow stairs from the cellar into pre-dawn gloom.)

**Pia:** (whispering as they climb) One day, we won't have to meet like this, hide like criminals for printing truth.

**Camus:** (softly) One day, we'll shout the truth from the rooftops in broad daylight.

**Jacques:** May that day come soon. (He carefully shuts the cellar door behind them and covers it with a false shelf)

**Pia:** It will. And if our words have any say in it, perhaps a little sooner.

**Camus:** (placing a hand on Pia's shoulder as the first grey hint of dawn seeps under the door) Courage. The night is nearly over – in more ways than one.

---

*They share a determined glance. In the silence, the printing press sits ink-stained and silent in the darkness below, having done its duty. Soon, all across the city, thin sheaves of clandestine newsprint will find their way into longing hands. The truth, painstakingly printed by night, will spark courage by daybreak.*

---

# Chapter 7
## Letters to the Unforgiven

---

*Lyon, winter, early 1944. Rain pelts the window of a cramped garret room overlooking the Rhône. Inside, by the light of a single lantern, two friends sit on the floor amid scattered pages and an old revolver. The city is tense under tightening German occupation, but in this small sanctuary, ideas and camaraderie flicker against the encroaching darkness. Albert Camus, on a rare journey outside Paris, has sought refuge with René Leynaud – poet, journalist, and Résistance member. Tonight, they speak in hushed tones that carry the weight of impending fate.*

---

**Leynaud:** (gazing at a half-written letter in Camus' hands) So you *are* going to write to him.

**Camus:** (nods, leaning against the foot of the bed) I already have, in a way. This is my third draft of a letter I'll never mail.

**Leynaud:** To that German friend of yours?

**Camus:** (smiles sadly) To the idea of him, at least. I doubt the actual man – Franz was his name – is anywhere I could reach. He might be in Russia with the Wehrmacht, or dead for all I know. But I write as if to him. It helps clarify my thoughts about this war.

**Leynaud:** May I? (He gestures to the pages)

**Camus:** Of course. (He hands them over)

**Leynaud:** (holds the pages up to the lantern light and reads softly) *"You used to say to me, 'The greatness of my country has no price... those who find meaning in the destiny of our nation must sacrifice* *everything for it.' I loved you then, but already I was distancing myself. I told you, 'No. Some means are inexcusable. I would like to love my country and still love justice. I don't want a greatness for France born of blood and falsehood. Only through upholding justice do I want my country to flourish.'"*

(Leynaud lowers the page, eyes shining.) Mon Dieu, Albert – you wrote that?

**Camus:** (quietly) It's what I told him five years ago, in 1939, before war broke out. Word for word, nearly. And I'm writing it now so I never forget why we chose this path.

**Leynaud:** "Love my country and still love justice" – that's a beautiful creed. And the only one that makes sense to me too.

**Camus:** (runs a hand through his hair) He accused me of not loving France because I wouldn't put France above moral law. To him, worship of country was absolute, even if it meant trampling truth or lives. I couldn't agree – which to him meant I was a traitor of sorts.

**Leynaud:** So many thought like him in Germany. And so many think like that in every nation – that patriotism means turning a blind eye to evil done in your nation's name.

**Camus:** Exactly. But real patriotism, in my view, is loving your country enough to speak out when it's wrong. To hold it to its best self, not indulge its worst.

**Leynaud:** (nods thoughtfully) You know, that is what we all did, in our own way. We said *no* when everyone else shouted *yes* to Pétain and Hitler. Some call us traitors to France, but we believe we're trying to save France's honor.

**Camus:** We are. Those who fight tyranny from within their own nation – they are the bravest patriots. As I wrote in that letter: *those men who, in your opinion, did not love their country, did more for it than you will ever do for yours.* I meant every word.

**Leynaud:** (smiles) That will make a stirring passage when these letters of yours see the light of day.

**Camus:** If they do. I sometimes doubt I'll ever publish them. Perhaps after victory – if I'm alive – I might.

**Leynaud:** You must. People should read this kind of honest reckoning. God knows after the war there will be a flood of lies about who did what and why. Your letters could stand as a truthful testimony of conscience.

**Camus:** (shrugs lightly) Maybe. Honestly, I write them also to keep myself sane. It's a conversation – even if one-sided – with someone I once cared for, who became ideological enemy. It helps me articulate why I fight, beyond just anger.

**Leynaud:** (continues reading another excerpt) *"I loathe none but executioners."* I like that line immensely.

**Camus:** (softly) I wanted to be clear that I do not hate Germans as a people. I hate the murderers, the fanatics – the executioners of any nation.

**Leynaud:** That distinction is crucial. Hatred without distinction is what got us here – the Nazis hate all Jews, all "inferior" peoples, indiscriminately. We must never mirror that.

**Camus:** Exactly. I refuse to become what I oppose. If I started hating every German, I'd be surrendering to the same moral poison. And then all this suffering will have taught us nothing.

**Leynaud:** (a shadow crosses his face) Not everyone in the Resistance sees it that way, though. There are those among us who *do* hate every German, every collaborator, with a passion that worries me. After the war… I fear how far their vengeance might go.

**Camus:** I share that fear. I've been thinking a lot about measured justice versus raw revenge. When France is free, we'll have to hold traitors accountable – yes. But how, without losing our own soul?

**Leynaud:** (looks at Camus keenly) You already have ideas about that, don't you?

**Camus:** (hesitates, then speaks) I believe in justice under law, not mob violence. Even for those who have done monstrous things. If we start executing people in a frenzy, summarily, we continue the cycle of violence. We must punish, but not out of blind hatred.

**Leynaud:** (sighs) It will be hard. Some comrades saw their families shot or sent to camps because of informers. I suspect forgiveness will be in short supply.

**Camus:** Forgiveness… (he gazes at the raindrops trailing down the window) Do you think we'll ever be able to forgive? The Germans, the collaborators – all of them?

**Leynaud:** (quiet for a moment, the lantern light carving gentle hollows on his face) As a Christian, I'm taught to forgive. But as a man who has seen what I've seen… I admit, I struggle with it. I can forgive weakness, even cowardice perhaps. But deliberate cruelty? The ones who tortured my friends… (he shakes his head) That, I cannot forgive. At least not now.

**Camus:** I feel the same. There are crimes for which I believe forgiveness isn't ours to give. Perhaps only God, if He exists, can forgive such things. For us, we must simply refuse to excuse them.

**Leynaud:** And that's alright. Maybe "forgive" is the wrong word. Maybe "move forward without hatred" is better. For our own sake.

**Camus:** Yes. Letting go of hatred eventually, so it doesn't corrode us – that's different from pardoning the guilty outright. We can remember without animosity, perhaps, someday.

**Leynaud:** You call this chapter "Letters to the Unforgiven" – are the "unforgiven" those executioners, the fascists, in your mind?

**Camus:** That title came to me thinking of those like my German friend – people who embraced something I can never excuse. I write these letters to him, but I know I cannot truly forgive what he stood for. These letters, in a sense, are my attempt to reach out and also to pronounce judgment. A paradox, I know.

**Leynaud:** Not entirely. You can reach out to explain your truth without absolving his sin. That's what you're doing.

**Camus:** (smiles gratefully) Thank you, René. You always help me untangle my moral knots.

**Leynaud:** (pats Camus' hand) That's what poet-journalists are for. Untangling knots with words. (He glances at the messy bundle of handwritten poems and articles in the corner) You know, I've been writing too. Some poems... maybe more feverishly than ever.

**Camus:** I'd love to read them, if you'll share.

**Leynaud:** (rummages and pulls out a thin sheaf of paper) Here. This one I wrote after my last mission smuggling Jews to the Alps. I was so shaken by what I saw – families hiding in barns, children quiet as mice with fear. I had to pour it out.

**Camus:** (takes the pages gently and reads a few lines under his breath) It's powerful, René. Raw and beautiful. The image of "the silent child with war in her eyes" – that pierced me.

**Leynaud:** (voice low) There were many such children. We try to save them, but how to save what's been broken inside them?

**Camus:** Perhaps by ensuring they grow up in a world where truth is cherished, and where adults aren't monsters. That's the only way to heal that inner break – to build a different world.

**Leynaud:** (smiles a little) Listen to us – two young men talking about how to heal the world, while everything's still burning.

**Camus:** (smiling back) Someone has to think of the afterwards, no? Otherwise, all this sacrifice is meaningless. We have to imagine what we're fighting *for*, not just what we're fighting against.

**Leynaud:** And what do you imagine for *après-guerre*, Albert?

**Camus:** (takes a deep breath) Honestly? I imagine a France that has confronted its own failures – the silence, the collaboration – and determined never to fall prey to them again. I imagine a Europe where Germans and French can talk as humans, once the Nazis' ideology is buried, though it feels impossibly distant now. I imagine trying to live without hate.

**Leynaud:** (a soft light in his eyes) A rebel's dream – rebellion not just against an enemy, but against hatred itself.

**Camus:** Yes. Against hatred, against lies. A rebellion for human dignity.

**Leynaud:** (reaches out and squeezes Camus' hand) You must survive this war, mon ami. We need voices like yours when the shooting stops.

**Camus:** (laughs quietly) You sound like Pascal. He made me promise to be careful too.

**Leynaud:** Wise man. Promise me as well.

**Camus:** I… (his voice catches slightly) I promise to try. But you know as well as I, in our work, tomorrow isn't guaranteed.

**Leynaud:** That's why I want your word that you won't take foolish risks.

**Camus:** (smiles ruefully) I'll avoid foolish risks. Only very calculated, absolutely necessary ones.

**Leynaud:** (chuckles) Fair enough.

**Camus:** On one condition: you do the same. I know you're in thicker danger than I – out there in the field more often.

**Leynaud:** (a shadow crosses his face briefly) I'll try. But if a time comes when something *must* be done, I won't shrink from it, even if it's dangerous.

**Camus:** Nor would I ask you to. Just — take care. You're one of the few truly transparent souls I've known. The world needs you after this nightmare.

**Leynaud:** (touched) And it needs you. So let's both make it through, eh?

**Camus:** (softly) Yes. Let's agree on that – rendezvous in Paris, when the city is free. We'll sit at the Café de Flore with Sartre and raise a toast to those who are gone and to the new day.

**Leynaud:** To those who are gone… (he trails off, expression distant)

**Camus:** René?

**Leynaud:** (quietly) Sometimes I feel... I won't see that day. I don't know why. A premonition, maybe. If I don't, Albert, I want you to promise something.

**Camus:** Don't talk like that. Of course you —

**Leynaud:** (insistent) *If* I don't. Promise me you'll write. Keep writing what we believed in. Tell people about friends like... like me, so we're not forgotten or misremembered.

**Camus:** (emotion in his throat) You *will* see the day, René. But... I promise. I'll testify to the truth of men like you. *Truth needs witnesses*, you said that once. You are one of those witnesses. If you cannot speak, I will speak for you.

**Leynaud:** (smiles warmly) Thank you. That eases my mind.

Camus: Let's not sink into gloom. Here – let's finish reading this letter draft. (He takes one page back from Leynaud and reads aloud) *"For five years I have thought of your words – 'You don't love your country.' And I've seen men in France who answered you by deeds, not words. Those men you said did not love their country – they have done more for her than you who proclaimed your love with guns. They conquered something in themselves: their fear, their silence, their resignation. And by that, they became heroes, though you will never know their names."*

**Leynaud:** (listening, eyes shining) That's beautiful. It honors those in the Resistance without bragging.

**Camus:** They deserve more honor than we can ever give. Too many already have been "stood up against the wall facing the twelve little black eyes of German guns," as I put it in another draft. So many good people executed.

**Leynaud:** Did you reference "twelve little black eyes"? (He shivers) That phrase... the muzzles of rifles?

**Camus:** Yes. It's morbid poetry, I suppose, but it stuck in my head. Because our friends who've been shot, that is literally what they faced — twelve rifle barrels, like twelve blind eyes staring at them.

**Leynaud:** (murmurs) I hope if that moment comes for me, I'll face it with courage.

**Camus:** (grips Leynaud's shoulder fiercely) Don't speak of that. I can't bear the thought... (He forces a smile) Let's speak instead of the future. You have a book of poems to publish when this is over. I expect to write a preface for it, if you'll let me.

**Leynaud:** (brightens) I would be honored. Perhaps in that better future, we'll have the freedom to write everything we truly think. No censorship, no need for pseudonyms.

**Camus:** And no need for secret letters to phantoms. (He sets the letter pages aside) Maybe by then I can publish these letters openly, and Franz — if alive — might read them. Even if he never speaks to me, he'll know what I thought.

**Leynaud:** Do you think he would feel remorse, if he read them?

**Camus:** (long pause) I don't know. I doubt the true believers feel remorse. They justify everything. But maybe, if Germany is defeated, some of the spell will break. Maybe he'll be ashamed of what he cheered for.

**Leynaud:** I hope so. Shame is an honest start for the guilty.

**Camus:** And if not — well, then these letters become part of the historical record at least. A warning for future generations about how one retains one's humanity in inhuman times.

**Leynaud:** (chuckles softly) Ever the idealist.

**Camus:** (smiles) Realist, I claim. It's pragmatic to remind people of humanity; otherwise, the next tyranny will find us unprepared.

**Leynaud:** True enough.

(A rumble of thunder outside. The rain intensifies.)

**Camus:** (yawns, suddenly weary) Is it near midnight?

**Leynaud:** Past. Closer to one in the morning. We should rest while we can.

**Camus:** (nods, rubbing his eyes) We've a long journey back tomorrow. Provided the trains run.

**Leynaud:** They often don't, these days. But we'll manage. If needed, I know a farmer with a cart who can take you partway to a safe zone.

**Camus:** You're not coming with me to Paris?

**Leynaud:** (shakes his head) My work keeps me here in Lyon. There's a big operation brewing – I'm in the midst of it. (He smiles reassuringly) But I'll see you in Paris when it's successful.

**Camus:** (concern knitting his brow) Operation? Can you share?

**Leynaud:** (winks) The less you know, the better, in case you're stopped. Just… hold a good thought for us. The next few months are going to be sharp-edged.

**Camus:** (holding Leynaud's gaze) I will. And you – take no unnecessary chances. You promised.

**Leynaud:** (raises three fingers playfully) Scout's honor.

**Camus:** (manages a grin) You were never a scout, René.

**Leynaud:** No, but I can pretend. (He blows out the lantern, plunging the room in darkness except for occasional flashes of lightning backlighting the rain-streaked window) You take the cot; I'll take the floor.

**Camus:** Nonsense, I'll take the floor.

**Leynaud:** You're my guest and you have a long trip tomorrow. The cot, please.

**Camus:** (too tired to argue) Fine. Merci.

(He lies on the narrow cot. Leynaud settles on a blanket on the floor. Silence but for rain.)

**Leynaud:** Albert?

**Camus:** Yes?

**Leynaud:** If... if something happens and I can't write anymore, would you consider writing a short preface for my poems anyway? They're hidden with a friend and will likely be published posthumously if I...

**Camus:** (sits up) René, stop. You'll write your own preface.

**Leynaud:** Humor me.

**Camus:** (voice thick) Yes. If – God forbid – it comes to that, I will make sure your poems see light, with the homage they deserve. But I fully expect to argue with you over every word of that preface in person.

**Leynaud:** (chuckles softly) I look forward to that argument.

**Camus:** (lies back down) Sleep now. We both need a few hours.

**Leynaud:** Bonne nuit, Albert.

**Camus:** Bonne nuit, René.

*They fall silent. Camus closes his eyes, listening to the rhythm of rain. In the darkness, he silently recites a line from his letter — an affirmation against despair: "We are fighting for a certain idea of justice… and even if you cannot understand it, we will show you through our victory that this idea is stronger than your iron cross." He doesn't notice that Leynaud, still awake on the floor, is quietly moving his lips in prayer — a prayer for France, for freedom, and perhaps for the soul of Camus' German friend. The two resistants, a philosopher and a poet, drift into an uneasy sleep as the storm rages. Outside, Lyon's streets glisten, waiting for dawn and whatever fate the coming weeks will bring.*

# Chapter 8
## The Shadow of the Guillotine

*Paris, September 1944. The city has been liberated, bursting into song and gunfire only weeks ago, but now a tense hush hangs in a back room of the Combat newspaper office. The lamps are lit though it's midday, as dark clouds threaten rain. In this dim room, recently used as a makeshift court for collaborators, echoes of shouted accusations still linger. Albert Camus stands by an open window overlooking rain-slick cobblestones, smoking thoughtfully, as Jean-Paul Sartre and a burly Resistance fighter named Bernard argue near a desk piled with files of denunciations. The joy of victory has given way to the grim aftermath – reckoning with those who served the enemy. And the specter of the guillotine hovers over their conversation, a shadow from France's past cast onto its uncertain future.*

**Bernard:** (slamming a folder onto the desk) This one signed dozens of arrest orders for the Gestapo. Dozens! Men, women dragged off because of his pen strokes. If that's not a death warrant for him, what is?

**Sartre:** (calm but firm) Bernard, no one denies his guilt. The question is who decides his fate. A legal court, or a few of us in a back room with a pistol?

**Bernard:** (scowling) Legal court? Half the judges under Vichy were collaborators too! We can't trust the old system. We *are* the justice now – the Resistance, the people. And the people demand blood for blood.

**Camus:** (turning from the window, flicking ash from his cigarette) The people demand justice, Bernard. Not blood for blood like some primitive code. We didn't sacrifice and suffer to institute lynch law in place of Nazi law.

Bernard: (face flushed) With respect, Camus, it's easy for you to preach. You were sheltered in writing and editing. Some of us were out there with guns, seeing our comrades butchered. (He points a finger at Camus) I held a friend as he died, shot by a Milice collaborator. I swore to him I'd make the bastards pay. All of them.

**Camus:** (voice gentle but steely) I also lost friends, Bernard. Some of my closest. One was executed just a few months ago – by the Nazis. Believe me, I know the ache for vengeance. But I also know that making promises to the dead can lead us to cruel places.

**Bernard:** Cruel places? (He laughs harshly) Cruel was the firing squads at Mont Valérien, the torture chambers on Rue Lauriston. We are *mild* in comparison. We're only asking for traitors to face the firing squad themselves. A quick death – far kinder than what they dealt us.

**Sartre:** But who is a traitor, and who decides? These days a personal enemy can be labeled a collaborator just to settle old scores. It's happening already. We must be careful.

**Bernard:** (crossing his arms) Careful? Were they careful when they denounced entire families? When they whipped people in the streets as "examples"? Non! Why should we be any gentler?

**Camus:** (steps closer to Bernard, eyes earnest) Because if we let revenge completely take the wheel, we will become what we hated. The Revolution of 1789 began with high ideals and descended into the Terror. The guillotine worked day and night in the name of Justice – but it was indiscriminate vengeance, much of it.

**Bernard:** You're comparing us to Robespierre now?

**Camus:** I'm warning that we could go down that road if we aren't vigilant. I've been reading history in our downtime. In 1793, they truly believed each execution was purifying society. In the end, they had killed so many that the Revolution devoured itself. I do not want a second Reign of Terror in France.

**Sartre:** Nor do I. We have to found the new France on something better than terror and reprisal.

**Bernard:** (paces angrily) So you'd just let these collaborators go free, then? A slap on the wrist? Prison at most?

**Camus:** (shakes his head) I didn't say that. They must be punished. But punished lawfully, after fair trials, and without torture or summary executions. Some deserve prison, yes. Some perhaps death – but only the truly heinous, and after due process, not a mob's verdict.

**Bernard:** (spits on the floor) Due process – for those who denied it to others? You think giving them a trial makes any difference? They'll get shot either way, at least the worst of them.

**Sartre:** It *does* make a difference. It shows the world, and ourselves, that we are not like the fascists. That we have principles. That we believe in law and reason, not just force.

**Bernard:** (snarls) Principles don't bring back the dead! Was it principle that stayed the hand of the Boche or the Milice? No – only resistance and fear. They feared us, finally, and that's why some ran. I want every remaining collaborator to feel that fear now. To know there's a guillotine or a noose waiting if they ever dare to betray France again.

**Camus:** (sadly) If we rule by fear, we continue the Nazi method under a new banner. That would mean they have *won* in a way, by making us like themselves.

**Bernard:** (points accusingly) Easy words for someone who didn't have to execute a friend turned traitor. Did you? I did, last week. A man from my own resistance network, caught passing information to the Germans in July. We confirmed it, he admitted it sobbing. We took him to an alley... I put a bullet in his skull myself. (His voice breaks slightly) He was my friend, but he had cost lives. I did what had to be done.

(A heavy silence. Camus closes his eyes for a moment.)

**Camus:** I'm sorry, Bernard. That's a terrible burden.

**Bernard:** (defensive) I don't need your pity. He betrayed us. I gave him a quicker death than he gave some of our comrades.

**Sartre:** How do you feel about it, if I may ask?

**Bernard:** (hesitates, anger faltering) How do I feel? I feel... (he rubs his chest) hollow. It had to be done, but it didn't feel like victory.

**Camus:** *"No good is done to men by killing their friends."* Someone wrote that recently.

**Sartre:** (glancing at Camus, recognizing the sentiment) Camus is quoting something – I think from an essay about a friend executed by the Nazis.

**Camus:** Yes. I wrote about my friend René Leynaud, who was shot in June. I said that his death did not make me nobler, it made my revolt blind; that no good is achieved by killing those we love. I must not let myself turn to that – then or now. And I truly believe – no good is achieved by killing at all, if we can find another way.

94

**Bernard:** (whispers) But sometimes there is no other way… is there?

**Camus:** During the fight, maybe not. During the occupation, you had to take that hard action – I understand. War forces those moments. But *now*, now the war here is over. We have options beyond the gun in the alley. We have courts, we have the possibility of deliberation. We must use them, flawed as they are, and improve them rather than bypass them.

**Sartre:** Otherwise, every man becomes judge, jury, and executioner by himself. That way lies anarchy and endless blood feuds.

**Bernard:** So you both believe even the worst collaborator deserves a formal trial?

**Sartre:** Yes. For the worst – say, those who directly committed murder or torture – I won't weep if a court sentences them to death. But it must be a court, not a mob or a rogue band of partisans.

**Camus:** I concur. And I'll add – even as we judge the worst, we should avoid casting too wide a net. Not everyone who worked a low-level Vichy job was a monster. Some were cowards, some just trying to survive. Punish those with bloody hands and those who led others to doom. But we should not execute people merely for having been misled or fearful.

**Bernard:** (scowling) You sound like de Gaulle's people. They're cautioning moderation too. Some even say we should forget and "move on" to unite against communism or some such. I can't stomach that.

**Camus:** I'm not suggesting forgetting or moving on without justice. I'm saying justice, not vengeance. That's harder, in fact, because it means weighing cases individually, resisting the easy satisfaction of lump condemnation.

**Bernard:** Harder – and slower. Meanwhile these traitors walk free, maybe escape.

**Sartre:** Some have already fled, to Spain or hiding in the countryside. But most of the big ones we've caught or they're known. We can afford a bit of deliberation.

**Camus:** Also, consider – if we turn the liberation into a bloodbath, executing people left and right, we will tarnish our own victory. The world will say, "See, the French are killing each other now as savagely as the Nazis did." It will sully the honor we've earned.

**Bernard:** (grudgingly) Perhaps. But frankly, I care less about world opinion and more about avenging my friends.

**Camus:** Bernard – (he steps closer and speaks with intense empathy) – I know how you feel. Truly. When I got word of René's execution, I wanted to *kill.* I wanted to line up every SS officer and collaborator in a square and mow them down. I fantasized about it. (He looks down) Hatred flooded me like a fever.

**Bernard:** (quietly) What did you do with that?

**Camus:** I sat with it. I wrote about it. And I realized if I gave in entirely to that hatred, René's death would end up turning me into something he wouldn't recognize. He once told me about a concept – that we all carry the plague inside us, the germs of violence and hate. And the true struggle is to never let them infect us completely.

**Sartre:** That's from your novel idea, isn't it? The plague metaphor.

**Camus:** (nods to Sartre) Yes. The plague as symbol of rampant evil. One fights it, but one also takes care not to catch it oneself.

**Bernard:** Are you saying my desire for revenge is a *plague?*

**Camus:** I'm saying it's an understandable human reaction, but if it becomes obsessive and indiscriminate, it's like a sickness. It consumes. Look at some of the purges happening in villages – people settling old grudges under the guise of patriotism, shaving women's heads publicly, humiliating them. Some of those women did little more than fall in love with a German soldier. Is that a crime worth such degradation? In my view, no. It's ugly and unjust, and it drags us down to barbarity.

**Sartre:** I saw one of those head-shaving "ceremonies." It was vile – a howling crowd, the poor girl weeping, her head shorn. There was such relish in the mob's eyes. It made me shudder.

**Bernard:** (frowns) I don't participate in that. That's small stuff. I'm focused on real collaborators – like policemen who handed Jews over, informers who got résistants killed, propagandists who spewed Nazi lies.

**Camus:** And those people should face consequences, yes. But do you truly think executing every one of them is necessary or right? Perhaps some yes, but all?

**Bernard:** (hesitates) The propagandists… maybe prison for some of them. The worst like that writer Brasillach who called for Jews to be killed – him I'd shoot without a second thought.

**Sartre:** Brasillach will have a trial. I suspect he will be sentenced to death; many are calling for it. Some intellectuals are actually uneasy about executing even a fascist writer – they argue words shouldn't be punished by death. It's a debate raging now.

**Camus:** I've heard. It's complicated. Brasillach's writings certainly abetted murder. But to execute a writer for writings alone – it sets a precedent I'm uncomfortable with, even though I despise him.

**Bernard:** (shakes head in disbelief) You'd spare that venomous snake? After all the poison he spread?

**Camus:** (raising a hand) I'm not saying spare without punishment. Perhaps a long imprisonment. I just worry about the principle – today we execute someone for writing fascist propaganda, tomorrow perhaps someone will want to execute a communist for writing something, or even a moralist for dissent. I fear the slippery slope.

**Bernard:** Hmph. Perhaps you philosophers overthink.

**Sartre:** It's our job to overthink, Bernard. (He smiles a little to soften the jab)

**Camus:** Think of it this way: We want a France where life is valued and law is respected. If we start chopping off heads left and right, we normalize state violence again, right after we got rid of an occupying regime built on violence.

**Bernard:** (rubs his temple) I admit… sometimes at night after one of these "deliveries of justice," I feel sick. I thought seeing a traitor fall would fill the emptiness of losing my friends. It doesn't. It's just another dead body, and I still feel empty.

**Camus:** (softly) *"With him here, I saw more clearly, and his death… made my revolt more blind."* I wrote that about René – that his death didn't make me nobler or happier, it just blinded me with anger ([commentary.org](commentary.org)). Killing those who caused his death hasn't brought him back, hasn't truly relieved the pain.

**Bernard:** (voice low) Yes. Yes, that's it. After I executed my friend-turned-informer, I went home and vomited. And then I cried like a baby. I didn't expect that. I felt I had killed a part of myself too.

**Sartre:** (puts a hand on Bernard's shoulder) War makes murderers of even decent men. And it scars the soul. We're trying to step back from that abyss now.

**Bernard:** (looks between Sartre and Camus) You both truly believe in mercy over retribution, don't you?

**Camus:** (carefully) I believe in measured retribution. Mercy where possible, punishment where truly deserved – but never cruelty for cruelty's sake. We must break the cycle. As I wrote in an essay draft: *"We must cease to be both victims and executioners."* We've been victims, we nearly became executioners. Let's stop the pendulum there.

**Sartre:** Neither victims nor executioners – a fine motto.

**Bernard:** (lets out a long breath) You make it sound noble, but it's damned hard. When I see those smug collaborationists, part of me still just wants to line them against a wall.

**Camus:** Then let someone else judge them. Step back if you can. You've done enough, Bernard. You helped liberate Paris. Now maybe let the courts and committees handle the traitors. At least the ones that are in custody. Focus on rebuilding the country, which is another battle itself.

**Bernard:** (gazes out the window at the dripping eaves) Rebuilding… (he laughs a little) I only ever learned to destroy – rail lines, enemy convoys. Building will be new.

**Sartre:** France needs builders now: of houses, of institutions, of trust. We all have to pivot.

**Bernard:** What about the Communists? They're pushing hard to take control in some areas. They have their own courts, and they're not exactly known for leniency.

**Camus:** I'm aware. I plan to write about that too – cautioning our compatriots not to trade one authoritarianism for another. Fascism is defeated here, but Stalinism is a temptation for some. We must defend liberty on all fronts now.

**Sartre:** (raises an eyebrow) Careful, Albert. Not everyone sees the Communist Party that way. They are heroes to many for their role in the Resistance.

**Camus:** They fought bravely, yes. But I won't ignore the threats of any totalitarian tendency, left or right. We already see how some of them want revolutionary tribunals and summary executions of "class enemies." I won't have it. I'll oppose them in print if need be.

**Bernard:** (half-smiles) You really are fearless, Camus. Ready to take on new enemies so soon?

**Camus:** (shrugs) My *only* enemies are those who oppose human dignity and freedom – the executioners of any stripe. I loathe none but those, remember.

**Bernard:** (extends a hand to Camus) I may not agree with all your softness, but… I respect you. And I hear you. Perhaps it's time I step back from being an executioner. (His voice trembles slightly) It's not a role I ever wanted in the first place.

**Camus:** (grips Bernard's hand firmly) It takes courage to lay down the gun, sometimes more than to pick it up.

**Sartre:** Indeed. The revolution is over; now comes the evolution – into something better.

**Bernard:** (nods and straightens his posture, as if a weight has shifted) Alright. I'll advocate formal trials in my sector, and I'll try to rein in the summary justice. Perhaps I'll even testify against some of the bastards to ensure they're convicted properly.

**Camus:** That's a good path. See it through, and you'll honor your fallen friends more profoundly than by a hundred summary executions.

**Bernard:** (manages a faint smile) Maybe so. Though some nights, I suspect their restless spirits whisper to me for revenge.

**Camus:** Then tell them – or tell yourself – that their deaths will not be made sacred by more death, but by a France that upholds what is right. A France where no one need fear a knock at the door in the night ever again.

**Bernard:** (looking at Camus intently) You truly believe that possible?

**Camus:** (with quiet passion) I have to believe it. Otherwise, everything we fought for is dust. We *can* build a society of laws and compassion, imperfect but striving, if we have the will.

**Sartre:** (lights his pipe, which had gone out) And with people like you, Bernard, who've seen the worst and still can choose something better – I think we have a chance.

**Bernard:** (blinks back a sudden wetness in his eyes) Merci, messieurs. I needed this conversation more than I knew.

**Camus:** (smiles kindly) As did we. These are the difficult dialogues of victory. It's easier to fight an enemy than to restrain oneself after the fight.

**Bernard:** Right. (He picks up the folder on the desk) I'll take these dossiers to the commission downtown. They're setting up proper courts for collaboration cases. I'll add my testimony to ensure justice is done.

**Sartre:** That's wise. And if you need any support from us – a statement from *Combat*, perhaps – I'm sure Camus can arrange it.

**Camus:** Absolutely. *Combat* will support fair trials and strongly condemn any attempted lynchings or illegal punishments. We'll urge the public to channel their anger into rebuilding and legal justice.

**Bernard:** Good. Might steady some nerves if they read that. Many still want to take matters into their own hands.

**Camus:** We'll try to persuade them otherwise – with *clear language*, no less.

**Sartre:** (grins) Always *clear language*, eh, Albert?

**Camus:** (grinning back) The least we owe our readers is clarity and honesty.

**Bernard:** I'll be going, then. (He opens the door, then pauses) Camus, Sartre... thank you. You may have saved me from... from losing myself.

**Sartre:** (nods) Take care, Bernard.

**Camus:** Au revoir, Bernard. You're doing the right thing.

(Bernard exits into the hallway. A distant rumble of thunder is heard as the rain picks up.)

**Sartre:** (walking over to the window, looking at the rain) Storm's coming.

**Camus:** (stands beside him) Paris has been through many storms. This one will pass.

**Sartre:** You handled that well. I wasn't sure he'd relent.

**Camus:** Nor was I. But I saw pain in his eyes, not just anger. He needed relief more than revenge, though he didn't realize it.

**Sartre:** You gave him a bit of relief by sharing your own pain. That was deft.

**Camus:** We all carry wounds, Jean-Paul. Sometimes speaking them out is the salve.

**Sartre:** (puffing his pipe) True. I sometimes worry I was too sanguine about *le purge* at first. Immediately after liberation, I wrote that severe justice was normal, even necessary. But seeing some excesses… I've moderated.

**Camus:** It's good that you have. We intellectuals must be consistent – we preached humanity during the war, we cannot abandon it now.

**Sartre:** Just wait, though – I suspect some will label you "soft on fascism" or naive for these views.

**Camus:** (shrugs) So be it. I'd rather be called naive than become cruel. Let them say what they want. I'll answer with my work.

**Sartre:** And I'll back you, publicly where I can. We may differ on some things, but on this I feel we agree profoundly.

Camus: Thank you, Jean-Paul.

**Sartre:** I think often of something you wrote a few weeks ago in *Combat*. You wrote that France entered this war not for conquest but for a certain idea of happiness. That struck me.

**Camus:** (smiles softly) Yes, I wrote: *"We entered this war not because of any love of conquest, but to defend a certain notion of happiness… Let us retain the memory of this happiness and of those who* *have lost it."* It was my way of reminding everyone why we fought.

**Sartre:** Exactly. For a notion of happiness – meaning a life of freedom and dignity. Not to perpetuate misery or vengeance.

**Camus:** And to honor those who lost their chance at that happiness by ensuring we don't squander ours on continuing hatred.

**Sartre:** Well, said, my friend.

**Camus:** (gazes out at the rain-washed street) The shadow of the guillotine will fade, if we ensure France chooses measured justice. I believe we have convinced at least one strong soul today. Perhaps others will follow.

**Sartre:** Little by little. Revolutions aren't won in a day, nor are hearts changed overnight. But the work goes on.

**Camus:** (places a hand on Sartre's shoulder) Yes. And we'll keep sowing these ideas – of mercy, of balance – in our papers, our books, our conversations. These are the seeds of a more humane future.

**Sartre:** (smiles and taps Camus' hand) You know, some might call you an idealist or even a moralist for all this.

**Camus:** (laughs lightly) They already do. I've been called "moraliste" as if it were an insult. It doesn't bother me. I'd rather try to be a moral voice than surrender to cynicism.

**Sartre:** I admire it. There's a real strength in holding to morals after such a brutal period. Many just become nihilistic.

**Camus:** Nihilism is the easy way out – saying nothing matters, so do as you will. But I can't accept that. I feel the weight of what we do, so it all matters deeply.

**Sartre:** Perhaps that's what makes you, *vous autres*, Camus, unique. (He smirks) The *absurd* man who still cares intensely.

**Camus:** (grins) The absurd only demands acknowledgment that the world is irrational. It doesn't require us to be indifferent. In fact, recognizing absurdity can compel us to solidarity, to defiance.

**Sartre:** Well, I for one am glad of your defiance.

**Camus:** (tilts his head appreciatively) Thank you, Jean-Paul.

**Sartre:** Come, the rain's easing. Shall we find a café and celebrate the *Liberation* properly, before the next crisis calls?

**Camus:** (smiles) Why not. We've earned a moment of respite.

(They grab their coats. As they head out, Camus lingers a second, looking back at the dim room where so many fateful decisions were debated in recent days. The desk lies empty now, the guillotine's shadow seemingly receding from the walls.)

**Camus:** (murmurs to himself) Neither victims nor executioners…

**Sartre:** (from the doorway) Did you say something?

**Camus:** (joining him) Just thinking out loud. Let's go, Jean-Paul.

---

*They exit together into the fragile light of post-storm Paris. The clouds are breaking. In the puddles on the street, the reflected sky shows patches of blue.*

---

# Chapter 9
## Return to Light

---

*Paris, early dawn, Late Summer 1945. On the balcony of a modest Montmartre apartment, two friends watch the city emerge slowly from the night. The streetlamps flicker off one by one. The air is cool, hinting at renewal. Albert Camus and Jean-Paul Sartre lean on the iron railing, side by side, their collars turned up against the morning chill. They have spent the whole night talking – about war, about what comes after. Now, in the stillness before sunrise, their conversation finds its most intimate, hopeful notes. Liberation is months past; the war in Europe is ending. The long shadow is lifting. It is a tentative return to light, and these two philosophers feel the glow and burden of a new day.*

---

**Camus:** (inhaling the crisp air) Look – the sky over the Seine, it's turning that pale gray-blue. Another minute and the sun will poke through.

**Sartre:** (rubs his bleary eyes, smiling) We've talked until dawn again. Some things never change.

**Camus:** At least now it's a free dawn. No curfew, no blackout curtains.

**Sartre:** Oui. You know, last night I actually forgot to feel afraid. All those years, a footstep in the hall at 3 AM meant terror. Tonight, just footsteps.

**Camus:** I noticed that too. I heard someone whistling *La Marseillaise* down on the street at 2 AM. Just a drunk reveler, I suppose. A year ago that would have been unthinkable.

**Sartre:** Small signs of normalcy returning. People dare to sing again.

**Camus:** (quietly) I wonder if we'll ever really be normal. After what we've lived through.

**Sartre:** Not the same *normal* as before, no. We're changed – perhaps for the better in some ways, worse in others.

**Camus:** "The tragedy of the war was the tragedy of separation," I wrote that once . And now I feel the tragedy of war's end is the tragedy of *reunion* – finding how to live together again, after such division and loss.

**Sartre:** You always did have a poetic way of seeing it. But it's true – reknitting the social fabric isn't easy. There's mistrust, grief, guilt.

**Camus:** Guilt, yes. So many small guilts and large ones. The former collaborators slink about hoping to be forgiven. The rest of us carry guilt too – survivor's guilt, or guilt at not having done more.

**Sartre:** Do you feel that, honestly? That you didn't do enough?

**Camus:** (hesitates) At times. I did what I could – wrote, edited, spoke out. But I wasn't on the barricades with a rifle during the liberation. My health kept me from physical combat. A part of me feels I didn't pay the same price others did.

**Sartre:** (shakes his head) Your words were bullets of a kind, Albert. Don't undervalue that. You rallied spirits, stiffened spines. Not all heroism is on the battlefield.

**Camus:** Perhaps. I try to accept that. Still, when I walk past the plaques on walls – you know, "Here fell so-and-so for the liberation of Paris" – I feel a pang. Why them, not me? Why am I allowed to see this dawn when they are not?

**Sartre:** (softly) I think every survivor of a war asks that. There's no answer except chance, fate, whatever you call it. We are alive; they are not. Our task is to live in such a way that honors their sacrifice.

**Camus:** Yes. That's how I quell the guilt – by telling myself to do something worthy with the life they safeguarded for me.

**Sartre:** And you will. You've already begun. Your essays in *Combat* since liberation – they've been a conscience for France. Many might prefer to just celebrate victory and forget the hard lessons, but you keep pressing them not to forget.

**Camus:** I can't help it. I carry those lessons like a fever. "We entered this war to defend a certain notion of happiness… Let us retain the memory of this happiness and of those who have lost it," I wrote, and I meant it. The happiness – by which I meant freedom, human dignity – that's what we fought for. We must not betray that by sliding into new tyranny or despair.

**Sartre:** I particularly liked your piece "Toward Dialogue" last fall – "Yes, we must raise our voices…" That series *Neither Victims nor Executioners*, it was called?

**Camus:** (nods) That was in the fall. I argued that our world had had enough of killing and should reject both roles – to neither be slaughtered like sheep nor slaughter others like butchers. It was my plea for a new humane era.

**Sartre:** Naïve to some, but I found it stirring. Maybe I wouldn't have written it myself – I sometimes relish a bit of righteous anger – but I saw the wisdom. And your words traveled; I heard echoes in café debates.

**Camus:** If even a few minds opened to the idea, I'm content. The great challenge ahead is preventing new fanaticisms from filling the void left by fascism's defeat.

**Sartre:** You're thinking of communism, naturally.

**Camus:** (half-smiles) Naturally. And other isms too. Blind nationalism could return as well. There's already tension brewing between former Résistance factions.

**Sartre:** True. De Gaulle's vision vs. the Communists vs. the Socialists – the unity is fracturing.

**Camus:** It was inevitable. The moment the common enemy was gone, differences resurfaced. But I hope we can handle them civilly, without cracking heads.

**Sartre:** That might be optimistic. Politics is a blood sport, perhaps figuratively again now but still vicious.

**Camus:** And yet, I must hope. If we could stand united under occupation, surely in freedom we can disagree without destroying each other.

**Sartre:** Theoretically. But the stakes feel high – how France rebuilds, how justice is served, whether colonial empires continue or not...

**Camus:** (frowns) Ah, the colonies. That's a whole other powder keg.

**Sartre:** I suspect that will be France's next moral test. The colonies endured French defeat and saw European weakness; now independence movements stir.

**Camus:** You know my heart is torn there. I am from Algeria – I love it – but I also abhor oppression.

**Sartre:** (gently) One day you may have to choose between your homeland and your principles.

**Camus:** *(distant)* Perhaps. If there's a way to reconcile them — reform, equality within a federation — I'll hold onto it. I fear violence. I don't want to see the land of my birth drowned in blood from both sides.

**Sartre:** (looks at Camus sympathetically) We will have tough debates on that, I suspect. I already lean toward supporting colonial liberation unequivocally, even if it's violent. You have more skin in the game, so to speak.

**Camus:** Indeed. But let's not open that front quite yet this morning. (He rubs his eyes, smiling sadly) There will be time enough for those arguments.

**Sartre:** Agreed. It's nice to share a calm moment, for once. The war in Europe is over, but peace still feels like a thread pulling tight.

**Camus**: And yet, curiously, I find peace still elusive. Perhaps the final shot has already been fired. But what comes after… still doesn't feel like peace. New fears already loom – the atomic bomb, tensions with the Soviets.

**Sartre:** (grimaces) The atomic bomb. Yes, your editorial on Hiroshima was spot on – calling it a "technical civilization's ultimate degree of savagery". I read it and shuddered.

**Camus:** That day – August 6th – I'll never forget the sick feeling when news came about Hiroshima. We had just celebrated the war's imminent end, then that. It felt like a warning from the future: *any average city can be wiped out by a bomb the size of a football.* The world became suddenly more fragile.

**Sartre:** And now East and West eye each other warily, both likely to seek those terrible weapons.

**Camus:** It's a troubling thought. Collective suicide or intelligent cooperation – that's the choice I wrote of.

**Sartre:** Let's hope wisdom prevails for once.

**Camus:** We must lend our voices to make it prevail. Otherwise all this – everything we fought for – could end in a flash of nuclear light. (He sighs) Pardon, I didn't mean to darken the mood.

**Sartre:** No, it's alright. The world remains dangerous. But at least, here and now, this city is free and waking up to peace.

**Camus:** Yes. (He gazes out as the first golden edge of sun peeks over the rooftops) Look, the sun.

**Sartre:** (smiles, taking a deep breath) How many dawns we saw in the war years that were gray or red with fire… This one's gentle.

**Camus:** *La vie recommence.* Life begins anew.

**Sartre:** Albert, do you recall that night in 1940 when we first crossed paths at the Café de Flore? Paris was darkened, occupied, our futures uncertain. If someone told us then that in five years we'd be standing here watching the sunrise of victory…

**Camus:** …we might've laughed or cried, depending on our mood.

**Sartre:** Indeed. But here we are. I'm grateful – for survival, for friendship, for the chance to continue our work.

**Camus:** Me too. (He turns to Sartre) Speaking of work – what now, Jean-Paul? What will you tackle in this new chapter?

**Sartre:** (puffs his cigarette) I have a mind to launch a new journal – a monthly review for literature and philosophy, to shape the intellectual debate of this reborn nation. I think I'll call it *Les Temps Modernes.*

**Camus:** (grins) "Modern Times" – like Chaplin's film, but plural.

**Sartre:** Ha, hadn't thought of Chaplin. Yes, times *are* modern and we must catch up. Would you consider writing something for it?

**Camus:** Possibly, if invited. Though I have my hands full at *Combat* still.

**Sartre:** True. And you? Will you stay at *Combat* much longer?

**Camus:** Not sure. Now that it's an above-ground daily and politics are professionalizing, I sometimes feel out of place. They want alignment with a party line, and you know me – I can't be a partisan mouthpiece.

**Sartre:** You value independence too much.

**Camus:** Exactly. I may step back and focus on my literary work again. Finish this novel I've been toiling on – the one about a plague in Oran.

**Sartre:** Ah yes, *La Peste*. How's it coming?

**Camus:** Nearly done, I think. Writing it during the war was strange – an allegory of plague to mirror Occupation, but also more universal. It's about human solidarity in the face of indifferent death.

**Sartre:** I look forward to reading it. Perhaps there's a role for me to review it in *Les Temps Modernes*? With due praise, of course.

**Camus:** (laughs) I'll hold you to that – if you like it, that is. If not, be honest; I can take it.

**Sartre:** Don't worry, I'll be fair. And after the novel?

**Camus:** I have an idea brewing for a long essay or book on rebellion. Not just political rebellion, but the spirit of rebellion as a fundamental human value. To articulate what distinguishes a rebellion that affirms human dignity from a revolution that ends in tyranny.

**Sartre:** (teasing) Sounds ambitious – and perhaps like a veiled critique of our Communist friends?

**Camus:** It will critique any ideology that justifies murder for a supposed paradise. I want to champion the rebel who says *no* to injustice but doesn't turn that *no* into a fanatic *yes* to destruction. A rebel who respects limits – who refuses to become an executioner even in revolt.

**Sartre:** A *measured* rebellion.

**Camus:** Precisely. One that, as you and I discussed before, doesn't become what it hates. I think the times demand such reflection. After all, we've seen how revolutions can go horribly wrong – the French Revolution's terror, the Russian Revolution's Stalinist purges.

**Sartre:** Careful – the latter example will earn you ire from the Left.

**Camus**: I'm aware. But truth is truth. If I learned one thing in these years, it's to speak out even if one stands alone.

**Sartre:** (clinks the last of his coffee in a cup against Camus') To speaking out alone, then.

**Camus:** (smiles) Hopefully not *alone* – I hope not to lose your friendly voice even if we debate fiercely.

**Sartre:** Don't worry, I suspect our friendship will endure some stormy debates yet. (He chuckles) We might spar in print, but we'll still share a drink after.

**Camus:** That's good. I value that – the ability to disagree and still respect each other. It's what I want for society at large as well.

**Sartre:** A noble wish. We must model it, perhaps.

**Camus:** We shall. (He tilts his head back, feeling the first rays of sun on his face) Do you feel that warmth? The sun's fully up.

**Sartre:** (closes his eyes briefly) Mmm. I'd almost forgotten how Paris can feel in a tranquil sunrise.

**Camus:** Hard-won tranquility.

**Sartre:** You know, Albert, in this light, you look less burdened. Almost youthful.

**Camus:** (raises an eyebrow) Are you saying I looked old and burdened before?

**Sartre:** We both did. War aged us. But maybe peace will restore a bit of youth.

**Camus:** (smiles) If not youth, then at least life. I do feel… lighter, at this moment. Like some heaviness in the air has lifted.

**Sartre:** That's hope you're feeling. We intellectuals are not used to that sensation, so we barely recognize it.

**Camus:** (laughs) Touché. Yes, maybe it is hope. In spite of everything, I have hope.

**Sartre:** So do I, I confess. The war taught me that people can surprise you – both in evil and in good. And I think we've learned too much to slide back without a fight.

**Camus:** We'll keep watch, you and I. Sound the alarm if needed, rally minds with pen and voice.

**Sartre:** Guardians at the gates of humanity's conscience – how grand that sounds.

**Camus:** (chuckles) Let's not get pompous. We're just writers. But sometimes, writers can influence the soul of a nation.

**Sartre:** I believe that. Words are powerful – we saw that in war, and we see it now in shaping peace.

**Camus:** Then we'll continue using words for what is true and just. It's the least – and the best – we can do.

**Sartre:** (extends his hand) To truth and justice, then. And to friendship.

**Camus:** (clasps Sartre's hand firmly) To friendship. And *happiness*, Jean-Paul – a notion of happiness that we defended and must now fulfill.

**Sartre:** Oui. A happiness that is not trivial pleasure, but the deep contentment of living free and equal with others.

**Camus:** Exactly. We owe it to those who died – to "retain the memory of this happiness and of those who have lost it". We must build a world worthy of their dreams.

**Sartre:** And to those who come after us – so they inherit something better, not just ashes and graves.

**Camus:** (looking out at Paris, now bathed in soft morning gold) I sometimes imagine — years from now — a child walking these streets, never knowing fear or hunger like we saw, living an ordinary life in a truly humane society. That image keeps me going.

**Sartre:** A beautiful image. Perhaps one of your children, even?

**Camus:** (smiling) Perhaps. My twins are still babies now, too young to remember war. Thank God.

**Sartre:** They'll grow up in a different world, if we have any say.

**Camus:** We will make sure of it.

116

**Sartre:** (releases Camus' hand and stretches) Mon ami, the city calls. We should get some sleep, but alas, I have a meeting at noon. Life accelerates.

**Camus:** I should head home too – Francine will wake soon, and wonder if I've been out carousing.

**Sartre:** (grins) In a sense we have – carousing in ideas all night.

**Camus:** The best kind of carouse for me.

**Sartre:** (as they turn to go inside) Albert, one last thing – do you think we'll keep this hope? This clarity of purpose? Or will it fade as normalcy returns?

**Camus:** It might fade, under daily trifles and new conflicts. But we can remind each other. That's why a friendship like ours – and a community of thinkers – is important. We'll remind France of what was learned, if forgetfulness sets in.

**Sartre:** Very true. We'll be the reminders-in-chief.

**Camus:** (laughs) Not an official title, but a calling.

**Sartre:** A calling, yes.

(They step back into the apartment. Camus picks up his coat, Sartre his hat.)

**Camus:** Look at us – alive, free, thinking about the future. It's almost miraculous.

**Sartre:** And yet entirely real. Sometimes reality exceeds our dreams.

**Camus:** (opens the door to leave) We should never cease dreaming better, though, and then trying to make it real.

**Sartre:** Hear, hear.

(They exit into the stairwell, footsteps echoing as they descend. Outside, the first vendors set up their carts, a milkman rings his bicycle bell. Paris is awakening in peace.)

**Camus:** (stepping onto the street, lifting his face to the sun) Good morning, Paris!

**Sartre:** Good morning, indeed.

---

*They share a grin like schoolboys on holiday. Then, with a warm clasp of hands and a parting of ways at the corner, they go off into the brightening day — two friends who have endured darkness and now walk in the light, carrying within them the philosophical seeds that will blossom in the works they have yet to write, and in the better world they hope to help shape.*

*In this new morning, Albert Camus feels the gentle weight of responsibility and hope. The war's night is over; the time of rebuilding has come. As he walks home, he silently recites a vow — to remember the happiness they fought for, to honor the dead by speaking truth, and to nurture the spirit of rebellion against injustice wherever it may arise. And with each step on the sunlit cobblestones, he steps further out of the long night and into the daybreak of freedom.*

---

# Part III:
# Recognition & Division

# Chapter 10
## The Acclaim and the Ache

---

*Late-afternoon sunlight slants through the windows of a quiet Parisian café, dust and smoke twirling in its beams. At a corner table, Albert Camus sits with a close friend amid the low murmur of patrons and clinking glasses. Outside, boulevard traffic hums in the glow of spring. Inside, the air is thick with the warmth of coffee and the unspoken weight of recent success.*

---

**Pascal:** (lifting a newspaper) They're still raving about *The Plague*, you know. Every paper in Paris has sung its praises this week. You're the toast of the town, Albert.

**Camus:** (smiles faintly, stirring his coffee) So it seems. Though I confess, I hardly recognize myself in their praise.

**Pascal:** Come now, don't be modest. Not everyone gets mentioned in Stockholm circles before forty. I even heard a Swedish poet has whispered your name among the Academy.

**Camus:** (arches an eyebrow) Stockholm gossip travels fast. In truth, I can't imagine it. A Nobel… at my age? (shakes his head) The notion is absurd. An honor like that… I'm not sure I *want* it.

**Pascal:** (grinning) Not want it? Why ever not? It would be vindication – recognition on the grandest scale. Isn't that what every writer dreams of?

**Camus:** Perhaps. But recognition can become its own kind of plague. I worry it might separate me from… myself. (pauses, choosing words) When I wrote *The Plague*, I hoped to convey something simple and true. Now all the noise around it — it

123

feels like standing outside oneself, watching strangers debate your soul.

**Pascal:** They call it a masterpiece, Albert. A triumph. Even Sartre said as much to me last week. Why shouldn't you accept that?

**Camus:** (softly) Because in my heart, I judged the book a failure.

**Pascal:** *(blinking in surprise)* A failure? *The Plague* – a failure? It's your most successful work by far, widely read across continents!

**Camus:** Successful, yes, in readers. But in execution… (sighs) I could not fully express what I meant. The depth of suffering, the collective courage – I feel I only scratched the surface. So, yes, I smile at the kind words, but inside I remain unsatisfied.

**Pascal:** You're a perfectionist. Perhaps that's why you're great. Still, failure or not, your *surface* moved millions. You've become a kind of hero, like your Dr. Rieux – a symbol of conscience.

**Camus:** A hero? (shakes his head firmly) No. I don't believe in heroism; I've seen enough people die for ideas. Heroism comes easy, and I've learned it can be murderous. What interests me is living and dying for what one loves.

**Pascal:** (studying Camus) Living and dying for what one loves… That does sound like you. And what is it you love most, my friend?

**Camus:** Perhaps decency. Simple human decency. All I've ever done is try to articulate that – that even amidst plague, war, whatever evil, the only thing that matters is that ordinary people do good, act with decency. No medals, no fanfare. Just the quiet courage to not bow to brutality.

**Pascal:** (raises his cup in a toast) To simple decency, then. Though the world gives you fanfare whether you like it or not! *(laughs)* Albert, you may shy from it, but you have become a voice people look to – a *moral* voice. France loves a moralist.

**Camus:** (wry smile) France loves them until they say something disagreeable. Then the mob can turn. Fame is fickle. One day I fear I'll offend the very people now praising me.

**Pascal:** Offend them? How? You've fought fascists, uplifted the resistance, written truth. What could turn them against you?

**Camus:** (gazing out the window) The truth itself, perhaps. If I continue to speak it. For example – now that fascism is defeated, many of our friends cheer the new revolutionary dreams from the East. They excuse tyrants of a different stripe. I cannot. Eventually, I'll be asked to take sides, East or West, red or blue. And I know already: I won't do it. I *can't*.

**Pascal:** You can't choose between communism and capitalism, between Moscow and Washington?

**Camus:** No. "We are asked to love or hate such and such a country," I wrote, "but some of us feel too strongly our common humanity to make such a choice". How can I applaud one power and demonize the other when both build arsenals and empires? How can I, who love the Russian people, turn a blind eye to their suffering under Stalin? Or ignore America's errors because I prefer its freedoms?

**Pascal:** (leans in, lowering his voice) Careful, Albert. That sounds dangerously neutral to some. Sartre and the others, they think we must choose the *correct* side – History with a capital H.

**Camus:** Yes, I've heard Jean-Paul on this. But to me, truth isn't a matter of sides. One does not decide the truth of a thought by whether it's labeled right-wing or left-wing. If an injustice is committed, I will oppose it – no matter who the culprit is.

**Pascal:** That stance... it could put you at odds with Sartre someday. With a lot of people.

**Camus:** So be it. I didn't survive the Nazis' censorship just to become silent or partisan now. If I must stand alone, I'll stand. (smiles a little) You know, Pascal, I keep thinking of an old Spanish proverb my mother likes: "To live well is to live hidden." There's wisdom in a quiet, ordinary life. Some days I envy those who live unseen.

**Pascal:** (grins) Unseen? That's not your fate, my friend. Like it or not, you're in the light now. And I suspect you'll only shine brighter. *(he lifts his cup again)* So if you won't celebrate yourself, allow me. To the *failure* that is *The Plague*, and the man who wrote it. May he remain as decent and stubborn as ever, whatever comes.

**Camus:** (clinks cups, a quiet chuckle) I'll drink to that. Whatever comes.

---

*They sip their coffee in companionable silence as the sun dips lower, each lost in thought.*

---

# Chapter 11
## Jasmine and Silence

*Evening falls gently over the old working-class quarter of Algiers. In a small courtyard behind a modest one-story house, the air is warm and still. Jasmine vines cling to sun-bleached walls, releasing a faint sweet scent. Albert sits on a low stool beside his mother, who shells peas into a bowl on her lap. The hush is broken only by the soft rustle of palm fronds and distant sounds of children at play. Mother and son share the quiet, the space between them filled with unspoken love and the ache of years apart.*

**Camus:** *(in a gentle Algerian French)* It's a beautiful evening, Maman. The sky — do you see? — all pink and gold. *(He smiles and touches her arm to get her attention.)*

**Mother:** (glancing up from the peas, she nods and smiles softly) Oui. Beau.

**Camus:** (after a pause) Thank you for letting me just sit here with you. I've longed for this quiet. In Paris everything is noise – words, arguments, accolades… (shrugs) Here, with you, it's simple.

**Mother:** (reaching to pat his hand, speaking slowly) You work too hard, Albert. Always thinking, writing… Tu es fatigué? *You're tired?*

**Camus:** (squeezes her hand) A little. Sometimes I feel old, though I'm only thirty-something. (chuckles) Paris has a way of tiring the soul. Everyone wants a piece of me there. Here, I can be your little boy again for a while.

**Mother:** (her cloudy eyes fixed on him fondly) My little one. (She brushes a curl of his hair aside, a gesture of habit and tenderness.)

**Camus:** (smiles with glistening eyes) Being here brings back everything – the smell of jasmine, the sound of your sewing late at night. (He looks around the courtyard) Do you remember how I'd do my schoolwork out here, reading by the last daylight? You would scold me to come inside…

**Mother:** (laughs softly, nodding) Always reading. Even by moonlight, you read.

**Camus:** Those were good days. We had nothing, but it didn't matter. "I was poised midway between poverty and sunshine," I wrote once of my childhood – do you know what I meant? Poverty kept me from believing all was well in the world, and the sun… the sun taught me that history isn't everything.

**Mother:** (tilts her head, catching fragments) Tu avais le soleil. *You had the sun.*

**Camus:** Oui, le soleil. We had the sun. (He gazes upward at the evening sky turning cobalt) Life was hard, but it glowed, somehow. Because of you, Maman. You gave me warmth in the little things – fresh bread, your gentle silence.

**Mother:** (smiles, her eyes moist though she doesn't fully understand all his words) Je suis contente que tu es ici. *I'm glad you're here.*

**Camus:** I'm glad too. (He falls quiet for a moment, then speaks hesitantly) Maman… do you ever feel I've left you behind? That I belong to a different world now?

**Mother:** (frowns in mild confusion) Différent?

128

**Camus:** Different life. Over there – France, fame… (he sighs) I fear I've become a stranger to my own family.

**Mother:** (slowly, deliberate) Tu restes mon fils. *You remain my son.* Toujours. *Always.* (She takes his hand, placing it on her heart.) Ici.

**Camus:** (his voice catches) Yes. I'm always your son. (He swallows, blinking back tears) Maman, people in France — they call me a spokesman for justice, for truth. But when I speak, it's your voice I want to honor – the voice of those who can't easily speak. Your silence taught me that poverty is anonymity, that the poor and quiet are so often unseen. I have tried to give voice to those without one – perhaps in speaking, I've been speaking for *you.*

**Mother:** (cups his cheek, looking faintly perplexed but moved by his tone) Mon bon garçon… *My good boy…*

**Camus:** (closing his eyes at her touch) I'm not always so good. I've made mistakes. But I keep that promise to myself – that I will defend people like you, ordinary, decent people, against those who'd hurt them in the name of some grand idea.

**Mother:** (simply) Tu as un bon cœur. *You have a good heart.*

**Camus:** (softly) I hope so. (He takes a breath, struggling with something unsaid) Maman… if ever the world asks me to choose between an abstract justice and you… I will choose you. Always.

**Mother:** (her hearing failed her; she reads the seriousness in his eyes instead and nods gently, unsure of his words but certain of his love)

**Camus:** (smiles through his emotion, switching to a lighter tone) Enough of my chatter. Tell me, do you still make couscous on Sundays? I've been dreaming of it.

**Mother:** (brightens, understanding this) Ah, couscous! Oui. Dimanche. *Yes, Sunday.* (She gestures eating with her hand and laughs quietly)

**Camus:** (laughs softly, relieved) Magnifique. I'll be here, Sunday, with a big appetite. (He wraps an arm around her shoulders carefully) It's good to be home, even for a little while.

**Mother:** (leans her head against his shoulder, content) Chez toi, ici. *Your home is here.*

Camus: Oui, ici. *Yes, here.*

---

*He falls silent, holding her close as the stars begin to emerge above, one by one. In the stillness, no philosophy is needed — only the steady rhythm of two hearts, reunited in the night.*

---

# Chapter 12
## The Threshold

*The office of Les Temps Modernes is half-empty in the late morning hush, the other staff off to lunch. Sunlight from a high window falls in pale rectangles on a clutter of manuscripts, books, and overflowing ashtrays. Jean-Paul Sartre stands by a desk, sleeves rolled up, lighting a cigarette, while Camus sits across from him, a copy of the latest issue in hand. The two friends, once inseparable, now study each other through a subtle veil of differing convictions. Outside, a typewriter clacks from another room, a faint metronome to the tension inside.*

**Sartre:** (exhaling smoke) Your essay series in *Combat* caused quite the stir, you know. The *Neither Victims nor Executioners* pieces – I've never seen so many letters to the editor. Half in admiration, half in fury.

**Camus:** (nods thoughtfully) I expected as much. Saying "no" to murder – not exactly a popular stance with ideologues of the day.

**Sartre:** (raises an eyebrow) It was a bit... absolute, Albert. "I will never again be one of those who compromise with murder" – I recall that line. Stirring, yes. But some would call it naïve. History is not so black-and-white.

**Camus:** Is refusing to condone murder naïve? I don't think so. We just emerged from a war where each side justified atrocities. Now new conflicts gather, and again we hear that killing is a necessary means to some glorious end. I reject that. Frankly, I *meant* every word: I will never be one of those, whoever they are, who compromise with murder.

131

**Sartre:** (paces slowly) Even if by refusing violence now, you allow greater violence later? What if *not* killing one tyrant leads to a thousand innocents dying under him? These are not classroom hypotheticals – this is the real world.

**Camus:** (leans forward, earnest) Yes, the real world – where each murder, each atrocity, is entirely real. I can't weigh lives on a scale of ideology. Once you start saying "this death is acceptable for future benefit," you're on the slippery slope. There are means which cannot be excused, Jean-Paul. I cannot believe that everything must be subordinated to one ultimate end – some means will poison even the purest ends.

**Sartre:** (frowns, flicking ash) That's easy to say when one's not in the shoes of the oppressed fighting for liberation. You speak of tyrants – what about the ones still ruling? The colonialists, the capitalists strangling workers? You wouldn't have fought the Nazis if you truly believed no violent ends justified, no?

**Camus:** I fought the Nazis to stop a greater violence – but even then, I never celebrated killing. In the Resistance I wrote that one must fight for truth *without* becoming an executioner oneself. We sought to "preserve in our hearts the memory of a happy sea, of a beloved face" even amid war. I despised what war made us do.

**Sartre:** Everyone hates war in theory. But sometimes war comes, regardless. The question is, what next? The proletariat today faces its own tyrants. Can we tell them to lay down arms and *reflect* on murder, as you suggest? History won't wait for our moral purity.

**Camus:** (sadly) Perhaps not. But I must *try*. I asked in that essay, must our world "be made still more miserable in order to achieve far-off ends," or can we avoid bloodshed so future generations might have a chance? I've chosen my stance. I'd rather be called naïve than quietly become an apologist for butchery.

**Sartre:** (folds arms, eyeing Camus) You fear becoming an apologist; I fear becoming irrelevant. The masses out there suffering injustice – they cry out for action, not moral hesitations. The Communists, for all their flaws, at least promise action. That's why so many of our friends lean that way.

**Camus:** I know. Action is intoxicating. But look at what we already know – Soviet labor camps, purges, show trials of old Bolsheviks. How can we ignore those? Because it's inconvenient? I can't. If I shouted against Hitler's camps, I'll shout against Stalin's camps too. My voice will be for those ordinary Russians, whom I love, who deserve better than another tyrant.

**Sartre:** (waves a hand) You're sounding like an editorial, Albert. Of course tyranny is bad. But you're focusing on the wrong side. American imperialism, colonialism – *that's* what progressive writers fight now. The Soviet excesses, many see as temporary, fixable within the grand march of progress.

**Camus:** (with a bitter chuckle) Temporary gulags? An interesting concept. Jean-Paul, if we close our eyes to one form of oppression because another offends us more, we're simply choosing hypocrisy. All this talk of "sides"… I tell you, I'm done with it. One does not decide the truth of a thought according to whether it's right or left. If the Communists are wrong about something, I'll say so — even if it puts me on the same side as *bourgeois* opinion for a moment.

**Sartre:** And if that moment stretches into a Cold War? If you find yourself aligned with reactionaries? They're already calling you soft on capitalism, you know.

**Camus:** Let them. I am not soft on anything – except perhaps on the value of a single human life. That I will defend, regardless of whose politics it inconveniences. If that brands me a reactionary in some eyes, so be it. I think it simply brands me *consistent.*

**Sartre:** (stares at him, then shakes his head) You always did prize consistency over... shall we say, effectiveness. (He takes a slow drag, then speaks quieter) You know, some of the younger writers whisper that you're starting to sound like a moralist scolding from the sidelines. They wonder what you *stand* for, if you reject both East and West.

**Camus:** I stand for the human being in front of me, over any idea or flag. That may be a feeble banner, but it's mine. I've said it before: some of us feel our common humanity too strongly to pick one tribe and betray all others.

**Sartre:** (sighs, sitting on edge of desk) I admire your humanism, Albert, I do. But history will force choices on us. Neutrality won't be tenable when the world splits in two.

**Camus:** Perhaps. I'm not neutral between freedom and tyranny, if that's what you mean. I just refuse to accept that I must support one tyranny to fight another. If that's an intellectual luxury, then call me a decadent, I suppose.

**Sartre:** (smiles thinly) Oh, I've heard other words, but let's not go there. We're still on the same side, broadly – for now. Both of us are concerned with justice, with human dignity. We differ on strategy, maybe.

**Camus:** I hope it's only that. (He stands, stretching) Jean-Paul, I appreciate this frank talk. I worry...it feels like a gulf is opening between my path and yours. But I hope, in the end, we won't be standing too far apart to still call across.

**Sartre:** (extinguishes his cigarette) That depends. If you keep publicly criticizing the comrades and harping on absolute morality… well, that could widen the gulf.

**Camus:** I suppose it could. (puts on his coat) Yet I can't do otherwise. You know me.

**Sartre:** (nods slowly) I do. Stubborn as ever. Just… watch yourself, Albert. The literary world, our world – it can turn ugly when schisms arise. I'd hate to see you isolated.

**Camus:** (with a faint sad smile) Isolation doesn't scare me as much as betrayal of myself. I'd rather be alone with the truth than in crowded error.

**Sartre:** (regards him in silence for a moment) I'll pretend you didn't just imply I'm in error.

**Camus:** (grinning, a flicker of their old camaraderie) I implied no such thing, mon ami. Only speaking generally.

**Sartre:** (extends his hand) Generally speaking, take care. And keep writing – *The Rebel*, is it? I look forward to it, even if I suspect I'll disagree with half of it.

**Camus:** You may. (shakes Sartre's hand firmly) Thank you, Jean-Paul. Until soon.

---

*He turns and walks out. Sartre watches his friend go, a troubled expression on his face as the afternoon light shifts, lengthening the shadows in the empty office.*

---

# Chapter 13
## In Transit

---

*The night train from Paris to Amsterdam snakes through the dark countryside with a steady iron rhythm. In a nearly deserted second-class compartment, Camus gazes out at the blur of moonlit fields. Opposite him sits a stranger – a middle-aged man with haunted eyes and a weathered overcoat. The faint glow of a single lamp casts gentle shadows as the train jostles on. Outside, a distant thunderstorm flickers on the horizon. Inside, two men share the solitude, drawn together by the quiet intimacy of travel.*

---

**Stranger:** (clears his throat softly) Excuse me... you wouldn't happen to have a light? My matches are spent.

**Camus:** (turning from the window) Of course. *(leans forward, cupping his hand to light the man's cigarette with his old metal lighter)* There you are.

**Stranger:** Thank you... (studies Camus' face in the dim light) Forgive me, but you look familiar. Have we met?

**Camus:** (smiles politely) Not that I recall. Perhaps I just have one of those faces.

**Stranger:** Perhaps... (he inhales, then sighs) Lovely night, isn't it? The fields under the moon like that – reminds me of summers long ago, before the war.

**Camus:** (nods) There's a peacefulness out there. Hard to imagine, in this darkness, the world's troubles.

**Stranger:** (a bitter chuckle) Hard to imagine? Not for me, monsieur. The darkness brings them right back. (taps ash

137

nervously) I was at Dunkirk in '40. Nights like this, I still hear the bombardments in my dreams.

**Camus:** (voice gentle) You served in the war?

**Stranger:** Oui. And lost more than I care to remember. Friends... my brother. And after coming home, I lost my wife to illness, just last year. (He looks down, ashamed of the tears welling in his eyes) Pardon, I... I don't mean to burden you with a stranger's sorrows.

**Camus:** You're not burdening me. (leans forward, hands clasped) I'm truly sorry for your losses. Life has been cruel to you.

**Stranger:** (wipes his eye) Life is cruel, period. I try to tell myself there's some meaning in it – the suffering – but I haven't found it. My priest says to keep faith, that suffering is part of God's plan. But I... (he trails off, shaking his head) I'm not sure I believe that anymore.

**Camus:** (quietly) I understand. I'm... not a man of faith myself. I've seen children die senselessly, good people cut down. I could never accept that any just God willed those things. In fact I once wrote, "I shall refuse to love a scheme of things in which children are put to torture". No paradise worth that price, in my view.

**Stranger:** (searches Camus' face) Those words... I've heard them. Wait, I... (sudden recognition dawns) My God, you're Albert Camus, aren't you? The writer.

**Camus:** (hesitates, then nods) I am.

Stranger: *(sits back, astonished)* Well. Forgive me for not realizing sooner. I read *The Plague* last year. It... it meant a great deal to me.

**Camus:** (smiling kindly) Thank you. I'm glad.

Stranger: The way you wrote about the plague as a collective ordeal – it felt like the war, like life itself. Honestly, it helped me a little, to know others feel as I do. That maybe there is… I don't know, some solidarity in suffering.

**Camus:** There is. We are none of us alone in suffering – even when we feel most alone. In Oran, when plague struck, Dr. Rieux and his friends found meaning in solidarity, in helping each other without hope of reward. That's all we can do, I think.

**Stranger:** But their victories were temporary, you wrote. The plague bacillus never dies; it waits in the shadows. Isn't that terribly futile? To struggle on, knowing evil will rise again?

**Camus:** (sighs softly, looking down at his hands) It can seem futile. But futility and hope aren't mutually exclusive. We fight even when we know we can't win definitively. Why? Because it's *right*. Because doing nothing is far worse. I have always believed, as Rieux says, there's no question of heroism in this – "the only means of fighting a plague is common decency". Decency may seem small, but it's what keeps us human in the darkest times.

**Stranger:** Decency… (he nods, turning the word over in his mouth) During the war, I saw both brutality and decency. Sometimes from the same people. I did things I regret, out of fear. I've tried to be a good man since, but… I don't know. Maybe there's a plague inside me too.

**Camus:** (regards him with empathy) You're not alone in that feeling. Believe me. We all carry the plague inside, in one form or another – the capacity for harm, for selfishness. I wrote that as well, though it was a hard truth to accept.

**Stranger:** If that's true, then what hope do we have? If everyone has the plague germ…

**Camus:** (gentle, firm) The hope is that we also carry its antidote: conscience, love. "What's natural is the microbe," one character observes, "all the rest – health, integrity, purity – is a product of the human will". Goodness is a choice, an attention that must never falter. The good person is the one who has the fewest lapses of attention, who infects as few others as possible.

**Stranger:** (thinking) A constant vigilance of the heart. Yes… yes, I see. And when we fail? As we inevitably do?

**Camus:** We acknowledge it, we repent in our actions by trying to make amends. We start again. There is no final victory – but there is also no final defeat as long as we refuse to give in to despair or cynicism.

**Stranger:** (meets Camus' eyes, a faint light of gratitude in his own) Hearing you say that… it lifts a weight, somehow. I've been so afraid my failures made me irredeemable.

**Camus:** No one is irredeemable who understands and regrets what they've done. I think genuine remorse already contains the seed of hope. It means the plague has not taken you over completely – part of you is fighting back.

**Stranger:** (smiles a little for the first time) That's a comforting thought. You know, Monsieur Camus, I boarded this train feeling utterly lost. Now… I feel I've met a friend.

**Camus:** As do I. (He reaches across and clasps the stranger's hand warmly) What is your name, friend?

**Stranger:** Jules. Jules Martel.

**Camus:** (reclining back) Jules, I'm grateful we shared this journey. Sometimes two strangers can understand each other better than old acquaintances.

**Stranger:** I'll be honest – part of me still struggles with the meaning of all this suffering. But at least now I feel I'm not carrying it alone.

**Camus:** You aren't. None of us are. That's one thing I've learned. Even in our deepest isolation, there's someone, somewhere, who feels as we do. And if we're lucky, we meet them – maybe in a train car on a moonlit night. *(smiles)*

**Stranger:** (with a chuckle) Fate, or chance, has been kind to me tonight.

**Camus:** (looks out at a flash of distant lightning) Chance… I've come to respect chance a great deal. It can be cruel, but also strangely benevolent at times. Perhaps there's a kind of grace in the random meetings it throws our way.

**Stranger:** Perhaps there is. (He stubs out his cigarette) Monsieur Camus – Albert – thank you. I won't forget this conversation.

**Camus:** Nor will I, Jules. And remember, the task before us is very simple, even if it's hard: do what good we can, in whatever corner of the world we find ourselves. That's all. No grand theories – just small decencies. Each day, each moment.

**Stranger:** (nods, eyes brighter) I will try. (The train whistle sounds in the distance; he notices) Your stop must be soon?

**Camus:** Yes, Amsterdam by dawn. And you?

**Stranger:** I continue on to Brussels. Long night yet. But I think I'll sleep easier now.

**Camus:** (stands and offers his hand once more as the train begins to slow) Safe travels, Jules. And good luck.

**Stranger:** Safe travels, Albert. And… merci. *Thank you.*

---

*They shake hands firmly. Camus takes his coat from the rack as the train pulls into the dimly lit station. With a final nod to the stranger, he departs into the night, leaving Jules with a lighter heart and the steady rhythm of the rails for company.*

---

# Chapter 14
## The Unforgiven

---

*Paris, early 1952. A crowded lecture hall at the Sorbonne slowly empties after a heated panel on "Revolution and Justice." Under flickering fluorescent lights, Camus lingers near the podium, folding notes into his battered briefcase. At the back of the hall, a young man in a cheap worker's jacket strides down the aisle toward him. His eyes shine with fervor and indignation. The remaining audience members hush their conversations, sensing an confrontation. Camus straightens, weary but calm, as the young communist approaches.*

---

**Young Man:** (voice raised) Monsieur Camus, may I have a word?

**Camus:** (turning to face him) Of course. You stayed until the end – thank you. What's on your mind?

**Young Man:** I listened to your talk… your *sermon*, rather. All that talk of morality, of not staining one's soul with blood. (He scoffs) You make it sound so noble to do nothing. Tell me, do your high principles feed the poor or free the oppressed?

**Camus:** (clasps his hands before him gently) I never suggested doing nothing. In fact, I argue we must act – but act without sacrificing our conscience. There are always alternatives to murder.

**Young Man:** Alternatives? Try telling that to those rotting under fascist regimes or colonial rule! You sit here in serene judgment, refusing to support violent uprising – that means you effectively support the oppressor. Your hands stay *clean*, but others continue to die.

**Camus:** The moment we allow murder for a cause, we hand our conscience to that cause — and history has shown us what it does with it.

**Young Man:** (steps closer, intensity in his face) Easy for you to say. You're not the one enslaved. You're a Frenchman, respected, safe. My parents were Algerian, Camus. I've seen my people treated as subhuman in our own land. The FLN fighters – they're willing to give their lives to end that. And you? You condemn them for spilling blood? Whose side are you on? France's?

**Camus:** I'm on the side of a just future where French and Algerians need not spill each other's blood. I'm on no one's "side" that demands I rejoice in murder.

**Young Man:** So you condemn the FLN. You've made that clear. You won't "compromise with murder" – yes, I've read your words . But you condemn colonial atrocities too, I assume?

**Camus:** Absolutely. I have never wavered in denouncing colonial injustices and the violence inflicted on Algerian civilians. Torture, executions – I oppose it with every fiber of my being.

**Young Man:** Yet you won't fully support our liberation struggle because some innocents may die for it. Do you know what they call you now? A bourgeois moralist. A coward. Even Sartre sees it – he said not long ago that *anti-colonial violence, while ugly, might be necessary.* History demands it.

**Camus:** (a shadow of pain crosses his face at Sartre's mention, but he remains composed) Names don't bother me. I'm concerned with *results*. Suppose your revolution succeeds by killing indiscriminately – what kind of freedom is built on slaughtered children and lynched farmers? You'd just trade one atrocity for another. "The slave begins by demanding justice and ends by wanting to wear a crown," I wrote in *The Rebel*, "he must dominate in his turn."

**Young Man:** (sneers) Yes, I know that book – your so-called *Rebel* that was more concerned with attacking Marx and our revolution than with attacking real tyrants. It's why Sartre's journal tore you apart. They said your vague humanism was politically useless. And they were right.

**Camus:** (takes a slow breath, the wound clearly felt) They have their view; I have mine. My "vague humanism" holds that the ends do not justify the means – that if in order to free men we must kill children, then we are no better than the tyrants we replace. I cannot budge on this.

**Young Man:** So you would have us do nothing? Offer our throats to the colonial executioner and say "at least I am morally pure"?

**Camus:** Not at all. Fight, yes – but fight *clean*. If that limits tactics, so be it. Perhaps it makes our struggle harder, slower. But it keeps our humanity intact. Perhaps we cannot prevent this world from being one in which children are tortured, but we can at least reduce the number of tortured children. That is *real* progress – not swapping which children get hurt.

**Young Man:** (shakes his head, voice rising) *Reduce the number?* That's reformist drivel. We want to eliminate injustice entirely! You think you can accomplish that with clean hands? Dream on. Every revolution makes sacrifices. It's tragic, yes, but necessary.

**Camus:** Necessary? I've heard that word too often from fanatics of all stripes. It's the excuse of every executioner – that his violence is "necessary" for a better world. I do not trust any paradise that requires war crimes to reach. *If that is justice, I prefer my mother* – meaning, I prefer the simple, immediate innocence of a single life over the bloodstained promises of some utopia.

**Young Man:** (stares at Camus, taken aback by the fervor in his statement) "Your mother" over justice... Yes, I've heard of that quote. Many in the anti-colonial movement found it outrageous – selfish even.

**Camus:** It was misunderstood. My point was that abstract *ideas* of justice mean nothing to me if they trample concrete human lives – like the life of my own mother, an impoverished, innocent woman who never harmed a soul. I won't abandon actual people for the sake of an idea.

**Young Man:** (quietly, with scorn) Then maybe you are not cut out for revolution. Revolutions are not won by sentiment.

**Camus:** (sadly) Perhaps I am not. But consider: if revolutions devour the innocent, they might sow the seeds of their own corruption. I'm trying to save our side's soul, if you will.

**Young Man:** (throws up his hands) Our soul? That's a luxury for those who aren't fighting for their lives. Tell the Algerian patriot facing a French firing squad about *his soul*. He'd rather have a rifle.

**Camus:** I would never fault a man for defending himself from death. I am speaking against the *ideology* of indiscriminate violence, of bombing civilians in the name of principle – which I see unfolding on all sides. I love justice, as you do, but I love it enough not to pervert it. *Murder in the service of virtue is still murder.*

**Young Man:** (voice thick with frustration) And virtue in the service of oppression is still oppression. Your pretty phrases change nothing for those under the boot.

**Camus:** (bows his head a moment, then looks the young man in the eye) What do you want from me? Endorsement of killing? You won't have it. If that isolates me – if former friends call me traitor – so be it. I'd rather stand alone in truth than join the chorus of lies.

**Young Man:** Alone is exactly how you'll end up. Can't you see? Sartre, the whole left bank, they've moved on without you. You're being left behind, irrelevant, with only your conscience for company.

**Camus:** (a faint, melancholic smile) I have noticed. The invitations grow fewer, the smiles colder. It is not easy – I won't pretend otherwise. It hurts to be estranged from old comrades.

**Young Man:** Then why not bend, just a little? Meet them half way. Otherwise you'll shout into the void, unheard. What good does that do anyone?

**Camus:** (his face lined with tiredness, but resolute) Perhaps none. But I cannot trade integrity for popularity. I carry a responsibility – to the victims of *both* sides, to the truth as I see it. Even if I'm a lone voice, I'll continue to speak. History will judge who was right, I suppose.

**Young Man:** (bitterly) History... History is written by those who win. And you, monsieur, you are choosing to lose.

**Camus:** (shrugs gently) Maybe so. Yet some defeats are better than unprincipled victories. Even if I lose every ally, I won't betray what I believe is right.

**Young Man:** (studies Camus, half-contemptuous, half-curious) Are you happy with that? To be solitary, "right" and ineffective?

**Camus:** Happy? (he thinks, then answers with a hint of sorrow) No, not happy. But at peace, perhaps. There's a kind of peace in knowing I won't cross certain lines. It simplifies things.

**Young Man:** (shakes his head) I can't understand you. And frankly, people like you – you stand in the way of real change with your moralizing.

**Camus:** If "real change" demands running over the innocent, then yes, I'll stand in the way. If that makes me an enemy in your eyes, so be it.

**Young Man:** (steps back, raising his voice to the room) At least Sartre and his lot aren't afraid to get their hands dirty for freedom! Enjoy your sterile solitude, Monsieur Camus. History will pass you by.

**Camus:** (softly, as the young man turns to go) It may. But my conscience will remain with me.

**Young Man:** (spins around one last time) Conscience! Try brandishing that at the barricades – see how much good it does. (He spits on the floor in disgust) We'll win *without* you.

**Camus:** (quietly) Perhaps you will. I genuinely hope the result is freedom, even if I can't approve of all your methods.

**Young Man:** Save your hope. We don't need it. (He marches up the aisle, his footsteps echoing. A few onlookers follow him out, their faces a mix of anger and uncertainty.)

*(Camus remains by the podium, nearly alone now. The confrontation has drained the color from his face. He closes his briefcase slowly. An elderly*

*professor, one of the event organizers, approaches with an apologetic expression.)*

**Professor:** Monsieur Camus, I'm terribly sorry about that scene... Are you all right?

**Camus:** (manages a faint smile) I'm all right, thank you. It's nothing I haven't heard before.

**Professor:** (shakes his head) Such disrespect. Your talk was profoundly moving. Some of us... (he clears his throat) Some of us still believe in what you said.

**Camus:** (with gratitude) That means a great deal to me. More than you know.

**Professor:** You are not as alone as you think.

**Camus:** (picks up his coat, gazing toward the empty doorway where the young man exited) Perhaps. Though it often feels that way.

**Professor:** History will have its say in time. In the meantime, please continue to speak your mind. Voices of principle are rare and sorely needed.

**Camus:** (nodding, shoulders straightening a little) I will. As long as I have breath.

**Professor:** Bon. *Good.* Can I walk you out?

**Camus:** Thank you. I'd appreciate the company. *(They walk slowly up the aisle together.)*

**Professor:** (softly, as they reach the doors) Your path is difficult, Monsieur Camus, but take heart. Integrity may be lonely, but it is not without its own honor.

**Camus:** (stepping out into the cool night, he looks up at the sky) Lonely and honorable... I can live with that. *(He offers the professor a parting handshake.)* Good night, my friend.

**Professor:** Good night.

---

*Camus pulls his coat tight against a chill breeze. As he walks off into the Parisian night, he is solitary — a figure etched in streetlamp glow — yet his stride is composed. Sorrow and defiance mingle in his eyes. He disappears down the quiet street, a man apart, upheld by nothing but the clear light of his own conscience. In the distance, the city lights shimmer, indifferent. Camus moves toward them, into the darkness, unbowed and unafraid.*

---

# Part IV:
# Isolation & Integrity

# Chapter 15
## Graveside Argument

---

*Dawn lifts its veil slowly over the Paris cemetery. A dim grey fog clings to the gravestones, beading them with moisture. In the silence, Albert Camus stands before a modest headstone, hands in coat pockets, shoulders bowed. The air tastes of wet earth and loss. Between black iron gates and rows of crosses, a lone woman in mourning clothes appears, like an apparition from the mist. The widow's silhouette moves toward Camus, and the fog swirls as if making way for this quiet convergence of the living among the dead.*

---

**Camus:** (softly, without turning) It's a cold morning, Madame. I didn't expect anyone else here so early.

**Widow:** (stepping closer, her voice low) Nor did I. But I come at dawn most days... when the world is quiet enough to remember.

**Camus:** (nods, eyes still on the headstone) You're here for Louis, aren't you? I thought I recognized you through the fog. It's been a long time.

**Widow:** Yes. Ten years since the war ended, ten years since he... since we won and I lost him. (She wraps her coat tighter) And you, M. Camus? You remember him too, I see.

**Camus:** "Comrade Louis," we called him in the Resistance. Of course I remember. We printed underground papers side by side, shared cigarettes under curfew... He believed in what we fought for, with a sincerity that kept me going on darker nights.

**Widow:** (with a faint, sad smile) He admired you, you know. He'd come home excited whenever you published another fiery editorial in *Combat*. Told me you gave hope a voice when hope was scarce.

**Camus:** (closing his eyes a moment) He never said that to me. I'm grateful... Though it sometimes feels like another life, when we all believed our sacrifices would build something better.

**Widow:** (gazes at the headstone) I used to believe that, too. But now — look at the world. France is free, yes, but how quickly new struggles replace the old. Factories on strike, new wars overseas, old injustices wearing new faces. (Her tone hardens) Louis died for *this*? For politicians to argue while widows tend graves in the fog?

**Camus:** (turns to her) His sacrifice wasn't for politicians. It was for *us*, for the people he loved and the country he cherished.

**Widow:** (bitterly) Big words. *Country. Love.* I loved one man — him. The country took him from me and gives me nothing in return except a pension and a folded flag. Do your ideals console me on long nights? Do philosophies keep me warm? (She meets his eyes) You wrote of justice and rebellion — tell me, where is the justice in *this*?

**Camus:** (his voice thick) There is none. There is no replacing a husband, no rationalizing a single death. Louis's absence is an injustice I feel in my bones every time I remember his laugh.

**Widow:** (her eyes soften slightly at his tone) Then what was the point? You, of all people, must have an answer. Otherwise everything we endured, everything he gave... it's meaningless.

**Camus:** (steps closer, gently) No, not meaningless. I won't say the usual words — that *his death had a purpose*. The truth is we create purpose after the fact, to bear the loss. Louis fought so fewer innocents would suffer. He died so others might not have to. That doesn't ease your pain — I know. But perhaps it can dignify it.

**Widow:** (tears in her voice) Dignify... my pain?

**Camus:** (carefully) Your pain comes from love. And Louis's life, and even his death, were expressions of love — love for you, for life, for a freedom he wanted others to taste. In the midst of war's madness, he held onto that love. *That* is not meaningless.

**Widow:** (shaking her head slowly) Love. (She brushes a hand over the cold headstone) Love didn't save him.

**Camus:** No. (He bows his head) We couldn't save him. I replay it often — the last mission, the warning I wish I'd given, the bullet I wish I could have stopped.

**Widow:** (whispers) You feel guilty.

**Camus:** (tightens his jaw) Every survivor feels the weight of guilt. That we are here and they are not. Sometimes I wonder — did I do enough? Could I have been braver, saved one more life? These questions haunt me in the early hours.

**Widow:** (studies him) I didn't know that. The newspapers always show you as confident, principled... I never imagined you kneeling in doubt.

**Camus:** (smiles sadly) I'm a human being before I'm a name in print. And like you, I mourn. I question. I rage quietly at tombstones in the dawn.

**Widow:** (her eyes fill) I'm sorry. Perhaps I judged you harshly. It's just... when Louis died, a part of me turned to stone. I have been angry for so long.

**Camus:** No apology necessary. (He tentatively reaches and places a warm hand over her cold, gloved hand on the headstone) Your anger is honest. It speaks to your love for him.

**Widow:** (closing her eyes) I don't want to be angry forever. But I can't pretend to share the hopes you and he shared. Not anymore.

**Camus:** We hoped for a better world, yes. We still do. But I understand — you carry the cost of that hope.

**Widow:** (faintly) Do you still believe it? That better world?

**Camus:** (looks up at the whitening sky) On days like this, I confess I doubt. But then I remind myself what Louis stood for. In our darkest hours, he insisted that even if we stand to lose, we must fight cruelty, so that *some* justice, however small, can exist in this absurd world. If I abandon that belief, then his death truly would be empty. I can't do that — to him or to myself.

**Widow:** And what do I do with my anger, M. Camus? What do I do with this *hole* in my life?

**Camus:** Maybe... maybe you keep talking to him. (He half-smiles at her surprised look) I mean it. Come here in the quiet mornings as you do, tell him your anger and your sorrow. And listen, too — in the way the mist moves or a bird sings, perhaps you'll sense what he might respond.

**Widow:** (tears slipping down) I only ever hear silence.

**Camus:** I know. But silence doesn't mean absence. (He looks around at the gravestones) These stones, this fog — they carry memory. In the stillness, sometimes I feel Louis's presence more vividly than in the noise of day.

**Widow:** (wipes her cheek and manages a small, wry smile) He was a quiet man, wasn't he? Perhaps silence *is* his way.

**Camus:** (smiling a little) He would let others shout and argue, and then he'd say one simple thing that cut to the heart of it all.

**Widow:** Yes. (She breathes deeply) I miss even the silence we shared.

**Camus:** (as the fog begins to brighten) Madame, I can't promise that anger will leave you. But maybe alongside it, if you allow, a bit of the love that Louis gave can grow. Enough to lighten the burden, if only by a feather's weight.

**Widow:** (studying him gently) You carry your own burden, I see that now. Perhaps... perhaps talking helps. Even to a dead husband — or an old friend. (She touches his hand briefly) Thank you.

**Camus:** (squeezes her hand) For what?

**Widow:** For not giving me cheap optimism. For sharing your doubt and pain. It feels... honest. Louis valued honesty above all, even when it hurt.

**Camus:** He taught me that. (Camus clears his throat, emotion heavy) We must be honest, yes — even about the grief and the anger. Only then can we find a path *through* them.

**Widow:** (nods, then looks toward the gates) The sun is fighting through the fog. I should go before the crowds and daytime noises come.

**Camus:** Take care, Madame.

**Widow:** (pauses) One more thing... Louis's ideals, the ones that you both fought for — don't let them die, even if I can't carry them now. Someone must.

**Camus:** I won't forget. I carry them, and I carry him, always. (He bows respectfully as she turns to leave) Goodbye... and my heartfelt good wishes.

**Widow:** (voice already a little distant in the mist) Goodbye, M. Camus.

---

*Camus watches her figure recede into the fog. Alone again among the gravestones, he places a hand on Louis's headstone. In the growing light, the letters of his friend's name glisten with dew. Camus closes his eyes as if in prayer, though no gods are invoked. Only the unspoken vow in his heart answers the silence: he will remember, and he will remain true.*

---

# Chapter 16
## The Empty Cathedral

---

*Late afternoon light filters through stained-glass windows, painting the empty pews of Saint-Julien church in hues of sapphire and blood-red. The vaulted ceiling soars into shadows; the air smells of melted wax and old incense. Camus steps quietly through the heavy wooden door, removing his hat as his eyes adjust to the dim sanctuary. A few votive candles flicker by a side altar. In a far corner, a grey-haired priest in a threadbare cassock tends to a rack of unlit candles, humming a plainchant under his breath. Footsteps echoing on stone, Camus wanders down the center aisle, drawn by the silence and the faint promise of warmth in this cavern of prayer. He slides into a pew near the middle, sitting as one might in a library, seeking hush and refuge rather than worship. The priest, noticing the solitary visitor, makes his way over, his wrinkled face kind under the flicker of holy light from above.*

---

**Priest:** (smiling gently) Good evening, my son. You look a bit lost. Are you seeking someone, or perhaps seeking *something?*

**Camus:** (glancing up at the stained-glass crucifixion scene) Good evening, Father. In truth... I'm not sure. I saw the door was open, and the emptiness inside drew me in. I hope that's alright.

**Priest:** Of course. Our doors are open to all. This is the hour when the church is often empty — save for God and the ghosts, as I like to joke. (He chuckles softly) Please, stay as long as you need.

**Camus:** (nods gratefully) Thank you. It's peaceful here. The city out there is so loud with argument lately; I needed a place to hear myself think.

**Priest:** Or to hear *Him* think, perhaps? (He gestures upward playfully) Forgive me, I mean no disrespect. Old habit of a priest, to gently point every wanderer toward God.

**Camus:** (smiles faintly) No offense taken. But I should be honest — I'm not here in search of God's voice. Silence itself is what I was looking for.

**Priest:** (leans on the pew in front of Camus) Silence can be a great healer. In our tradition, we say God often speaks most clearly in the silence. Even if one does not believe, quiet can still reveal truths, don't you think?

**Camus:** (exhales, looking at his hands) I do. Silence strips away the day's noise and the slogans everyone shouts. In silence, I can finally confront my own thoughts... and doubts.

**Priest:** Doubt, yes. That faithful companion of belief. (He studies Camus' face) You are Albert Camus, are you not?

**Camus:** (a little surprised) I am.

**Priest:** I've read your work. This may surprise you, but your novel *The Stranger* and some of your essays — I found them deeply engaging, even as a man of faith. You write of a kind of moral integrity even without God.

**Camus:** (quietly) I try to, at least. I appreciate that you read them with an open mind.

**Priest:** (smiling) Open mind, open heart — that's what I preach. Though some in my position condemned you as an apostate influence on the young, I never saw you as an enemy of the Church. Merely a soul in search of light, albeit one who does not call it God.

**Camus:** (perhaps a bit embarrassed) Father, I... I was raised without religion. But I have always respected those who live their faith with compassion. I hope I haven't offended that compassion in anything I've written.

**Priest:** No offense. In fact, I sense in you *une inquiétude*, a kind of holy unrest. You remind me of some of our best believers, strangely enough — wrestling with angels even if you won't name them.

**Camus:** (smiles) "Holy unrest" is a kind way to put it. I have been wrestling, certainly — though not with angels. With men, with my own conscience, with the state of the world.

**Priest:** (nods) These are heavy burdens. Would you care to talk about it? Sometimes a conversation in an empty church can be as confidential as a confession. I offer only a listening ear, not judgment.

**Camus:** (rubs his chin, then gestures lightly) Very well. Lately, I feel... estranged. Alienated from the intellectual currents swirling outside these walls. Many of my old companions see me as a traitor or a fool because I will not march in step with their ideologies.

**Priest:** You speak of the political quarrels? The famous falling-out with M. Sartre and his circle?

**Camus:** (looks down) That, and more. Ever since I dared question whether any end — however noble — justifies the means of killing, I've been cast out to the margins. It's as if refusing to applaud murder — no matter who commits it — made me a heretic in their secular church.

**Priest:** (smiles sadly) In that sense, you *are* a heretic of the age. You won't bow to their god of ideology.

**Camus:** I can't. I believe there are things no cause should force us to betray: our common humanity, the innocent among us. I've said simply that one cannot make oneself God to play judge and executioner, that *no one* has that right. For this I was scorned by those who once called me friend.

**Priest:** And that wounds you. (He sits in the pew across the aisle, facing Camus) Despite your public poise, it is clear the estrangement causes you pain.

**Camus:** (admitting quietly) Yes. I do feel pain. And a sense of shame, oddly — a shame at being publicly attacked as naive, or as lacking *engagement*. Perhaps it's pride, but I never thought defending basic human values would make me unpopular among those who also fought tyranny.

**Priest:** People can be zealous, especially when they convince themselves they alone know the path to salvation — earthly or heavenly. Or, worse yet, they fear that they have long been on the wrong path. They become inquisitors. It has happened in the Church's history too, tragically.

**Camus:** (nods) I opposed them for that very reason — the inquisition of one's peers in the name of dogma. And now I find myself a target of a new inquisition. (He lets out a dry chuckle) Life has a cruel sense of irony.

**Priest:** The prophets were often without honor in their own country. In a way, by insisting on mercy and limits, you challenge the new orthodoxy. They react as people often do to heresy: with anger and ostracism.

**Camus:** Perhaps. I don't claim to be a prophet — far from it. I've no revelation, only the conviction that we must not become what we oppose.

**Priest:** That is a profoundly moral stance. And might I add, quite Christian in spirit, even if you arrived at it through secular means. "Love thine enemies" and "thou shalt not kill" resonate in what you say.

**Camus:** (raises an eyebrow) I hadn't thought of it that way. I came to it simply because I've seen death — my father's, my comrades' — and I cannot accept any reasoning that coldly sacrifices a living person on the altar of some utopia. It strikes me as... blasphemy, if I may borrow your language.

**Priest:** Borrow it freely. Many tongues, one truth. (He clasps his hands) It heartens me to hear this. Often I worry that as faith recedes in our society, so too will the basic regard for life and neighbor. But you show that conscience can burn bright even outside these church walls.

**Camus:** I appreciate that. Still, Father, without faith, I find it hard to locate hope some days. The silence here is soothing, but out there — (he gestures toward the door) — out there the silence is God's. And He remains mute to the injustices and absurdities. How do you reconcile that?

**Priest:** (looks thoughtfully at the stained-glass) It is the oldest question. *The silence of God.* I have lived long, and I confess I have no final answer. Only this: if God is silent, perhaps He entrusts us to be His voice. To speak for justice, to console, to stand with the suffering.

**Camus:** A *coordinate* of God on earth, rather than a subject?

Priest: Exactly. If you will humor an old man's musings — maybe God prefers to work through human hearts. So the voice of your conscience championing mercy... could that not be a spark of the divine working anonymously?

**Camus:** (chuckles) Father, you're assigning me heavenly importance I surely lack.

**Priest:** (smiling) Not importance — responsibility. We say humans are made in God's image. I interpret that as a charge to act as a mirror of the highest good we can envision. You, without belief, still act with a fervor for good, for human dignity. In my eyes, that is godly work, whether you call it that or not.

**Camus:** (falls silent, moved, after a pause) I have never thought to hear a priest calling my work "godly."

**Priest:** Perhaps I'm a heretic in my own order. (He laughs softly) But truth is truth. One doesn't decide the truth of an idea based on whether it comes from a believer or an unbeliever.

**Camus:** (thoughtful) How liberating it would be if everyone thought so. Father, may I ask — have you ever doubted your path? Ever felt, as I do, utterly alone in your convictions?

**Priest:** (closes his eyes a moment) Oh yes. There was a time during the last war, when I saw children killed in bombings despite all my prayers. I nearly lost my faith. I shouted at God's silence. I felt abandoned.

**Camus:** What pulled you back?

**Priest:** One broken mother in my parish, who had lost her child in those bombings. I had no answers for her, no miracles. But I sat with her in her grief. I simply shared her silence and tears. Over time, I realized — that was my role. Not to *solve* the silence of God, but to be present in it, with others. My faith became less about expecting answers and more about offering presence, love, in a world often devoid of it.

**Camus:** (nods slowly) Offering presence in the silence... There's profound meaning in that. In a way, that's what I have left too. I cannot change the world as I wish, but I can be present — through words, through small acts — so that those who suffer know they're not alone.

**Priest:** And that, my son, is hope. (He smiles kindly) You see, you **have not abandoned the ethic of hope after all.**

**Camus:** (smiles back faintly) Perhaps not entirely. It's a quieter hope now, though. Not the trumpet of victory we imagined in our youth, but a small candle in a long night.

**Priest:** Often, a candle is all that's needed to show someone the way home in the dark.

**Camus:** (looking around the dim church, the colorful light dancing on stone pillars) This place... it reminds me of the caves where the early Christians huddled, keeping a flame alive in the darkness of empire. I sometimes feel like I'm huddling around a tiny flame of my own, trying to protect it from the winds of fanaticism and despair.

**Priest:** You are not as alone as you think. Even here, every morning I light candles for the same reason. And there are others out there, secular or faithful, guarding their little lights. In the end, those lights together may illumine more than we imagine.

**Camus:** (stands, moved to shake the priest's hand) Thank you, Father. You've given me something unexpected today — understanding.

**Priest:** (rising and clasping Camus' hand in both of his) Go with my blessing — though I know you don't seek it formally. Consider it the blessing of one flawed human to another: that you find peace in your solitude, and strength to keep that flame alive.

**Camus:** Softly, *merci*. I will try. (He releases the priest's hands) Perhaps I'll visit again — if only to enjoy this splendid silence.

**Priest:** (smiling) Our silence is always here for you, Monsieur Camus. God be with you — spoken as a hope, not a doctrine.

**Camus:** And you as well, Father.

---

*Camus places his hat back on and walks up the aisle, each footstep echoing. At the threshold he pauses to glance back: the priest stands in a shaft of colored light beneath the rose window, a solitary figure waving gently. Camus offers a grateful nod, then steps out into the city's dusk. The heavy door swings shut, snuffing out the candle-glow behind him. Outside, the noises of Paris resume — but something quiet and steady now glows within him, a small courage against the coming night.*

---

# Chapter 17
## Under the Streetlamp

---

*Night has fallen in a narrow back alley of Montparnasse. Rain drips from rusty fire escapes and puddles around the garbage bins. Under a lone streetlamp, Camus stands with collar upturned against the drizzle, a cigarette glowing between his fingers. The cobblestones shine slick underfoot. Across from him, leaning against a graffiti-stained wall, is a man about Camus' age with stormy eyes and a hard-set jaw. Henri's coat is frayed, his once-vibrant face worn by years of disappointment. They have chanced upon each other after a heated public debate at a nearby café, and now, away from prying eyes, a more personal confrontation brews in the damp, enclosed quiet of the alley. The distant hum of traffic and a neon sign's flicker provide the only backdrop as two former comrades face each other, shadows stretching long beneath the lamp.*

---

**Henri:** (flicking the ash from his cigarette) So, the great moralist emerges from his cave. I thought you'd slip away before I could catch you, Camus.

**Camus:** (calmy) I wasn't avoiding you, Henri. I stepped out for air — things got stuffy in there with all the shouting.

**Henri:** Stuffed with *words*, you mean. You and those professors... debating theory while real people bleed. (He spits rainwater aside) What a farce.

**Camus:** I came to discuss ideas, not to trade insults. If you have something to say to me, say it plainly.

**Henri:** Alright. (He stares hard at Camus) How can you live with yourself these days? How can you preach from the sidelines about what's right and wrong, when you've abandoned the very fight we once agreed mattered?

**Camus:** (steady gaze) I haven't abandoned any fight, unless you define "fight" as blind obedience to a party line. I'm true to the principles we shared in the Resistance.

**Henri:** Aha, the *Resistance*. We were brothers-in-arms then. But look at you now — standing apart, wringing your hands about "means and ends," refusing to support the oppressed because one side of the barricade doesn't meet your purity test.

**Camus:** (low, firm) Is that what you think? That I refuse to support the oppressed? Henri, I have spent years writing and speaking on behalf of the oppressed — whether under fascism or communism or colonialism. I have not changed that.

**Henri:** Oh? You condemned the fascists, yes. But now when colonial authorities massacre Algerian protesters, you stay silent. When socialist revolutionaries rise up, you scold them for violence. You've made yourself a man in the middle of every issue — smug and aloof.

**Camus:** Aloof? I bleed with every act of injustice, but I will not cheer for one form of terror simply because it calls itself revolutionary. I lost friends to Nazi firing squads; I won't justify a firing squad run by *anyone*, Red or otherwise.

**Henri:** Our world isn't that simple, Camus! Perhaps we *need* terror now and then — how else to shatter a rotten system? Sartre understands that, why can't you? The status quo won't fall with gentle protests and pretty words.

**Camus:** (voice rising) I know the world isn't simple. But if you start believing that *any* means are acceptable, you become what we once stood against. We fought Nazis who believed the ends justified the means — do you really want to mirror them under a different flag?

**Henri:** (smirks) There it is: the high-minded refrain. You're infamous for it now. Tell me, do you feel superior when you refuse to dirty your hands? Does your conscience glow white while others wade through blood?

**Camus:** (taking a slow drag, then exhaling) I don't feel superior. I feel sick — sick that people I respect have grown intoxicated on abstract causes and forgotten the value of a single human life. I'm trying to remind them, and myself, that *no ideal* is worth more than a child's tear. That's not superiority, Henri. It's humility in the face of the suffering I've seen.

**Henri:** And yet you *judged* us, judged me, for choosing a side. You wrote that those of us who advocate violent revolt for justice are morally in the wrong. Easy for you to say — you got your fame, your Nobel prize, and now you lecture us about moderation from your cozy study. Meanwhile, people are dying in the streets of Algiers and Budapest.

**Camus:** (coiled anger) Don't you dare imply I'm indifferent to those deaths. I spoke out for a truce in Algeria, for humane solutions — no one listened. I condemned the Soviet tanks in Budapest and pleaded for help to that city. What more do you want? Should I encourage young men to strap on bombs in markets? Should I endorse execution squads? Tell me, at what point does justice become indistinguishable from atrocity?

**Henri:** Justice *isn't* gentle, Camus. Look at history. The American and French revolutions spilled blood to uproot old orders. That's reality. The oppressed cannot win by playing nice; their oppressors certainly never do.

**Camus:** I'm not naive about history. But revolutions that begin by slaughtering innocents end as nightmares. I refuse to celebrate a guillotine, no matter whose neck lies beneath it.

**Henri:** (slams his fist lightly against the wall) So we do nothing? We let tyrants reign because we're too moral to fight?

**Camus:** Through terror, yes. Through other means — solidarity, truth, pressure — I still fight. I haven't given up on change, Henri. I've given up on the illusion that one can create freedom by murder.

**Henri:** Freedom by murder... You always twist it like that. What about self-defense? What about a people rising because they can't breathe under a boot? Is every violent act equally condemnable to you, no matter context?

**Camus:** (somberly) Context matters, absolutely. I understand why desperate people strike back. In their place, who knows what I'd do? I'm not above the fray — I'm painfully aware I too could be driven by anger to hatred. That is exactly why I will not justify it in advance with pretty words. The moment we start excusing killing, we unleash something uncontrollable.

**Henri:** (containing a tremor of emotion) Then what did Louis die for, hmm? (Camus flinches at the name.) Yes, I spoke to his widow. She told me you met her. What did he die for if not so that someday others might have the courage to take up arms against injustice?

**Camus:** (softly) Louis died to defeat a tyranny that had invaded our home. And we honor him best by never becoming tyrants ourselves in the name of liberty.

**Henri:** But we *are* tyrants — Frenchmen in Algeria, for example. Doesn't that outrage you? Or does your famous humanism stop at the Mediterranean?

**Camus:** (anguished) You know it outrages me! I was born there; those streets, Arab and French, are my home. I've wept for Algeria every day of this war. But I also fear for my mother, my family — civilians on both sides. That war is tearing me in two. I have publicly called for a ceasefire, for dialogue, anything to stop the slaughter.

**Henri:** But you haven't endorsed independence outright. That's what people wanted to hear, Camus. Instead, you delivered that unfortunate line at the Nobel press conference — what was it? "I believe in justice, but I will defend my mother before justice".

**Camus:** (bitterly) Yes. A clumsy, heartfelt truth — and for it I was branded a colonialist sympathizer. What I meant was exactly what we're arguing: abstract justice means nothing if it demands I condone the murder of innocents — *my mother* being the symbol of an innocent. I will never apologize for protecting the innocent before any cause, even my own.

**Henri:** So in practice, you protect your own tribe first. How convenient for the moralist to retreat to something as primal as blood.

**Camus:** (voice low) Have you ever heard your mother's voice cry out in fear? I have not, and I pray I never do, not for any ideology. Call that weakness, call it bourgeois sentiment — I call it the basic line of sanity. There are lines I will not cross.

**Henri:** (sneers) Lines, lines — while others are in trenches. You know what people say about you now? That you're yesterday's hero. A moderate, a *centriste* who couldn't stomach the true battle for the future.

**Camus:** I've heard worse. They also say I'm a hypocrite, a prude, a closet reactionary. It's fine. Let them say it. If refusing to join their chorus makes me "yesterday's hero," so be it. I did not seek to be anyone's hero, only to remain myself.

**Henri:** Your *pure self*, unsullied by history's blood. (He flicks his cigarette away, stepping closer) But guess what — history moves on without you. While you write lonely essays, others are making the new world, dirty hands and all. And they'll win.

**Camus:** (stares at him) They might. Tyranny often wins in the short run — wrapped in whatever flag, even red. But winning doesn't make them right.

**Henri:** It's easy to be "right" and dead, or irrelevant. I'd rather be on the side of those who make a difference.

**Camus:** And I'd rather not celebrate executions or gulags for the sake of a difference that poisons itself. I haven't changed, Henri — I still want a world of justice and freedom. I just don't believe the road there runs through a river of blood. We must build on something clean, or the house will collapse.

**Henri:** (shaking his head, a mix of anger and sadness) I miss the Camus who inspired us during the Occupation. You had fire then. Now all I see is doubt and hesitation.

**Camus:** The fire is still there, but it's tempered. War taught me the cost of unchecked fire. I carry every death with me. Perhaps you're right — I hesitate. Because I know each step into violence leaves footprints that never fade.

**Henri:** Then maybe you're already dead, old friend. Because the world won't wait for your philosophical purity. (He turns as if to leave, then stops) I'll fight on, with or without you. And if we achieve something, don't expect a share in the victory you shunned.

**Camus:** (softly) I expect nothing, Henri. Only that you remember, when this "victory" comes, to look at what it cost you — and whether it was worth the price of your soul.

**Henri:** (snorts) My soul? Luxuries. Ask the wretched of the earth about souls when they have no bread.

**Camus:** I have. And they told me they want bread *and* respect for their lives, not one at the cost of the other.

**Henri:** Enough. This is pointless. We're repeating ourselves, as always. (He steps back into the shadows) Goodbye, Camus. I hope your candle keeps you warm in the dark.

**Camus:** Goodbye, Henri. Take care... *mon ami.* Despite everything.

**Henri:** (pauses at that, an old warmth in his eyes glimmering, then hardening again) We chose different roads. Pray that mine doesn't lead to hell — since you don't believe in it, I'll bear that risk.

---

*Henri turns abruptly and strides off into the alley's darkness, footsteps splashing through puddles. Camus stands under the streetlamp a moment longer, watching his friend disappear around a corner. The rain has slowed to a mist. He drops his spent cigarette into the puddle and pulls his coat tighter. Alone in the chill alley, Camus feels the weight of the encounter pressing on his chest. He whispers something — a name, a fragment of a prayer, lost to the dripping silence — then walks out toward the faint lights of the boulevard, leaving only the dim streetlamp halo behind.*

---

# Chapter 18
## The Mirror in the Field

---

*A dense fog rolls in off the canals at midnight, shrouding the Amsterdam waterfront in a pale glow. In a dimly lit tavern by the water's edge, Camus pushes open a heavy door marked Mexico City Bar, entering a world of smoke and quiet jazz. The air smells of stale beer and saltwater. He finds a corner table by a rain-streaked window; outside, canal lights shimmer in the mist like drowned stars. A stranger sits alone at the next table — a gaunt man in a frayed suit, hat tilted low. There's an amber bottle of jenever in front of him and an empty glass in his hand. The stranger's eyes, sharp and weary, slide over to Camus as he takes a seat. In this nearly empty bar, their proximity invites an exchange. A single bartender polishes glasses by a rack of dusty bottles, paying them no mind. From somewhere in the haze, a saxophone croons a slow, melancholic tune. Camus lights a cigarette, and the stranger lets out a soft, ironic chuckle as if he recognizes an old acquaintance.*

---

**Stranger:** (smiling thinly) Well, well. A fellow traveler in the fog. What brings a man like you to a place like this at such an hour?

**Camus:** (exhales smoke, glancing at the man) Perhaps the same thing that brings you — a bit of solitude among people. And you seem to know what kind of man I am without ever meeting me.

**Stranger:** Oh, I have a guess or two. (He tips his glass in a mock toast) You carry yourself with that unmistakable weight — someone who's seen too much, felt too much. Am I wrong?

**Camus:** (smiles quietly) No, you're not wrong. Though I suspect many carry that weight nowadays.

**Stranger:** True. But some of us acknowledge it. Others go on pretending. I sense you're the former. (He gestures to the chair opposite him) Care to join me? There's a certain relief in not pretending, and I could use the company of an honest face.

**Camus:** (after a moment, he stands and moves to the stranger's table, sitting down) Alright. Honesty it is, then.

**Stranger:** (offering the bottle) A drink? It's Dutch courage — literally.

**Camus:** (pours a finger into a spare glass) Merci. To honesty, then.

**Stranger:** (lifting his drink) To honesty — or whatever remains of it in our tattered souls. (They drink) So, have you also been judged by the world and found lacking? Or are you among the judges?

**Camus:** (chuckles dryly) I've been on both sides, I think. Judged by many, and regrettably, I've done my share of judging too.

**Stranger:** Aha. (He lights a cigarette of his own, eyes glinting) As have I. You see, I was once a respectable man — respected by others and by myself. A *do-gooder*, charitable, high-minded. I imagine you might relate.

**Camus:** (surveys him) Perhaps a little. And now?

**Stranger:** (smoke curling from his lips) Now I find myself in a place like this, half drunk in the middle of the night, with no company but strangers. What does that tell you?

**Camus:** That something happened along the way.

**Stranger:** Oh yes. Something always happens, doesn't it? The fall from grace, the moment one's image of oneself cracks. (He taps ash into an ashtray) Tell me, friend — have you ever had that moment? When you looked in the mirror and no longer recognized the idealistic fool staring back?

**Camus:** (quietly) I have looked in the mirror and seen a stranger, yes.

**Stranger:** (laughs softly) Poetic. That's exactly it. For me, the mirror was literal. I used to be a lawyer, you know — a champion of noble causes, helping the oppressed, speaking lofty words in court. One night, not far from here, I heard a woman's scream and a splash. Someone drowning in the canal. And do you know what I did?

**Camus:** (frowns, leaning in) What?

**Stranger:** Nothing. I kept walking. (He gives a crooked grin) Monsieur, I kept walking and did not turn my head. The champion of justice, the defender of the helpless, slunk away. Cowardice? Indifference? Who knows. But in that single moment, all my fine self-opinion drowned in that canal with her.

**Camus:** (brows knit with sympathy and alarm) That's... a terrible burden to live with.

**Stranger:** Oh, it is. It is indeed. And ever since, I've made it my mission to strip away the pretensions — from myself and others. You see, I decided that night that we are all hypocrites. Every last one of us. (He points the cigarette at Camus) Even you, monsieur.

**Camus:** (meets his gaze steadily) I won't claim I've never been hypocritical. I'm human. I have my contradictions.

**Stranger:** Good. An honest response. But let's test how far your honesty goes. *(His voice takes on a razor edge)* You speak as though you value human life and moral purity — I've read your work. Your essays, your editorials. I remember the tone.

Righteous, yes. But also trembling, as if you were trying to convince yourself as much as others.

**Camus:** (tense) You've read my work?

**Stranger:** Of course. You were one of the last moral voices in France who tried to steer between the slogans. I remember the paper. *Combat.* I remember a particular piece on executions. Clear, even noble — until the blood dried.

**Camus:** (flatly) I meant every word.

**Stranger:** Perhaps you did. But allow me to play judge for a moment. *(He leans forward, eyes glinting)* You say no ideal justifies killing innocents. Yet, during the war, you supported the Allied bombings, the executions of Nazi collaborators, did you not? Blood was shed for liberty — your liberty.

**Camus:** (voice low) I supported fighting the Nazis, yes. I did not revel in any death. Even then, I tried to argue against revenge killings after the liberation, against excess. I wrote against the death penalty for collaborators when passions ran hottest.

**Stranger:** True, true, you did. And you were derided for it even then. I recall an editorial — yours, perhaps — urging France not to become what it hated.

**Camus:** (raises an eyebrow) You have a sharp memory indeed.

**Stranger:** I do. It's my curse. And here's what my memory whispers now: even you have had blood on your hands by proxy. You fought with words, but those words stirred men to fight with guns. You can't deny that, can you?

**Camus:** (falls silent, jaw tight) During the Resistance, yes, I knew my words in *Combat* might spur violence. I accepted that as the price to defeat a monstrosity. That decision still weighs on me. War leaves none of us unstained.

**Stranger:** (smiles with a hint of triumph) Ah, so you admit it. The idealist's compromise. You aren't so different from your comrade Henri after all only perhaps more fastidious about where to draw the line.

**Camus:** (defensive) I *am* different in that I draw the line at a point where my conscience can live with it and no further. Perhaps I failed at perfect consistency, but one must try to limit the damage.

**Stranger:** Limit the damage... (he savors the phrase) And yet, damage is done. Always. You limit it here, it pops up elsewhere. The world runs on damage.

**Camus:** (frowning) What are you saying?

**Stranger:** That the sooner we accept our own complicity in the world's evil, the more honest we become. I, for one, have accepted it. I've stopped fighting it. I drink my jenever, I laugh at virtue, I play the penitent and the judge at once — because who better to judge than one who is guilty too?

**Camus:** (quietly horrified) You've abandoned hope entirely, then.

**Stranger:** Hope? (He laughs — a brittle, echoing sound) My dear man, hope is a luxury for those who have not yet looked into their own abyss. You have a name for it, don't you? The absurd. The gap between our ideals and reality.

**Camus:** Yes... the absurd, the confrontation between human longing for meaning and the indifferent silence of the universe.

**Stranger:** Exactly. Some, like you, see it and still talk of humanism, of pushing the boulder up the hill like Sisyphus.

Me? I laugh. I laugh because I finally understand that all our righteousness is a performance to avoid being judged. We hasten to judge others so we won't be judged ourselves, eh?

**Camus:** (cold realization in his eyes) That sounds disturbingly familiar. I've imagined such a voice before — half confessor, half executioner.

**Stranger:** (raises his glass) Then perhaps you and I have met in thought, if not on paper. Some truths are too old to be original. But admit it, you recognize me — not my face, but the echo.

**Camus:** (quietly) Yes. I recognize the echo. And I dread what it becomes.

**Stranger:** But you followed, nonetheless. All this time preaching from the margins — has it not made you even a little self-satisfied? Be honest. Don't you secretly think yourself better than those who hate you?

**Camus:** (winces, then after a pause) Yes. In moments of anger... I've felt that poisonous pride — that illusion that I alone remained true. It's a lie I know too well. One I must keep rooting out. I'm no better than anyone — just obstinate in what I believe. And I've betrayed even that, in quiet, personal ways.

**Stranger:** (leaps at that confession) Betrayed, you say? Personally? Do tell!

**Camus:** (hesitant, haunted) I've hurt people I love. I've been unfaithful to my wife, the mother of my children, chasing my own selfish passions. I speak of loyalty and humanism, yet I created suffering in my own home. That guilt weighs on me more than the political storms.

**Stranger:** So the idealist is also an adulterer. (He clasps his hands in mock prayer) Oh, the complexity! Delicious. And does the great moralist ask forgiveness?

**Camus:** (with sorrow) Every day, though not in a confessional. I ask it silently, through small acts, through trying to be better. Whether I'll be granted it — I don't know. My wife has endured a lot. Perhaps more than she should have.

**Stranger:** And yet you did it. Why? Did your own philosophy not hold up when faced with the temptations of flesh and ego?

**Camus:** (bitterly) Perhaps not. Or perhaps I am simply weak, craving affirmation and warmth beyond what I had. It's not something I'm proud of. If anything, it humbles me — I know I'm no paragon.

**Stranger:** So then why persist in lecturing others? Why not admit you too are a hypocrite and join me in this sweet abyss of irony?

**Camus:** (looks directly at him, a clear calm in his voice) Because acknowledging my failures doesn't erase my responsibility to keep striving for what's right. Yes, I'm flawed — deeply. But if I give up hope for myself, I'd be giving up on all I've fought for. The answer to hypocrisy isn't to revel in it; it's to try to lessen it, step by step.

**Stranger:** (scoffs) Spoken like a true penitent who still hopes to be a saint.

**Camus:** (smiles sadly) No, not a saint. In fact, I wrote once that there's no humble sainthood for me — I know I'll never be one. I'll settle for being a decent human being, on good days.

**Stranger:** But you see, that's where we differ. I've abandoned the attempt. I'm free now — free to admit I'm wretched and so is everyone else. It's... strangely liberating to stand in the mud and say, "Yes, here I am."

**Camus:** And does it make you happy, this liberation?

**Stranger:** (pauses, eyes unfocused) Happy? (He lets out a slow breath) It spares me the disappointment of hope. Happiness... no. I wouldn't call it that. It's more like a numb contentment. Like a man who's stopped struggling and floats downstream with the current.

**Camus:** That is one form of peace, I suppose. But forgive me, it sounds like a living death.

**Stranger:** (smiles thinly) You really are incorrigible. Anyone else with your life — vilified by peers, plagued by illness, haunted by guilt — might have joined me in laughing at it all by now. Yet you cling to this *ethic of hope*, as you call it. Why? What keeps that ember alive in you?

**Camus:** (ponders, swirling the liquor in his glass) I ask myself that often. Part of it is sheer obstinacy — I simply refuse to let the world's absurdity have the final say. Part is memory: I remember moments of genuine beauty and solidarity, even in dark times, and I cannot betray them by giving in to cynicism. And part... part is love, I suppose.

Stranger: Love? (He raises an eyebrow skeptically) The romantic in you speaks.

**Camus:** Not just romantic love — though I have felt that deeply too — but love for *life*. For this world with all its sorrow. I was born in sunlight by the Mediterranean; there's a part of me that will always recall the simple joy of being alive on a bright morning, the sea stretching beyond the horizon. That memory, that love, it outlasts the despair.

**Stranger:** (rolls his eyes lightly, but there's a trace of genuine curiosity) The invincible summer, eh?

**Camus:** (looks at him sharply) Yes… exactly. In the depths of winter, I learned there lay in me an invincible summer. I wrote that once, and I still believe it. Even now.

**Stranger:** (snorts softly) Optimism from the mouth of the defeated. Incredible.

**Camus:** Call it optimism if you like. I call it fidelity — to the few things in life that made me want to be alive in the first place. I may have lost faith in revolutions and manifestos, but I haven't lost faith in the taste of bread, in the laughter of children, in the loyalty of a friend, in the gentle light of a winter sun. These humble things… they keep me from total despair.

**Stranger:** (finishes his drink, regarding Camus with an inscrutable expression) Perhaps you and I are not so different after all. We both see the world's grotesque comedy. But where I chose to play the clown, you choose to remain — what, the compassionate witness?

**Camus:** If I can, yes. To bear witness to suffering yet still celebrate whatever is worthy in us. To say, *"This is our lot, but we will not be lesser for it."* That's the closest I come to a credo.

**Stranger:** (shakes his head slowly) Listening to you, I almost feel… wistful. As if I glimpsed a man I might have become had I turned left instead of right on a certain night.

**Camus:** It's never too late, you know. One can always turn back toward that part of oneself that cared.

**Stranger:** (smiling sadly) For me it might be. I've sunk too deep, and I've grown comfortable here. But you — perhaps you'll prove me wrong about everyone. (He stands unsteadily, placing coins on the table) It's been a pleasure, truly.

**Camus:** (rising as well) Must you go?

**Stranger:** Yes. I prefer to wander before the dawn scatters this lovely fog. (He extends his hand unexpectedly) Albert Camus, thank you — for the company, and the argument.

**Camus:** (grips his hand firmly) Thank *you*. I won't soon forget this conversation.

**Stranger:** (smiles with a hint of warmth) Nor will I. Au revoir, monsieur.

**Camus:** Au revoir. And... good luck.

**Stranger:** (chuckles as he walks to the door) I'm beyond luck, but I appreciate the sentiment. *(The stranger tips his hat and exits into the misty night.*

**Camus:** (watches the door swing shut, then turns back to the empty table. He notices the stranger's half-full bottle left behind; he pours a final sip into his glass. Lifting it toward the vacant seat across from him, Camus whispers to the silence) Adieu, mon semblable, mon frère. (He downs the bitter liquid, sets the glass down, and gathers his coat.)

---

*Outside, the fog presses against the window. Camus leaves a few francs on the table and steps back out into the cold, where the canal's dark water flows quietly under the bridge. The fog swallows his figure as he heads toward his hotel, a solitary man walking but not yet lost, the echo of jazz and confessions trailing behind him like a fading beacon.*

---

# Chapter 19
## Return to Tipasa

---

*Winter sunlight bathes the ancient Roman ruins of Tipasa in a gentle gold, taking the chill out of the December air. Camus walks among tumbled columns and crumbling arches overlooking the glittering Mediterranean Sea. Here, the world feels timeless: olive trees twist up from broken marble, and the distant cry of a seabird echoes against amphitheater stones. He has returned to this Algerian shore to seek something he lost in the clamor of Europe — perhaps an innocence, or a clarity only the open sky and sea can grant. As he pauses by a fragment of mosaic floor, he breathes deeply of the salt-tinged breeze. In the bright noon light, the fog of past days is a memory; here all is stark and clean. An old caretaker of the site, a local man in a simple djellaba robe, approaches slowly with a kind smile, his sandaled feet silent on the worn path. He recognizes the visitor — Camus had been here years ago — and without ceremony falls into step beside him. Among the sun-warmed ruins, two men, different in origin yet oddly united by the space between words, wander toward a low wall where the waves can be heard thrashing gently against the rocks below.*

---

**Old Man:** (in Arabic-accented French) It does the heart good, doesn't it? This sun. These ruins. I remember you, monsieur — you came here in winter many years ago, no?

**Camus:** (smiling softly) Yes. I was here over a decade back, one bright winter day much like this. You have a good memory.

**Old Man:** I remember those who stop and truly look, truly breathe this place in. Many tourists come, but few really *absorb*

Tipasa. You did. You sat and closed your eyes to feel the sun
— just as you were doing now.

**Camus:** It's true. (He runs a hand along a rough stone) I was
desperate to feel alive then. And this place... gave me that, if
only for a moment. I've carried that moment with me.

**Old Man:** (smiles) Welcome home, then. You seem older now
— more burden on your shoulders.

**Camus:** I am older. The burdens... I hope to lay some of them
down here, even briefly. There's a kind of forgiveness in the sea
and sky, isn't there?

**Old Man:** Perhaps. Nature doesn't judge us, at least. It just is.
The sea is the sea. The sun is the sun. They outlast our little
triumphs and tragedies.

**Camus:** Yes. When I'm here, I remember that beyond all our
arguments and sorrows, the world itself has a simple purity. It
puts things in perspective.

**Old Man:** (nods, looking at the sea) I've watched many come
and go — warriors, poets, lovers — over these stones. Some
leave heavy, some leave light. It pleases me to see you back; I
think you left a bit of your spirit here last time and maybe came
to reclaim it?

**Camus:** Perhaps I did. (He gazes at the horizon) The last time
I came, I wrote afterwards that in the midst of winter I found
within me an invincible summer. That feeling... I feared I had
lost it in the years between. So I've returned, hoping to touch it
again.

**Old Man:** Everything changes, monsieur. You cannot step in
the same river twice, as the saying goes. But maybe you'll find a
new truth rhyming with the old one.

**Camus:** (turns to him) And what truth do you find living among these ruins, my friend? You must have thought a lot, tending this silent city of the past.

**Old Man:** Oh, I am no philosopher — just a simple man. But I have learned this: Empires rise and fall, men come and go, but life continues in cycles. What was once in ruins can blossom again in time, differently. See, look — (he points to a cluster of wildflowers growing between two cracked stones) — even here, life finds a way to bloom.

**Camus:** (kneels briefly to touch the delicate purple flower) Wild cyclamen... pushing out of a tombstone. (He smiles) It's beautiful, isn't it? Fragile and stubborn at once.

**Old Man:** Yes. Like hope. You don't plant it, it just appears, even in forgotten places.

**Camus:** (rising) I needed to see this. In my country — France, I mean — I've been surrounded by noise: arguments, polemics, people calling me traitor or saint or fool. I nearly forgot the silent truth that life persists beyond all that. A flower doesn't know our quarrels; it just reaches for the sun.

**Old Man:** Just so. You intellectuals complicate life. Out here, we have simpler wisdom: Love your family, take joy in the sun and sea, stand upright before God or fate, and when death comes, meet it with dignity.

**Camus:** (simple, earnest) That's wisdom I crave. I've spent so much time analyzing what ails the world, fighting and mourning. Perhaps I lost sight of those simple things.

**Old Man:** (offering a date fruit from his pocket) Here, have something sweet. Grown in my own garden.

**Camus:** (accepts the date and tastes it) Thank you... it's delicious.

**Old Man:** (smiling) Sweetness in winter — that's something, no? (He looks at Camus shrewdly) You know, I read the papers. I know you've had a heavy burden, speaking about Algeria's troubles. Many here have been angry with you, others praise you.

**Camus:** (braces slightly) I imagine I've displeased people on all sides.

**Old Man:** True. You tried to stop the bloodshed and please everyone — impossible task. But I think you did it because you love this place and its people, both Arab and French. Not everyone understands that.

**Camus:** (voice catching) It's true. They're both my people — the soil of Algeria nurtured me, and yet I carry French blood and tongue. It tears me apart to see the hatred, the pain on both sides. I only wanted them to remember each other's humanity.

**Old Man:** A hard thing in times of war. People prefer to forget humanity then; it makes fighting easier.

**Camus:** Yes. They call it necessity, but it feels like a great betrayal — of our common life.

**Old Man:** Perhaps when the anger passes, they'll recall voices like yours. If not now, then later, to heal.

**Camus:** I hope so. Even if I'm gone by then... I hope something I tried to say will make sense to someone.

**Old Man:** It will. Words have echoes. Sometimes they just take time to be heard. (He pats Camus' arm) In any case, you did what your conscience demanded. Here under the sun, that's all any man can answer for, no?

**Camus:** (relaxes, a gentle smile warming his face) You're right. Here under the sun, I feel no need to justify further. I simply... *am*.

**Old Man:** (laughs kindly) Exactly! You see, you're becoming a simple man too, if only for an afternoon.

**Camus:** Perhaps that is the final wisdom for me — to be at peace with just living, not forever arguing my existence.

**Old Man:** You've earned that peace, I'd say.

**Camus:** (quietly) I feel it here. A quiet, mythic coherence, as if all the scattered pieces of me come together under this light.

**Old Man:** Mythic coherence... (chuckles) Those are grand words, but I think I understand.

**Camus:** (looking out at the sea) It's like standing on this ancient ground, I sense all the stories that came before — heroes, lovers, rebels — and I'm just one more man passing through. I don't need to raise my voice so much anymore. The ruins speak for themselves. The waves, the wind — they whisper truths that will be here long after I'm gone.

**Old Man:** And that doesn't sadden you?

**Camus:** (shakes his head) No. It humbles and comforts me. I have been arguing from the margins for so long, trying to be heard over the crowd. Here, I realize it's enough to have *lived* by what I value. To embody it quietly is better than to shout it.

**Old Man:** (nods approvingly) You've found something today, I think.

**Camus:** (smiling through bright, unshed tears) Yes... I feel I have. A kind of clarity, simple and clean.

**Old Man:** Good. Carry it with you when you return to the noise. And whenever you need, come back. The sun and sea will still be here, God willing.

**Camus:** Thank you, my friend. I will come back, I promise.

**Old Man:** Now, I must attend to another visitor over there. Will you be alright on your own?

**Camus:** I'll be fine. I think I'll sit a while and just listen to the waves.

**Old Man:** (smiles) Enjoy, monsieur. Peace be with you.

**Camus:** And with you.

---

*The old man walks off toward a distant tourist, leaving Camus alone at the low sea wall. Camus takes a seat on a sun-warmed slab of stone, facing the endless blue expanse. He closes his eyes as the sun washes over his face. The sound of the surf fills his ears — a steady, rhythmic heartbeat of the world. In this moment, he releases the weight of argument and alienation. He simply exists, a man alive beneath the Algerian sky, feeling at one with the ruin and the flower, the sea and the shining air. He breathes, and within that breath, there is quiet resolution. Albert Camus, older now, scarred by history but unbroken in spirit, sits in solitude by the glittering water — no longer speaking from the margins, but living, fully, in the center of his own hard-won integrity.*

---

# Part V:
# The Final Dialogue

# Chapter 20
## The Door to Everything I Love

---

*Autumn sunlight drapes the quiet garden in gold. It is late 1957 in the Provence countryside, and a light breeze carries the scent of dry leaves and distant chimney smoke. Albert Camus sits at a small table under an old fig tree, a pot of tea and two cups between him and his former teacher, Jean Grenier. The afternoon is warm for late October; golden light filters through the leaves, casting gentle shadows. Camus' face is peaceful, reflective, as he savors the simple comfort of his mentor's presence. Grenier, hair gone mostly white, regards his onetime pupil with fond, wise eyes. In this stillness, time itself seems to pause, allowing two friends a moment outside of history.*

---

**Camus:** (pouring tea) It's good to see you again, Monsieur Grenier. I cherish these quiet afternoons. In Paris I'm surrounded by noise, but here… (smiles faintly) here I remember who I am.

**Grenier:** (warmly) And who are you these days, Albert? You've come a long way from the earnest student I knew in Algiers. Nobel Prize, fame… yet I sense the same gentle soul beneath it all. (He cradles the tea cup, peering over it.) Are you well, truly?

**Camus:** (shrugs lightly) As well as one can be. The world weighs heavy at times. Expectations, controversies… and the solitude of writing. But I have learned to accept certain burdens. Perhaps I've even made peace with them.

**Grenier:** I recall the young man who was always questioning, always wrestling with injustices. You've carried a great deal on your shoulders, *mon petit*. Sometimes I worry that solitude has become your only companion.

**Camus:** Not my only companion. (He meets Grenier's eyes gratefully.) I have friends, my family, and mentors who never truly leave me. Solitude – yes, I've known it. In youth it felt like exile. Now, I find it can be welcome, even necessary, for the work… and for honesty with oneself. I'm less afraid of being alone.

**Grenier:** There is a kind of reconciliation with solitude that comes with age, isn't there? (He smiles thoughtfully.) I remember you as a boy – the brightness in you. You had so little in material terms, but you brimmed with life. It was clear even then that you carried an "invincible summer" within you, even in the depths of hardship.

**Camus:** (laughing softly) *"Invincible summer"* – I wrote that once, years ago, perhaps to remind myself. And you, perhaps without knowing, nurtured that warmth. (He looks out at the sun-soaked garden.) I wrote to Monsieur Germain after the Nobel, you know. I needed to thank my first teacher while I still could. Without him – without you – I'd have remained in the dark.

**Grenier:** He was very proud of you. We all are. What did you tell him?

**Camus:** I told him what I feel for you as well: that when I was a small, foolish, lonely boy, a teacher noticed me and "without seeming to, opened for me the door to everything I love in the world". (His voice catches slightly, full of affection.) That door has never closed. Every book I've written, every idea I've explored – in some way I walked through the door you opened.

**Grenier:** (quiet, moved) And he replied calling you *his little Camus*, did he not? I can imagine the look on your face when you read that.

**Camus:** (smiling broadly) He did. "My little Camus" – as if I were still that schoolboy. It made me unreasonably happy. For all my *philosophe* posturing, I suppose I remain someone's student, someone's child, at heart.

**Grenier:** We are all children when loved in such a way. (He reaches across to pat Camus' hand.) You know, Albert, just as your teachers helped you live, *you* have helped others live – simply by being yourself. There are people who feel the world is vindicated by your presence, who carry on because of your words and example.

**Camus:** (ducking his head, embarrassed) You flatter me, Monsieur. I don't know if I deserve that thought. I've tried to speak for justice, for truth as I saw it… but I also know my limits now.

**Grenier:** Limits? From where I stand, you've done as much as one man could – perhaps more. Who else of your generation has given such voice to conscience? Not that awards matter, but the Nobel committee cited "the problems of the human conscience in our times." That was you.

**Camus:** (frowns gently, stirring his tea) I only ever spoke what I felt necessary. Yet, I confess, in recent years I've realized I cannot be the spokesman people wanted. The *position* of moral guide grew heavy. I became keenly aware that I'm just a man, full of doubts. In fact, in my last interview I finally admitted it: *"I speak for no one: I have enough difficulty speaking for myself. I am no one's guide. I don't know, or only dimly, where I am headed."* It was a relief to say it aloud.

**Grenier:** I saw that interview. It was startling, and yet – honest. Profoundly honest. Many of us were relieved *for* you, that you freed yourself from that pedestal. Even a prophet needs to lay down his burden.

**Camus:** (smiles wryly) Prophet – I never was that. I simply refused to lie. And I refused to give up on the idea that we must treat each other decently, even when the world seems absurd. But I learned that saying *less* can sometimes speak more. Silence can carry integrity, when words are corrupted.

**Grenier:** You withdrew from the tumult in these last years – I know. Especially with the Algerian tragedy, you were caught in a vise between sides. Silence was a stance, though not everyone understood.

**Camus:** How could they? (A shadow crosses his face.) I hurt for Algeria – my mother, my memories, *and* the injustices I railed against since my youth. But when the choices became terror or blind repression, I could not join either chorus. So I stepped back. It cost me, in reputation. But my conscience… I had to keep that intact.

**Grenier:** History will judge kindly, I believe. You tried to find a just middle in an impossible situation. One day, perhaps, they'll see the courage in that.

**Camus:** Perhaps. And if not, well… (He shrugs.) One does not do what's right to be praised later. I can live with misunderstanding. What I could not live with was betraying the truth as I saw it, or betraying those I love. Even if it made me solitary in certain circles.

**Grenier:** There is a kind of heroism in that solitude. You've embodied the principles you once only wrote about. In *The Rebel* you spoke of limits and moderation in the face of revolution's excess; when the time came, you lived that moderation, alone if need be. It's a quieter form of revolt, perhaps – but not a lesser one.

**Camus:** (meets his mentor's gaze) That means a great deal to hear. In my youth I shouted about revolt and absurdity. Now… I don't shout. I listen. I act when I can, quietly, and I write what feels true. With age I ask less of the world. Even of friendship – I used to demand everything of others: perfect loyalty, endless understanding. But no one can give that. Now I ask far less and find grace in what *is* given. Every simple act of companionship feels miraculous to me, a gift of grace.

**Grenier:** (smiling) Growing older has its benefits. Lower expectations, greater appreciation. Life becomes more precious in its small moments. Like this one – two friends sharing an afternoon. It *is* miraculous, in its way.

**Camus:** (breathes deeply, looking around) Yes. You know, I spent so many years chasing meaning – grappling with the absurd, insisting life is still worth living. Now I find meaning creeping up quietly in moments like this. A sunny garden, the sound of a friend's voice… (he closes his eyes briefly). Perhaps that's what my philosophy — if I have one — has led me to: the beauty and love in the everyday, waiting all along

**Grenier:** (softly) The absurd is still there too, of course.

**Camus:** Of course. The world's still absurd, unjust, often cruel. But perhaps I've learned, finally, what you tried to teach me long ago: that one must imagine Sisyphus happy – not by ignoring the rock and hill, but by loving the very struggle, the very earth underfoot. I embrace this imperfect life now, rather than rail at it. There's still rebellion in that embrace, I think. A defiant joy.

**Grenier:** Well said. (He tilts his head, studying Camus' face.) And what of your work? You once mentioned — was it last spring? — that you were circling something personal. A novel of your father? Your youth?

**Camus:** *Le Premier Homme.* The First Man. Yes, I've been circling it like a wary animal. It's slow going — even to begin. Returning to my father, whom I never knew, to my mother's silence... It feels like trying to dig into the past with bare hands. I don't know if I'll manage it.

**Grenier:** But you will. You must. If anyone can find the shape of truth in silence, it's you. I imagine it already — something warmer, more grounded than your earlier work. As if you've stopped struggling to explain yourself to others, and started listening to the boy inside.

**Camus:** (quietly) That's close to it. It feels important — more than anything else. If I could ever write it fully... I sometimes imagine it could be my *grand livre*. Not in fame, but in essence.

**Grenier:** (smiling) Then let it be that. Your *grand livre*. Not Tolstoy's, not anyone's. Just yours. And promise me this: don't let the perfect chase you off the page. It doesn't have to be your War and Peace. It only needs to be *true*.

**Camus:** Yours, Monsieur Germain's... my mother's. (He chuckles softly.) There are so many ghosts I'd like to write home to. But yes — I'll try to remember that.

**Grenier:** Good. We old teachers live for this: not to be proven right, but to watch our students come into themselves. Even if they've become world-famous authors along the way.

**Camus:** (reaches over and grips Grenier's hand) Whatever I've become, you're part of it. I remain — always — your grateful pupil.

**Grenier:** Then I'll be carried forward with you. That's all a teacher could ask. (He pats Camus' hand and then releases it, gazing at the glowing late-afternoon sky.) Look how the light is softening. Evening will be here soon.

**Camus:** Time for you to catch the train back to Aix, unfortunately. I wish you could stay for dinner. Catherine would have loved to see you, but she's at school today.

**Grenier:** Another time, certainly. There will be other afternoons.

**Camus:** (with a gentle smile) I hope so. (He stands, Grenier following suit. They begin to walk slowly toward the cottage.) Thank you for coming, Monsieur Grenier. These conversations mean a great deal to me – more than any interview or award ceremony.

**Grenier:** To me as well, Albert. Few things are as rewarding to a teacher as seeing the *whole* man his student becomes. And you have become a man of conscience *and* compassion. I could ask for no better legacy.

**Camus:** *Votre œuvre, c'est moi*, isn't that what one of your generation said? "Your work is me." If I am a legacy of yours, I hope I have not disappointed.

**Grenier:** Not for a moment. (He stops and turns to Camus, placing a hand on his shoulder.) Take care of yourself, my boy. The world needs you – but more importantly, your children need you, your friends need you. *I* need you, selfish as that sounds, to know that the values we share endure. So be kind to yourself, will you?

**Camus:** (with emotion) I will try. I promise. (They embrace briefly.) Safe travels, and give my regards to Madame Grenier.

**Grenier:** I shall. À bientôt, dear friend.

*Grenier walks slowly down the garden path and out the gate toward the small village station. Camus remains by the gate, watching until the older man disappears beyond the rows of plane trees. The sun dips lower, and the first hint of evening chill brushes the air. Camus pulls his jacket tighter and smiles softly to himself, a mix of melancholy and gratitude in his eyes. In the quiet that returns, he finds he is not lonely at all.*

# Chapter 21
## Invincible Summer

*Night has fallen over Lourmarin. Inside the cottage, a fire crackles in the hearth, painting the walls with flickering amber light. Albert Camus sits on a worn rug with his back against the couch, and beside him, his daughter Catherine curls up, her head resting on his shoulder. She is fifteen, caught in that tender cusp between childhood and adulthood, with her father's dark hair and her mother's eyes. Outside, a mistral wind rustles the shutters, but in here it is warm. On the low table, a single lamp casts a gentle glow over an open book and two mugs of hot cocoa. There's a comfortable silence — the kind only family can share — as father and daughter watch the dancing flames.*

**Catherine:** (softly) Papa?

**Camus:** Yes, ma chérie?

**Catherine:** You were far away just now. What were you thinking about?

**Camus:** (smiles, wrapping an arm around her shoulders) Honestly? I was just thinking how happy I am in this moment. Having you here with me, safe and warm… it's a simple thing, but it fills my heart.

**Catherine:** (nudges him playfully) You're not *that* old yet, to be talking like an old grand-père reminiscing!

**Camus:** (chuckles) I feel older some days. But you're right — I should not sound so solemn. Blame the fire, it makes philosophers of us all. (He looks at her fondly.) And how about you? What goes on in that busy mind of yours?

**Catherine:** Oh… school, friends… life. (She pauses, choosing her words.) Sometimes I try to understand you, you know. The world knows Albert Camus, the writer, the famous man with big ideas. But to me you're just Papa – a bit shy, often quiet… sometimes sad.

**Camus:** (his brow creases with concern) Sad? Do I seem sad to you, Cat?

**Catherine:** Not right now. But sometimes when you think I'm not looking, I see it. A sort of… distance in your eyes. Maman sees it too, I think.

**Camus:** (sighs softly) You're very observant, like your mother. There are moments, yes, when I feel a heaviness. It's hard to explain – it's not because of you or your brother, or your mother. It's more… (he struggles) a weight of the world, perhaps. Responsibilities, unfinished work, memories. But you must know, none of that diminishes my joy in you.

**Catherine:** I know you love us. (She sits up a bit straighter, turning to face him.) But I worry that you carry burdens alone. You hardly talk about your troubles. Even to me.

**Camus:** (brushes a stray lock of hair from her face) It's a father's instinct to shield his children from worry. When you're grown, you'll understand.

**Catherine:** I'm not a child anymore, Papa. I can handle it.

**Camus:** (smiling ruefully) You're right. You're not a little child. Forgive me. Perhaps I underestimate you – or overestimate my ability to hide my feelings. (He gazes into the fire, gathering his thoughts.) Let me try to explain one thing that might be on my mind… Something I've learned.

**Catherine:** I'm listening.

**Camus:** When I was younger – younger than you even – I thought suffering was the worst thing in life. Growing up poor, losing my father to the war, watching Maman struggle in silence... I felt pain and hardship everywhere. I steeled myself against it. Pain, injustice – those hardened me, made me want to fight, to resist. But do you know what has truly undone me, time and again?

**Catherine:** (quietly) What?

**Camus:** Kindness. Love. (He looks at her earnestly.) Whenever someone shows me genuine kindness or love, it moves me to my core. Far more than cruelty or pain ever did. Cruelty I can withstand – it only strengthens my resolve. But love... (his voice catches) love has the power to make me cry. Always. In my life, it's been "kindness and love that made me cry, never pain or persecution," which only stiffened my spirit.

**Catherine:** (eyes shining) I've seen that. Like when Uncle Étienne thanked you at his birthday dinner – you had tears. And I didn't understand why.

**Camus:** I remember. It was just a few heartfelt words he spoke, but they pierced me. I suppose because I never feel I deserve such love, and when it's given, it humbles me.

**Catherine:** (lays her hand on his arm) You do deserve it, Papa. You're always so humble about yourself, but I see how you treat people – with such care. Of course they love you.

**Camus:** (smiling) You might be biased.

**Catherine:** Maybe a little. (She grins) But it's true. You know, at school we learned about your books. It was strange hearing *my* father discussed. Some of my classmates didn't realize I was your daughter until the teacher mentioned it. They had so many questions for me after!

**Camus:** (groans in mock dismay) Ah, my worlds collide. I'm sorry you were put on the spot.

**Catherine:** It's okay. I was proud, actually. But what I wanted to say is — one of my friends asked, "What's he *really* like?" And I told her: you're kind. That was the first thing that came to mind. Not "famous" or "brilliant" or any of that. Just *kind*.

**Camus:** (his face softens, touched) Out of the mouths of babes... Kind. I think I like that most of all. Thank you.

**Catherine:** (leans her head back on his shoulder) Papa, can I ask something... a bit serious?

**Camus:** Of course. Anything.

**Catherine:** Are you happy? Truly? I know it's a big question. But sometimes I wonder — with everything you've been through, with the world being so complicated — have you found happiness?

**Camus:** (wraps both arms around her in a gentle hug from the side, pondering) You ask the question everyone asks themselves eventually. Am I happy... (He gazes into the flames.) I have moments of pure happiness, like right now with you. And moments of struggle, doubt — even despair. But overall... Yes, I think so. In my own way. I would perhaps choose the word *content* or *fulfilled* rather than an unbroken happy. Life isn't a constant state; it's a collage of moments. Some dark, some light. But I've learned that even in the depths of winter, within me has always lived an invincible summer. A warmth, a light that keeps me going. Part of that light is love — love for you and Jean, for your mother, for friends. Part is my work, which gives me a sense of meaning. And part is simply the beauty of being alive — the sea, the sun, the taste of good bread, the laugh of a friend. All that is happiness to me, woven with the sorrow.

**Catherine:** (nods slowly) I like that. I feel that way too sometimes, without knowing how to say it – that I can be sad about something but still… glad to be alive. Is that weird?

**Camus:** Not weird at all. That's exactly it. We must hold both things. As I've gotten older, I talk less about the grand ideas like *The Absurd* or *Revolt*, and care more about whether I kissed my daughter goodnight, or whether I watched the sunset. (He chuckles.) Perhaps I've become simple. But maybe in simplicity there is wisdom.

**Catherine:** (smiling) You're not simple, Papa. But I'm glad you're allowing yourself some rest from… being *Camus* all the time. I like you as just my father.

**Camus:** (kisses the top of her head) That might be the only role I ever truly wanted, deep down. To be a good father – better than mine got to be.

**Catherine:** You never talk about your father. My grandfather.

**Camus:** (falls silent for a moment, the fire crackling) It's hard to talk about someone you never knew. He died in the war when I was a baby. But I've been trying to know him, through writing this novel I mentioned. It's as much for you and your brother as it is for me – so that you might know where you come from.

**Catherine:** What have you discovered?

**Camus:** That he was very young, and brave in some obscure way. That he loved my mother. That he was the first man in my life, and yet left almost no trace in me except an ache. (He sighs.) I visited his grave, you know, in Saint-Brieuc, years ago. It was… overwhelming. To stand before the resting place of a man who gave me life and nothing else. I cried that day more than I ever have.

**Catherine:** (softly) Maman told me. She said that trip changed you.

**Camus:** It opened something in me. A door I had kept shut. Only then did I realize how much I missed having a father, how much every child – even a grown man – longs for the guidance and love of a parent. And I vowed then to give my children all the love I could, for as long as I live. If I have failed in that, it's my deepest regret.

**Catherine:** You haven't failed. (She turns and hugs him tightly.) I feel your love, always. Even when you're away, I never doubt it.

**Camus:** (hugs her back, closing his eyes) Merci, ma fille. You don't know what that means to me.

**Catherine:** (after a moment, pulling back to look at him) Just promise me one thing, Papa.

**Camus:** If I can.

**Catherine:** Promise me you'll take care of yourself. You drive too fast sometimes, you smoke too much, you work too late at night... (she laughs a little through her tears) I sound like Grand-mère scolding you, I know.

**Camus:** (smiling through a sudden mist in his eyes) You sound like someone who loves me.

**Catherine:** I do. So please, for me and Jean, be careful. We want you around for a very long time.

**Camus:** I promise to try, my dear. I'll try to live a long, *annoyingly* long life, just to pester you when you're my age.

**Catherine:** (laughs) Good. By then I'll be pestering you to take your medicine.

**Camus:** And I'll stubbornly quote some absurdist logic at you about freedom.

**Catherine:** And I'll roll my eyes and hug you anyway.

**Camus:** (leans back, drawing her with him into a comfortable lean against the couch again) Deal. (He gazes at the fire, then down at her.) Are you sleepy?

**Catherine:** A little. It's so cozy here, I could doze off.

**Camus:** Rest then. We don't have to talk. We can just watch the fire.

**Catherine:** Will you stay here if I fall asleep?

**Camus:** Always.

---

*Father and daughter fall into a gentle silence. Catherine's eyes flutter closed, her hand resting in her father's. Camus remains awake, staring into the dancing flames. His face is calm. At this moment, all the philosophies of the world wane before the simple, luminous fact of a loved one sleeping on his shoulder. In the quiet of the night, Albert Camus feels the invincible summer glowing warmly within, warding off every darkness.*

---

# Chapter 22
## Shared Journey

*Late afternoon on a slow train heading north from Lourmarin. The carriage is nearly empty — just a few travelers spread out in the old-fashioned compartment with worn blue seats. Albert Camus sits by the window, a book open on his lap that he isn't really reading. The winter countryside glides by: leafless trees, patches of snow, occasional lights of distant farmhouses as dusk approaches. Across from Camus sits an older woman bundled in a neat coat and hat, a small valise by her side. She has a gentle, lived-in face and holds a knitting project, though at the moment she's gazing out the window. The atmosphere is calm and intimate in that peculiar way of long train rides. Camus absently turns a page, then notices the woman shivering slightly. He offers a warm smile across the compartment.*

**Camus:** Excuse me, Madame — are you cold? I can ask the conductor to adjust the heat.

**Woman:** (smiles gratefully) Oh, you're kind. It is a bit chilly, but don't trouble yourself. I think it will warm once we're further along.

**Camus:** (closes his book, giving her his attention) Sometimes the old cars take a while to heat up. This reminds me of my childhood trains — drafty but reliable.

**Woman:** You sound as if you traveled a lot as a child.

**Camus:** Not too much. I grew up in Algeria, and we were poor, so train journeys were a luxury. But I did take one or two memorable ones. Now they've become more frequent in my life.

**Woman:** Algeria – how interesting. I've never been, but I've seen pictures of the sunlight there. Very bright, yes?

**Camus:** Bright and golden, especially in Algiers by the sea. Quite unlike this pale winter light here. (He glances fondly at the dusk outside.) Each has its beauty, though.

**Woman:** True. I'm content to be watching France roll by. It's funny, at my age I notice the details more – a smoke curl from a chimney, the shape of a lonely tree on a hill. When I was young I'd have likely ignored it all, nose in a magazine.

**Camus:** (chuckles) Age teaches us to slow down, doesn't it? To appreciate the small things.

**Woman:** It does. Though in my case, it was also loss that taught me that. My husband passed three years ago. After that, every small thing became dear – because I wished he were there to share it.

**Camus:** (softly) I'm very sorry.

**Woman:** Thank you. He was a good man. A railway man, in fact, which is why I still often take trains – it makes me feel closer to him. Silly, perhaps.

**Camus:** Not silly at all. I think it's a lovely way to honor him. Sharing the journey, in a sense.

**Woman:** (eyes brighten) Yes, exactly. Oh listen to me, carrying on. I hope I'm not boring you.

**Camus:** Not in the least. I find real lives far more engaging than my book just now. (He closes the book gently and sets it aside.)

**Woman:** You're very kind. Are you traveling to Paris?

**Camus:** Yes, heading home after the holidays. And you?

**Woman:** The same. I spent New Year's with my sister's family in Dijon. Now back to the capital. Paris is home for me too.

**Camus:** Perhaps we're neighbors and don't even know it. Paris can be surprisingly small that way.

**Woman:** (smiles) Perhaps. You have the air of a Left Bank monsieur, if you don't mind me saying – maybe a professor?

**Camus:** (laughs lightly) Not a professor, no. I have friends who are. I'm… a writer.

**Woman:** Oh! How wonderful. Would I know any of your books?

**Camus:** It's possible. I wrote *The Stranger, The Plague*… a few others.

**Woman:** (eyes widen in recognition) *L'Étranger* – of course! My late husband adored that book. And *La Peste* – I read that during the war. Such a powerful story. (She peers at him more closely.) Forgive me, I didn't realize I was speaking to *that* Albert Camus.

**Camus:** (raises a gentle hand) Please, there's no need for formality. I'm just another traveler today, I promise.

**Woman:** (with genuine warmth) Well, Monsieur Camus, it's an honor. Jacques – my husband – always said you wrote about the human condition like no one else. He'd have been tickled to know I shared a train with you.

**Camus:** (touched) Thank you. Meeting a reader who connects with my work means more to me than any prize.

**Woman:** I imagine it must. You know, Jacques and I often discussed your books. We argued about the ending of *The Plague* – he was more optimistic, I was more pessimistic, ironically! But we both agreed it captured something true about people.

**Camus:** The capacity for decency, even in dark times – that's what I hoped to show.

**Woman:** Yes. And that one must keep fighting even if one cannot win definitively. That gave us comfort in those Occupation years.

**Camus:** (nods, silence falling briefly as memories flit by) Those were difficult years. I'm glad if my story offered some solace.

**Woman:** It did. I wonder, are you writing something new now?

**Camus:** I am, actually. A novel about my father and my childhood. Quite different from the others – more personal, grounded in memories.

**Woman:** That sounds beautiful. I'll look forward to it.

Camus: (smiles) I have to finish it first. It's been slow going.

**Woman:** You'll manage. Writers always fret, don't they? But something tells me you'll bring it to completion. Perhaps a little luck from the new year will help.

**Camus:** From your lips to God's ears, as they say.

**Woman:** I don't mean to pry, but how do you find life these days? You've had so much acclaim, and also some harsh criticism, I recall. It cannot be easy.

**Camus:** Life… (he reflects, watching the dusk deepen) Life has been generous to me, and also stern. I've known love, friendship, success – and also controversy, loneliness, and doubt. In the end, I'm grateful for all of it. Even the hardships taught me something. I think I am more *myself* now than I ever was in youth. More at ease in my own skin.

**Woman:** That in itself is a great success, if I may say so. So many never achieve that peace.

**Camus:** I had help – from good people, from late-night conversations, even from the silence of the Provencal nights where I live part-time now. I learned to slow down and listen to life, rather than always shouting at it.

**Woman:** (laughs) That's wisdom. I should take that advice too, in my own modest life.

**Camus:** Something tells me you already have. I sense a serenity in you that I envy a little.

**Woman:** Me? Serenity? (She chuckles.) That's mostly age, dear. At a certain point, you realize fretting changes nothing, and you learn to *be*. When I knit, for example, I enter a calm state. (She picks up her needles and yarn, which had fallen idle.) The rhythm of it… it's like a meditation.

**Camus:** My mother used to knit in silence. I often think of her when I see someone knitting quietly. There's love in every stitch, she always believed that, though she said it not in words but in how she made our sweaters.

**Woman:** Your mother sounds lovely. Is she still in Algeria?

**Camus:** Yes, in Algiers. I visited her last year. She's aging, and still mostly silent – she's hard of hearing – but her presence is… how to describe? Pure. There's no pretense or artifice to her. Being with her is like sitting by a calm sea.

**Woman:** That's a beautiful image. You must miss her.

**Camus:** I do. And I regret that circumstances have kept us apart much of my adult life. If things settle in Algeria, I'd like to bring her to live with me in France, at least for a while. But one never knows.

**Woman:** I pray peace comes. So much blood has been shed.

**Camus:** As do I. I pray in my own atheist way, I suppose – through hoping and small acts. But yes, may peace come.

*The train begins to slow as it approaches a station. The woman starts gathering her things.*

**Woman:** This is my stop coming up – a smaller station before Paris. I'll catch a local connection home.

**Camus:** (smiling warmly) It was truly a pleasure to meet you. Thank you for sharing your journey and your stories with me.

**Woman:** The pleasure was mine. You made this leg of the trip very special. (She hesitates, then reaches into her bag and pulls out a folded piece of paper.) Could I trouble you for an autograph? My niece admires you greatly – it would thrill her.

**Camus:** Of course. (He takes the paper and pen, and writes a brief line and signature.) There.

**Woman:** (reads it and her eyes well slightly) "In the midst of winter, an invincible summer – to brighten your life. – Albert Camus." Oh, that quote of yours is a favorite of mine. Thank you, monsieur.

**Camus:** Thank *you*. And I meant it for you as well, not just your niece. I see that invincible summer in you.

**Woman:** (blushes gently) You're too kind. Well... (the train is nearly stopped) I must go. Safe travels, Monsieur Camus.

**Camus:** Safe travels, Madame. Be well.

*She stands, and Camus helps her with the valise. As she exits the compartment, she turns and offers a final warm smile. Camus watches her depart down the corridor, then the train jolts lightly as it comes to a full stop. He glances out the window and sees her on the platform, turning to wave. He raises his hand in return. A moment later, the train gives a whistle and lurches forward again, pulling away from the station. Camus settles back into his seat. Twilight has deepened into early night; a few stars peek through the veil of clouds. He reaches for his book, then decides against it. Instead, he gazes out at the passing lights of farmhouses and villages, reflections flickering across his face.*

*In the quiet of the nearly empty carriage, Albert Camus feels an unexpected welling of contentment. The companionship of a stranger — simple, genuine — has warmed him. He thinks of his friend Michel, of Catherine and Jean, of his mother far away, of Grenier and the dialogues of his youth and the recent gentle meeting of minds. All the threads of his life seem to converge in this hush. He closes his eyes for a moment, listening to the steady rhythm of the train on the tracks — a lullaby of motion. When he opens them, he catches his own faint reflection in the window: a man at peace, neither clinging to the past nor afraid of the future.*

*The train chugs onward toward Paris. In this moving, ephemeral space — between departure and destination — Camus senses the quiet companionship of all humanity, each person on their own journey yet somehow together. He leans his head against the window, and as the first city lights of the outskirts appear, he whispers to no one and to everyone:*

**Camus:** We are all fellow travelers… and it is enough.

---

*The wheels click beneath him. Night embraces the train, carrying Albert Camus toward home, toward tomorrow. In this gentle, unrehearsed moment, he feels the warmth of human connection — a final, most human truth he has been seeking all along. Not closure, but coherence. Not an ending, but an open road, shared in quiet solidarity.*

---

# Chapter 23
## No One's Guide

---

*Early December, 1959. A gray morning in Paris, cold with a promise of rain. Albert Camus sits at a corner table in a small Left Bank café that smells of Gauloises and strong coffee. Across from him is a young man in his twenties clutching a notebook – an aspiring journalist or perhaps a philosophy student, visibly nervous but determined. The café is nearly empty at this hour; only the clink of a spoon and the distant hum of traffic punctuate the quiet. Camus stirs a sugar into his espresso, offering a reassuring half-smile to the earnest youth who has requested this meeting. The scene is intimate, subdued – two figures leaning in over a tiny marble table, as if conspiring.*

---

**Interviewer:** (clearing his throat) Monsieur Camus, thank you for agreeing to meet. I — I can't quite believe I have this chance.

**Camus:** (gently) I'm just a man having his morning coffee. No need to be nervous. What shall I call you?

**Interviewer:** Julien, sir.

**Camus:** Bien, Julien. You said on the phone you're writing an article for your university journal?

**Interviewer:** Yes. It's an end-of-year piece. The topic is, um, "Intellectuals at the Crossroads." We... I wanted to ask you about where you see yourself and your work heading, especially after all the – well, everything that's happened in recent years.

**Camus:** (nods, takes a sip of coffee) That's a broad question. Perhaps you could narrow it down for me?

**Interviewer:** Certainly. (He glances at his notes, then decides to set them aside and speak plainly.) Monsieur Camus – Albert – you were the voice of a generation, the moral compass for many in France after the war. But lately, some say you've grown silent, or irrelevant. Others, like myself, feel your voice is needed more than ever. How do you see your role today? Do you still speak for the causes you once championed?

**Camus:** (exhales slowly, looking into his cup) I see you aren't pulling any punches, Julien. Good. (He looks up, meeting the young man's eyes kindly.) I will answer you honestly: I no longer see myself as a spokesman for anything or anyone. In fact, I never truly did, but circumstances placed me in that role. The burden of being *"Camus"* – the public figure – became hard to bear. I've stepped back, as you noticed. And I intend to stay back.

**Interviewer:** But why? Your readers – especially young people like me – we *need* guidance. We need voices like yours to make sense of the world's absurdities and injustices.

**Camus:** (shakes his head gently) I understand the longing for guidance. I felt it too at your age. But please believe me: I am no one's guide. I actually said as much in an interview not long ago: *"I speak for no one; I have enough difficulty speaking for myself. I am no one's guide. I don't know, or know only dimly, where I am headed."* Those were my words, and I meant them.

**Interviewer:** I remember reading that – it caused quite a stir. Some thought you were abandoning your ideals.

**Camus:** Not abandoning. Just refusing the pedestal. My ideals remain, but I refuse to posture as the beacon for others. I'm human – flawed, searching, as confused at times as you might be. To hold myself up as certain or authoritative would be dishonest.

**Interviewer:** (frowning) But your *ideas* — the philosophy of the Absurd, the call to revolt against meaninglessness — those have guided so many of us. Are you saying those were mistaken?

**Camus:** Not mistaken. But perhaps incomplete. When I wrote of the Absurd — the contradiction between our search for meaning and a world that offers none — I was a young man hungry for clarity. I declared that one must imagine Sisyphus happy, that our rebellion against absurdity itself gives life meaning. I still believe there's truth in that. Life *is* absurd in many ways. We mustn't lie about that. And yet… (he folds his hands, choosing his words) and yet, as I've grown older, I have seen meaning emerge in spite of absurdity. In human connection, in love, in small acts of kindness. These things don't *solve* the absurd — but they transcend it. They make it irrelevant, at least for a moment.

**Interviewer:** So, would you say you've found *faith* in something? I know you rejected religious hope in your early work.

**Camus:** I have not turned religious, if that's what you mean. I still do not and cannot rely on a divine answer. My "faith," if I have one, is in humankind — or certain humans, anyway — and in the simple joys of living. Perhaps that sounds trite. But it took me decades to admit that to myself.

**Interviewer:** It doesn't sound trite at all. It sounds… hopeful.

**Camus:** (smiles) Yes. I suppose I am more hopeful now, oddly enough, than when I proclaimed the Absurd with such fervor. Don't misunderstand: the world's problems have not improved — in many ways, 1959 feels darker than 1945. We have new conflicts, new fears (glancing at the window as a light drizzle begins). But my capacity to see light in the cracks has grown.

**Interviewer:** If you don't mind, may I ask about your current work? I think many of us are eager to know what you'll publish next.

**Camus:** (leans back, one arm over his chair) Ah, *la curiosité*. Well, I've been working – slowly – on a novel. An autobiographical novel, actually, about my father and my childhood in Algeria. It's called *The First Man*. It's unlike anything I've done before – very personal, not overtly philosophical. Writing it has been an emotional journey.

**Interviewer:** That sounds fascinating. Will it address the themes of your earlier essays – the Absurd, revolt, etc. – through your life story?

**Camus:** In a way, everything one writes is of a piece. I'm certain those themes are present, but quietly. Mostly, it's about a boy and his search for his father's memory, his place in the world. It touches on poverty, on innocence, on how a child perceives great historical forces without understanding them. There's a lot about my mother – her silence, her kindness. She barely spoke, you know, because of her partial deafness. But her presence shaped me more than any philosophy.

**Interviewer:** It's sounding like your most intimate work. And perhaps your most ambitious, too?

**Camus:** (with a modest laugh) Possibly. Sometimes I feel I want it to be *the* book – you know, the big one that justifies everything. I joked to a friend that I hoped it would be my *War and Peace*. But that's the kind of grand statement a writer makes to psych himself up. In truth, I'll be content if it rings true and if, when I'm gone, my children read it and feel they've recovered a part of their heritage.

**Interviewer:** You speak of when you're gone… but that's decades away, surely! (He smiles eagerly.) After this novel, do you have other projects in mind? Perhaps returning to theater, since your adaptation of Dostoevsky was such a success last year?

**Camus:** (his face brightens at the topic) Ah, yes, *Les Possédés*. I loved working on that. Dostoevsky has been a mentor to me across time. Actually, since you ask – I've been toying with another stage project. Shakespeare, this time.

**Interviewer:** Shakespeare? Truly? Which play?

**Camus:** *Othello.* I've been studying a French translation and making notes, thinking about how to adapt it for modern theater. The themes fascinate me – jealousy, trust, fate. And that sense of inexorable tragedy... (he trails off, then smiles) Anyway, it's in the exploratory phase. But I admit, I've scribbled on the margins of an *Othello* transcript quite a bit. Don't quote me on it as a promise, though! It may come to nothing.

**Interviewer:** (jotting this down excitedly) I won't hold you to it, but it's wonderful to imagine. Camus meets Shakespeare...

**Camus:** (chuckles) Sounds like a bad café joke.

**Interviewer:** Hardly! And what about essays or political writing? You've not written directly about the Algerian conflict or the Cold War in some time.

**Camus:** I think I've said what I could on those matters. Perhaps history will find some use in my calls for moderation, for a ceasefire of hatred. Perhaps not. I grow weary of polemics. There are others better suited for it now. My friend Sartre thrives on it, as you know.

**Interviewer:** You two... haven't reconciled, I take it?

**Camus:** (shrugs lightly) We traveled such different paths after our break. I bear him no ill will, if that's what you mean. He did what he felt right, and I did what I felt right. Sometimes those diverge starkly. It's all right. Not all friends walk the same road forever.

**Interviewer:** That's oddly comforting, in a bittersweet way.

**Camus:** It is bittersweet. But life has taught me to accept the mix of sweet and bitter. The *"benign indifference of the universe,"* as I once wrote in *L'Étranger*, is something I accept more peacefully now. Indifferent the universe may be – but we, tiny as we are, do care for each other. I care deeply, and that's why I had to step back when my involvement only fueled more hatred.

**Interviewer:** Monsieur Camus… I have to confess something.

**Camus:** (raises an eyebrow) Go on.

Interviewer: (earnest, leaning forward) People like me – we *need* figures like you. Perhaps you don't want to be a guide, but knowingly or not, you have guided us. When I read *The Myth of Sisyphus*, it saved me from despair. When I read *The Rebel*, it gave me a moral compass beyond political ideologies. We don't expect you to be perfect – at least I don't. I just… I fear your silence. I fear a world where Albert Camus falls quiet.

**Camus:** (listening intently, a look of deep compassion on his face) Julien, thank you for trusting me with that. (He places a hand on the young man's forearm reassuringly.) Let me respond. First, I am touched that my words meant so much to you. A writer can hope for no greater reward. Second, my silence is not absolute. I am still here, speaking through what I write – even if it's not an editorial or a manifesto. A novel can guide one's soul as much as a speech, sometimes more gently. And third… if I can offer you guidance even as I renounce being a guide, it would be this: trust yourself. Do not idolize any public figure — especially not me. I try to shed such things. I'm afraid they might freeze me in place. Take what resonates from my work, yes, but then walk on your own two feet. *You* must shape the world now. My generation did what it could – we had war and resistance, then disillusionment. Yours will face its own trials. Perhaps your role will be to find new answers we could not.

**Interviewer:** (quietly) That's a daunting thought.

**Camus:** All grown-up thoughts are daunting, I'm afraid. But I believe in you – in the new generation. I've seen young Algerian and French students talk in my travels; I've read your journals. There is a spirit that wants neither tyranny nor terror, that wants humans simply to live with dignity. Nurture that. You don't actually need me to tell you what's right. You know it in your conscience.

**Interviewer:** (smiles a little) You *are* giving a kind of guidance now, you realize.

**Camus:** (laughs softly) Perhaps I can't help it. But note, I'm guiding you *away* from me. Towards yourself.

**Interviewer:** It's ironic but I think I understand. One more question, if I may – a bit more personal.

**Camus:** Certainly.

**Interviewer:** Are you at peace with how your life has turned out? With the legacy you've built?

**Camus:** (takes a long pause, considering) *At peace…* that might be too strong. I have many regrets. I feel I haven't finished what I started – my novel, certain projects, and on the personal front, I have made mistakes that caused pain to those I love. I carry those burdens. But I also feel, in my better moments, a deep gratitude. Life has given me more than I ever thought I'd have – more success, yes, but also more love, more beauty. (He glances around the humble café, as if encompassing the world outside it.) As a boy, I thought life was mainly struggle. Now, I see it as a tapestry – struggle woven with joy. If I died tomorrow, I would die with the knowledge that I loved this world, even in its absurdity. That, I think, is as much peace as one can ask for.

**Interviewer:** (visibly moved) Monsieur Camus… thank you. This conversation turned out very differently from the formal interview I had in mind, but I think it's far more valuable.

**Camus:** (stands and extends his hand) I'm glad, Julien. And please – call me Albert.

**Interviewer:** (rises and shakes his hand) Albert. Merci, mille fois. I will carry your words with me… always.

**Camus:** (puts a friendly hand on his shoulder) Take care. Write honestly. Live generously. That's all the advice this false prophet can offer.

**Interviewer:** It's more than enough. Au revoir, Albert.

**Camus:** Au revoir, Julien. And good luck.

*The young man gathers his notebook, eyes shining, and departs into the chilly Paris morning. Camus remains a moment, watching through the window as Julien disappears around a corner. The rain has begun to fall, speckling the glass with tiny drops. Camus takes a final sip of his coffee, now gone cold. He leaves a few francs on the table and steps outside, flipping up his collar against the rain. He walks alone down the boulevard, anonymous in the city's flow, a solitary figure who has, unknowingly, lit a flame in another's heart. And though he walks alone, he does not feel lonely — for he carries within him that quiet resolve, content to embody his truths without need to proclaim them.*

# Chapter 24
## Unfinished Manuscript

*New Year's Day, 1960. Dusk settles over a grand old estate in the Burgundy countryside. Inside a cozy library adorned with rows of leather-bound books, Albert Camus and Michel Gallimard stand by a tall window, looking out at the last orange sliver of sun sinking beyond winter-bare trees. Michel, Camus' close friend and publisher, holds two glasses of burgundy wine, one of which he hands to Camus. The room smells of aged paper, wood smoke from the fireplace, and the rich earthiness of the wine. A soft lamplight mingles with the dim twilight outside. They have spent the holiday together with their families, and now, in a quiet hour stolen from the festivities, the two men talk as friends do at the turn of a year — with candor, warmth, and a touch of nostalgia.*

**Michel:** (raising his glass) To the New Year, Albert. May it bring you inspiration – and perhaps even a finished manuscript. (He winks.)

**Camus:** (clinks glasses and chuckles) Hear, hear. Though I fear your optimism might be misplaced. *The First Man* still has a long way to go.

**Michel:** I don't doubt it. Great projects often do. But I'm patient – and I believe in this book. From the pages you shared, I can tell it's something special.

**Camus:** (sipping, then gazing at the wine's color) You think so? Sometimes I'm too close to it to know anymore. Writing about one's family… it blurs the line between truth and fiction in a way that unnerves me.

**Michel:** Perhaps that's why it feels alive. There's blood in it, not just ink. You're not dissecting an idea this time; you're opening a vein from your past. Readers will feel that authenticity, I'm sure of it.

**Camus:** If I manage to finish. Lately I struggle. The words come slowly. I sit at my desk in Lourmarin and sometimes... nothing. Just the sound of my pen scratching nonsense.

**Michel:** (nods sympathetically) It happens. You put enormous pressure on yourself. You always have. Maybe you need a change of scenery, or a break.

**Camus:** A break? (He laughs ruefully.) I had one for years – after the Nobel, I practically froze, wrote so little. This novel was the thaw. I can't afford to freeze again.

**Michel:** I meant a short break. A little adventure to refresh you. You know, Janine and I are delighted you decided to ride back to Paris with us by car instead of taking the train. We'll have a leisurely drive, stop at inns, enjoy the countryside. Consider it a mini-vacation.

**Camus:** (smiles) I admit, I was tempted by the idea of seeing more of France in winter. And the company, of course. A train is efficient, but a car with friends is an adventure.

**Michel:** Exactly. Maybe it'll shake some ideas loose for you.

**Camus:** Perhaps. (He pauses, swirling his wine gently.) Michel, can I share something with you, as a friend?

**Michel:** Of course. Anything.

**Camus:** I don't often voice this, but... I have this nagging fear that I won't live to finish *The First Man*.

**Michel:** (frowns) Don't say that, Albert. You're only 46, and aside from that pesky old tuberculosis, you're healthy. You'll finish it – and write many more after, God willing.

**Camus:** (half-smiles) I hope you're right. It's just a superstition I need to beat back. Perhaps because it's such a *big* project – my entire life's meaning poured in – I irrationally feel fate might interfere. Silly, I know.

**Michel:** (places a hand on Camus' shoulder firmly) Listen to me. You will finish it. And I will publish it. And it will be your masterpiece. None of this doom-talk. The New Year demands optimism!

**Camus:** (laughs softly) You're a good friend, Michel. Thank you.

**Michel:** And as your publisher, I selfishly need that book to be done – it's going to be a bestseller! (He grins.) So there's no way you're allowed to bow out early, understand?

**Camus:** Understood. I'm under contract with life itself, it seems, with you as the enforcer.

**Michel:** Damn right. (He clinks his glass to Camus' again lightly.) But really – how can I help? Would you like me to arrange anything? Perhaps some time in a quiet place to write, or a research trip to Algiers? We could even get someone to assist with transcribing your drafts.

**Camus:** It's kind of you. I don't think a research trip is wise at the moment – Algeria is… well, you know. And I was just there last year. As for transcribing, I rather enjoy writing longhand. My scribbles and crossings-out are part of the process.

**Michel:** I recall seeing that manuscript in your briefcase – pages covered in that tiny handwriting of yours, no margins to spare. I sometimes wonder how any typist manages to decipher it.

**Camus:** (smirks) I'm sure I'll have to rewrite it myself; it's barely legible. I actually carry those pages with me everywhere I travel now — irrationally afraid to lose them. They're in my briefcase upstairs as we speak.

**Michel:** Guard them well, then. That case is more valuable than any bank vault.

**Camus:** (a flicker of melancholy passes over his face) Yes... it holds something of my soul.

**Michel:** You know, Francine mentioned you've been writing letters again — to that actress, Catherine Sellers. She said you wrote something about work and death? Francine worries when you talk like that.

**Camus:** (waves a hand) Ah, she saw that, did she? It was a moment of frustration. I wrote to Catherine — we've become friends during *Les Possédés* — I wrote that *"to work, one must deprive oneself, and die without aid. So let's die, because I don't want to live without working..."*. A dramatic flourish in a private letter, nothing more. I was cursing my own block.

**Michel:** *Mon Dieu*, Albert. That's quite an expression. No wonder Francine got alarmed.

**Camus:** I didn't literally mean I wish to die. Only that a life without creative work feels like a kind of death to me. If I can't write, I don't feel truly alive. But I assure you, I have no death wish. On the contrary, I'm full of plans.

**Michel:** (relieved) Good. That's good. You had me worried for a second there.

**Camus:** I'm sorry. Sometimes I forget how my words, even offhand ones, can affect those who care about me. I'll apologize to Francine and clarify.

**Michel:** She knows you have a penchant for intensity. She just loves you, as do we all, and wants you around.

**Camus:** I am extravagantly loved, it seems. More than I ever expected. (He smiles gently.) Did I ever tell you, Michel — when I was young, I demanded too much of love and friendship. I expected absolute, eternal devotion from people, more than they could ever give. I was always disappointed. But now... now I ask for little and am astonished by generosity. Every friendship, every kind act seems like a miracle to me.

**Michel:** You have grown wiser, then. And perhaps softer.

**Camus:** Softer, yes. Fatherhood did that, among other things. And failure. Failure teaches softness, I think.

**Michel:** Failure? In what universe are you a failure?

**Camus:** (shrugs) I've failed in personal ways. My marriage suffered, my ideals sometimes outpaced my actions. And even publicly — remember *The Rebel* and how I was lambasted by Sartre and his friends? I felt I'd failed to communicate. But surviving that "failure" made me less rigid. I'm grateful in a strange way.

**Michel:** You stood your ground in *The Rebel*. History, I suspect, will vindicate you on that. But regardless, I'm glad you're at peace with it.

**Camus:** I am. (He drains the last of his wine.) Michel, do you ever think about... legacy? The mark we leave, or hope to leave?

**Michel:** (considers) Sometimes. In my case, publishing great books is my legacy – helping bring voices like yours to the world. I'm content with that supporting role. Why do you ask?

**Camus:** Because I wonder what mine will be. I didn't seek the role of moralist or hero; I stumbled into it by speaking my truth during and after the war. I wrote some books that touched people. But when I'm gone, what remains? A handful of novels and essays, an unfinished manuscript… and perhaps an example of a man who tried to live according to his conscience, even if clumsily.

**Michel:** That's more than most, Albert. You'll be remembered for both your words and your character. For the stands you took – against nihilism, against injustice – and how you carried yourself with integrity.

**Camus:** (smiling wistfully) Perhaps. And if I'm lucky, someone will finish editing *The First Man* and publish it posthumously, so the world can meet my father through my eyes, and my mother, and the Algeria I loved. That would be a parting gift to readers, and to my children.

**Michel:** Posthumously? Enough, enough. You'll publish it yourself in a year or two. Don't indulge these morbid hypotheticals.

**Camus:** (holds up a hand in surrender) You're right. I'm speaking like an old man tonight. Maybe the New Year has me reflective.

**Michel:** Then reflect on life, *mon ami*, not death. We have a new decade just around the corner. What do you hope for, in the 1960s?

**Camus:** (stares out at the first evening stars) I hope for peace – in Algeria, above all. A true peace, with reconciliation, though it may be a dream. I hope to see my children grow tall and strong, unshadowed by war or want. I hope to write a few more good books. And I hope to grow even quieter in my soul – to accept whatever comes with the calm I see in some of my elders.

**Michel:** A modest list… (he smiles). And I share those hopes, especially peace. We've had enough of blood for one lifetime.

**Camus:** Indeed. (He reaches into his coat pocket and produces a folded paper.) Speaking of peace – I wrote something on Christmas Eve, a kind of note to myself. May I read it to you?

**Michel:** Of course.

**Camus:** (unfolds the paper and reads softly) "What pleases me is that I have finally found the cemetery where I will be buried. I will be fine there."

**Michel:** (blinks, taken aback) Albert… that's what pleases you?

**Camus:** (laughs gently) I knew it would sound shocking. Let me explain. It's not a death wish. It's contentment. That cemetery is in Lourmarin, the village I now call home. When I bought the house there, I visited the little graveyard on a hill. It's quiet, overlooking fields and vineyards. I imagined resting there one day, among the local people who accepted me as a neighbor. And I felt… peace. For the first time, the idea of death didn't frighten me. I thought, "Yes, I'll be fine there when the time comes – hopefully many years from now." It was a strangely liberating realization.

**Michel:** (slowly nods) I think I understand. You've found a home, so even the thought of an eternal home doesn't scare you.

**Camus:** Exactly. It's not morbid, it's… *harmonious*. Like finishing a long journey and seeing a lovely inn at the end of the road, knowing you'll rest there. But I shared this with you to say: I am not afraid anymore. Whatever happens, I have made my peace with life.

**Michel:** (clinks his empty glass lightly against Camus' as a gesture) I'm glad, though I hope that rest is a long way off. In the meantime, you're stuck with us and with this messy, beautiful life.

**Camus:** (smiling) And I wouldn't have it any other way.

**Michel:** Good. Now, shall we rejoin the others? Janine is probably wondering what deep secrets we're trading in here.

**Camus:** In a moment. (He takes one last look at the darkening sky.) Michel, thank you — for your friendship, your faith in me. That's meant more than I've ever said aloud.

**Michel:** (slips an arm around Camus in a brief, brotherly embrace) It's mutual, Albert. And we're not done — not by a long shot. There's more to write. More to argue about. More to live.

**Camus:** (smiling) Good. Then let's just keep going, one road at a time.

**Michel:** (grinning) No promises on direction — but I'll try to keep the wheels turning.

**Camus:** As long as you don't lose your way, I'll be in good hands.

*They set their glasses down and head out of the library, their footsteps echoing lightly on the parquet floor. The fire in the hearth crackles on, unattended, warming the room where moments ago two friends spoke of life and death, hope and fear. On the table by the armchair lies Camus' folded note. The words on it are no longer ominous to Michel — instead they mark a man's quiet acceptance of his journey. As the house fills with the muffled sound of laughter from the family gathering, the last ember in the library fireplace pops softly, sending a small plume of sparks up the chimney, toward the winter night sky.*

# Epilogue
## The Last Drive

*A tree-lined stretch of the Route Nationale 5 near Villeblevin, France —
the road of Camus's final journey.*

A pale winter sun hung low in the sky as the car sped
northward along the straight ribbon of the Route Nationale.
Bare plane trees flanked the road, their trunks flashing by in a
rhythmic procession of light and shadow. In the passenger seat,
Albert Camus rested his head back, eyes half-closed against the
brightness that filtered through the windshield. The countryside
of Burgundy drifted past him – frost-laced fields, occasional
farmhouses, and villages still shaking off the holiday quiet.

He had spent the New Year's holiday in Provence, in the gentle
sun of Lourmarin, and a trace of that warmth lingered within
him now. The days in the south had been filled with family,
conversation, and the serene routine of writing each morning.
On an impulse, Camus had decided to ride home to Paris with
his friend Michel Gallimard instead of taking the train. The
unused return ticket sat folded in his coat pocket — a forgotten
slip of paper that marked the road not taken.

Beside him at the wheel, Gallimard drove with easy
concentration, the powerful Facel Vega gliding over the
asphalt. In the back, Janine and little Anne Gallimard sat
quietly, wrapped in blankets against the chill, lulled by the
engine's hum. The group traveled mostly in companionable
silence, as if the morning's conversations had given way to
personal reveries in the early afternoon light.

Camus watched the pale sunlight flicker across the dashboard and thought of the journey ahead. Less than a hundred kilometers now separated them from Paris. He imagined the city's grey winter skyline emerging in a couple of hours, the familiar streets waiting. He would soon be home, embracing his wife Francine and their children, Catherine and Jean, who had already returned by train. A faint smile touched his lips at the thought of the twins and the stories he would tell them of Christmas in Lourmarin.

In the trunk and at his feet were bags filled with the modest gifts and letters from the holiday, and one battered leather briefcase that he kept close by. Inside that case lay his newest manuscript, *Le Premier Homme (The First Man)* – 144 handwritten pages in which he had poured so many memories of Algeria, of the father he never knew, of childhood streets under an African sun. He had confided to friends that he hoped this work would be his finest yet. Now it rested beside him, quietly awaiting its completion.

The road ahead stretched out straight and empty, a glinting line of pale asphalt flanked by sleeping fields and leafless trees. Camus glanced at his friend – the calm profile of his face, the wool scarf snug around his neck against the cold. There was an unspoken contentment in the car, the simple feeling of moving forward on a clear day.

Camus closed his eyes for a moment, feeling the winter sun warm his face through the glass. Even in the depths of January, he carried within him a memory of summer — an invincible summer of Mediterranean light that no season could extinguish.

A sudden jerk disturbed the stillness. The car gave a violent shudder. Camus' eyes snapped open. Michel's knuckles had gone white on the wheel as he fought it — the Facel Vega was veering without warning, its tires crying against the asphalt.

The trees ahead seemed to lunge forward. In the backseat Janine gasped and clutched her daughter. There was no time for words. In one silent, heart-stopping instant, the car left the road and hurtled toward the trunks of the plane trees lining the shoulder.

Camus had often written that an absurd fate could strike at any moment, without rhyme or reason. Now, as the world tilted and metal screamed, he felt a curious calm even amid the swift rush of events. Perhaps it was only a fraction of a second, a flash of clarity: the pure blue of an Algerian sky, the taste of salt on his lips as a boy by the sea, his mother's face in lamplight. A warm memory flared and vanished. Then came impact – abrupt and thunderous – and with it, darkness.

When the noise ceased, a profound quiet fell over the roadside. The wrecked car steamed in the cold air beneath the avenue of plane trees. Twisted metal and shattered glass glittered in the afternoon sun that crept between the branches.

Michel Gallimard lay slumped over the wheel, alive but gravely still. Camus did not stir in the passenger seat. His eyes were closed, as if in gentle repose, his scarf still wrapped snugly at the neck. A trickle of blood on his temple was the only sign of violence. The winter breeze moved through the tall grass and gently through the open car door.

Janine and Anne Gallimard were miraculously unharmed, and they stumbled out into the light, dazed but alive. The mother held her daughter tight, both numb to the scene before them, unable to comprehend how abruptly fortune had turned. In the distance, a village clock struck two, its chime carrying through the crisp air.

Before long, a local farmer and his wife arrived, drawn by the sound of the crash. They approached with hesitant steps, their breath visible in the chill. Madame Choquart, who had been tending her garden nearby, recognized the wreck and let out a soft cry.

With trembling hands, the farmer checked on the passengers. Gallimard was breathing, faintly. Camus had no pulse. A life that had burned so brightly in letters and ideas had been snuffed out in an instant of silence.

The police and ambulance came, bringing motion and voices to that silent country road. As responders carefully pulled Albert Camus from the car, a leather briefcase tumbled onto the pale winter ground. A paramedic later retrieved it and opened it gently, finding the pages inside intact.

There, neatly stacked, was the manuscript Camus had been working on: *The First Man*, its 144 handwritten pages unmarred and still clasped together as one complete bundle. The pages had survived even though the man had not. In that small miracle, something of him remained.

By evening, the news would spread that Albert Camus, the Nobel laureate and voice of a generation, was dead at 46. But in this moment at the edge of a quiet village, there was only the fading daylight and the stunned hush of those around the wreck. The manuscript was placed back in Camus' briefcase and set aside, its cover closed over the unwritten chapters that the author would never see through. It rested beside him as attendants lifted his body, as though guarding the words he left behind.

Far above, the winter sky was beginning to glow with the first hints of dusk. The plane trees stood witness, their long shadows stretching over the road. There was no grand last pronouncement, no final bow – only a gentle departure amid the ordinary rhythms of an ordinary day. In the still air, one could almost imagine that time had paused again, just for a breath, as it had in the quiet moments of Camus' life.

The drive had ended in an unforeseen silence, but its finality was not absolute. Though the man was gone, the truth he sought and the questions he had pressed into those pages remained. Unfinished and unresolved, they endured beyond the crash, carried forward in the words he left and the lives he touched. In the fading light of that January afternoon, the closed manuscript in Albert Camus' briefcase lay waiting — a promise that the dialogue between the man and the world would continue, even in his absence.

# Closing Reflection

Camus once wrote that "real generosity toward the future lies in giving all to the present."

In these final pages, we glimpse a man who did just that — through his friendships, his writing, his convictions, and his refusal to betray what he believed.

His life ended suddenly. But it did not end in silence.

The questions remain.
The words remain.

And so does the quiet echo of a final drive under a winter sun — where even in death, Albert Camus bore witness to life.

# Appendix:
# Notes, Sources, and Context

# Introduction

The following material is provided for those who wish to examine the sources and reasoning behind the work.

This companion guide offers historical context, thematic commentary, and source-based insights for each chapter of *Beneath an Indifferent Sky*. While the novel blends documented events with imaginative reconstruction, every scene remains anchored in Albert Camus's life, letters, and published works. Where characters share names with historical figures, their dialogue represents a composite of documented tensions rather than an attempt at literal reconstruction

The purpose of this guide is twofold: first, to distinguish what is historically verifiable from what is artistically inferred; and second, to provide readers — whether casual or scholarly — with pathways into Camus's world, ideas, and evolving conscience.

Each chapter entry includes:

- A brief summary of historical basis vs. imagined content, clarifying how the narrative aligns with documented moments in Camus's biography.

- Thematic notes exploring Camus's philosophical evolution, especially in relation to rebellion, absurdity, exile, and ethical integrity.

- Suggested readings drawn from Camus's own writings, contemporary accounts, and credible biographical sources that deepen understanding of the events, relationships, and moral dilemmas portrayed.

Taken together, these notes serve as an annotated map of Camus's intellectual and emotional terrain — one that honors his resistance to ideological simplification and his lifelong pursuit of human dignity in an often indifferent world.

# Prologue: The Empty Bench

The prologue establishes the tone and method of *Beneath an Indifferent Sky*: an imagined encounter, intimate and reflective, in which a solitary speaker addresses a stranger at twilight. It is not a historically reconstructed scene from Camus' life, nor is it intended to depict a documented event. Rather, it serves as a threshold into the book's form — a sequence of imagined dialogues grounded in Camus' moral, emotional, and philosophical world.

The voice of the prologue draws most directly on the confessional mode of *The Fall*, Camus' final completed novel. Like Jean-Baptiste Clamence, the speaker reveals himself indirectly through conversation, circling questions of cowardice, judgment, responsibility, silence, and moral self-recognition. The bench becomes a quiet stage for confession: not a place of doctrine, but of self-disclosure.

The unnamed woman recalled in the monologue is not meant to correspond exactly to a single documented figure. She functions as an emotional shadow — a remembered failure, a lost possibility, and a symbol of the human cost of inaction. The passage reflects a recurring Camusian concern: that silence is not always neutral, and that failure to act can become its own form of betrayal.

At the same time, the prologue is not despairing. Its movement is toward humility, compassion, and renewed attention to life. The speaker does not offer answers. Instead, he invites the reader to continue down the path, listening for other voices. In this way, the prologue quietly prepares the reader for the structure of the book itself: not a lecture about Camus, but a series of encounters in which questions are lived rather than solved.

## Historical Accuracy and Narrative Framing

Because the prologue is deliberately symbolic and introductory, its "accuracy" lies not in event reconstruction but in fidelity of tone. It does not claim to record something Camus said or did. Its imagined form is consistent with the book's stated purpose: to create dialogues that are historically informed, but not documentary.

The chapter's atmosphere — twilight, solitude, confession, moral reckoning — is indebted to Camus' late style, especially *The Fall*, while its final invitation anticipates the book's larger movement through Camus' life. The reader is not being placed at the scene of Camus' death, but at the entrance to a reflective journey.

## Themes: Confession, Silence, and the Edge of Meaning

The prologue introduces several themes that will recur throughout the book: the burden of memory, the moral danger of silence, the ache of regret, and the possibility of beginning again without illusion. Its central insight is not that life provides answers, but that human beings may still speak honestly, listen carefully, and continue together.

The closing image — "the edge of silence" — is especially important. It frames the entire work as an act of listening. Camus' life and writings are not presented as a system to be explained, but as a voice to be encountered. The prologue therefore prepares the reader not to study Camus from a distance, but to sit beside him, as one human being beside another.

**Character Note**

The unnamed woman in the prologue should not be read as a direct fictionalization of Maria Casarès, Francine Camus, or any other single figure. However, the emotional terrain of the passage is consistent with the tensions that marked Camus' private life: divided loyalties, difficult silences, and the painful awareness that love sometimes demands action one fails to take.

If Maria Casarès casts a shadow over this material, it is thematic rather than literal. Her long and complicated relationship with Camus represents one of the great emotional tensions of his life. But the prologue wisely avoids direct identification. Its power depends on remaining more universal: a remembered failure, a wound carried in silence, and the possibility that confession may become the first movement toward compassion.

**Suggestions for Further Reading**

- Camus, Albert. *The Fall*. Translated by Justin O'Brien. New York: Vintage International, 1991.
  Camus' final completed novel and the clearest formal influence on the prologue's confessional voice. Its monologic structure, moral self-examination, and themes of judgment and guilt provide the best interpretive lens for "The Empty Bench."

- Camus, Albert. *The Myth of Sisyphus*. Translated by Justin O'Brien. New York: Alfred A. Knopf, 1955.
  The philosophical groundwork for Camus' lifelong refusal of despair. The prologue's movement from self-reproach toward renewed life echoes Camus' insistence that one may live lucidly without final answers.

- Camus, Albert. *The Stranger.* Translated by Matthew Ward. New York: Vintage Books, 1989.
  The novel's closing vision of the world's indifference informs the atmosphere of the prologue, though the prologue gives that indifference a warmer, more dialogic form.

- Camus, Albert, and Maria Casarès. *Correspondance, 1944–1959.* Paris: Gallimard, 2017.
  A deeply personal record of Camus' emotional life, useful for understanding the tensions of love, silence, separation, and divided loyalty that may inform the prologue's emotional undertone.

- Todd, Olivier. *Albert Camus: A Life.* Translated by Benjamin Ivry. New York: Alfred A. Knopf, 1997.
  A major English-language biography of Camus, especially useful for understanding his relationships, later isolation, and the personal conflicts that shaped the emotional atmosphere of his final years.

# Part I: Youth & First Fire

Part I introduces Camus's origins in Algeria and the formative "first fire" of his convictions. These opening chapters balance historical truth with imaginative reconstruction, showing how a boy from an impoverished pied-noir family rose to find purpose. Camus later wrote that he grew up "poised midway between poverty and sunshine". The harsh reality of colonial poverty never left him complacent, even as the North African sun filled him with a love of life's simple pleasures. This section explores that dual inheritance. Historically, Camus was born in 1913 to a poor French-Algerian household; his father died in World War I, and he was raised by his illiterate mother in a working-class Algiers neighborhood. The novel vividly imagines scenes of young Camus at home in Belcourt, at play in the Mediterranean light, and at school under the guidance of a mentor. These episodes distinguish clearly between known fact and creative embellishment. For instance, Camus's deep bond with his elementary school teacher, Louis Germain, is well documented, though the dialogue the novel assigns to their classroom interactions is necessarily invented. What remains true is the spirit of those interactions: Germain's encouragement set Camus on a path out of poverty and into intellectual life.

Throughout Part I, the historical context is enriched by letters, notebooks, and biographical details from Camus's early years. We see the youthful "fire" of idealism kindling in Camus — first in his love of literature and nature, and later in his brief flirtation with political causes. The chapters show him grappling with personal and moral awakenings: the humiliation of poverty, the exhilaration of academic success, the discovery of classical authors and new ideas. Camus's own notebooks from the 1930s reveal a young man already preoccupied with questions of identity and justice, even as he delighted in football matches and swimming in the sea. Part I connects these motifs to recurring themes in Camus's life: a sense of exile and belonging, the dignity of the ordinary, and a commitment to integrity born from lived experience. Readers wishing to delve further can consult Camus's early essay collection The Wrong Side and the Right Side (1937) or his posthumously published autobiographical novel The First Man, which both illuminate the real-life experiences behind the novel's youthful episodes. In sum, "Youth & First Fire" sets the stage by showing how Camus's character was forged in hardship and hope, carefully distinguishing the bedrock of fact from the sparks of fiction.

# Chapter 1: Under the Algerian Sun

Chapter 1 introduces the formative landscape of Albert Camus's youth in French Algeria. Camus was born in 1913 to a pied-noir (French settler) family and spent his childhood in a working-class Algiers neighborhood. The intense Mediterranean sun and the stark poverty of his upbringing profoundly shaped his outlook. He later wrote, *"I was poised midway between poverty and sunshine. Poverty prevented me from judging that all was well in the world and in history; the sun taught me that history is not everything"*. In other words, hardship made him skeptical of easy optimism, while the Algerian sun instilled in him a love of life beyond history's shadows. Camus's early years were marked by simple pleasures – days of swimming, sunshine and soccer despite material want – which he recalled as "a kind of sensual delight" lived alongside destitution. This chapter's vivid evocation of sun-soaked Algeria reflects that dual legacy of poverty and natural beauty in Camus's life.

### Historical vs. Imagined Elements

Much of the chapter's background is rooted in Camus's real childhood, even as specific scenes are fictionalized. Historically, Camus lost his father to World War I as an infant and was raised by his widowed mother, Catherine, in his grandmother's cramped flat in Belcourt (a poor district of Algiers). Catherine Camus was of Spanish (Minorcán) heritage, worked as a cleaning woman, and was almost deaf-mute, so Camus grew up in an unusually quiet household. His Uncle Étienne, who lived with them, was likewise nearly mute due to deafness. These factual details – a childhood of silence, poverty, and bright Algerian skies – form the canvas for *Under the Algerian Sun*. The novelistic narrative, however, necessarily imagines dialogues and episodes to illustrate Camus's inner growth. For example, any flowing conversations with his mother or uncle are an invention (in reality, his mother rarely spoke, and neither relative could easily converse). Likewise, if the chapter portrays a composite day of play or a formative incident under the blazing sun, it serves as a creative synthesis of Camus's real youthful experiences (such as playing football, roaming the beach, or simply observing the Algerian light) rather than a literal event. In short, the chapter paints an authentic atmosphere of Camus's youth while using fiction to fill in personal details that history only sketches.

## Themes and Significance

Several key themes emerge from this chapter's context. One is the balance of joy and struggle in Camus's early life. Immersed in the natural splendor of Algeria, young Camus learned to savor the present moment – a trait reflected in his later lyrical essays celebrating sun and sea – even as he became aware of deprivation and injustice around him. This blend of "solar" exuberance and social consciousness became a hallmark of Camus's mindset. The very title *Under an Indifferent Sky* (the novel's name) echoes Camus's belief in an ultimately indifferent universe: the notion that the sun-lit world cares nothing for human affairs, a core idea in his philosophy of the Absurd. In The Stranger, for instance, the Algerian sun symbolizes an indifferent fate that the protagonist must come to accept. Chapter 1 foreshadows this outlook by highlighting the relentless Algerian sunshine as both life-affirming and indifferent – a backdrop against which human values must be created.

Another theme is Camus's feeling of being an outsider in his own land. As a poor, mixed-heritage French Algerian, he did not fully belong to the colonial French elite, who "rejected him absolutely because of his poverty", nor to the Muslim Arab majority. This in-between status gave Camus a unique *dual perspective.* He was fiercely attached to Algeria and its people, yet skeptical of all forms of prejudice and extremism. The seeds of Camus's later humanism and advocacy for justice can be traced to these early insights. He saw dignity in ordinary, humble individuals – a view reinforced by figures like his primary-school teacher, Louis Germain, who recognized the bright boy's potential and helped him secure a scholarship to the lycée. Camus never forgot this debt and would later acknowledge such kindness in his 1957 Nobel Prize speech. The chapter's thematic undercurrents of gratitude, humility, and moral independence pay homage to the real influences of Camus's youth: the nurturing sun, the silence of his home, and the mentorship that set him on his path. Together, these themes set the stage for Camus's development into a writer who embraced life's simple pleasures while challenging injustice in an absurd world.

**Suggestions for Further Reding:**

- Camus, Albert. *The First Man.* Translated by David Hapgood. New York: Alfred A. Knopf, 1995. – Camus's posthumously published novel *The First Man* provides a vivid account of his childhood in Belcourt and the profound influence of his teacher (Jacques Cormery, the protagonist, is a fictional stand-in for young Camus). The appendix of *The First Man* even includes the full text of Camus's 1957 letter to Louis Germain, a moving document of gratitude.

- Camus, Albert. "Letter to Monsieur Germain, November 19, 1957." In *More Letters of Note*, edited by Shaun Usher, 194–195. San Francisco: Chronicle Books, 2015. – Upon winning the Nobel Prize, Camus wrote a heartfelt letter thanking his former teacher for "the affectionate hand" that guided him. This touching primary source underscores the real-life bond and gratitude dramatized in Chapter 1.

- *Nuptials* (**Noces**, 1938) – Camus's early set of four lyrical essays celebrating the **landscape of Algeria** and the **ecstasy of youth**. In "Nuptials at Tipasa," for example, he revels in "a world of sunshine and sensual pleasure" amidst ancient ruins, reflecting the reverence for nature seen in Chapter 1.

- Camus' Nobel Prize banquet speech (available through the Nobel Foundation archives) and the accompanying correspondence shed light on Camus's mature reflections about the artist's role in society and the enduring debt he felt to the ordinary, upright people – like his mother and his schoolteacher – who shaped him. Each of these sources enriches our understanding of Chapter 1, illuminating how the novel's imagined scene rests on a firm foundation of historical truth and carries forward the enduring light of Camus's ideas.

- *Algerian Chronicles* – A collection of Camus's journalism and essays on Algerian realities. Notably, it includes his 1939 investigative reports on the famine and poverty in Kabylia that exposed colonial injustices, as well as later pieces grappling with the Algerian independence crisis.

- Camus's essays in *Lyrical and Critical Essays* (particularly the preface to *The Wrong Side and the Right Side*) offer further insight into how he viewed the "poverty and sunlight" of his youth as the dual wellspring of his philosophy.

- *The Stranger* (1942) – Camus's famous novel set under the Algerian sun. Its protagonist's journey exemplifies the "joyful sensuality" of the locale combined with an awareness of an "indifferent universe," a duality shaped by Camus's Algerian upbringing. Reading this work illuminates how the blinding Algerian sun in fiction became a symbol for existential truth.

- *Albert Camus: A Life* by Olivier Todd – A comprehensive biography of Camus that covers his Algerian origins in depth. Todd's research (drawing on personal interviews and archival material) richly details Camus's family background, education, and the colonial context, providing scholarly context to the people and places featured in Chapter 1.

- Lottman, Herbert R. *Albert Camus: A Biography*. Garden City, NY: Doubleday, 1979. – Lottman's biography details Camus' childhood in Belcourt, Algiers, and the crucial mentorship of Louis Germain. It provides historical context for the scene in Chapter 1, showing how education offered Camus a "door out of poverty" and ignited his lifelong intellectual journey.

## Chapter 2: A Sudden Chill

This chapter marks a turning point in both the novel and Camus's own life. At age 17, in 1930, Albert Camus suffered a severe and unexpected hemorrhage during a football match — an episode that led to the diagnosis of tuberculosis, a condition that would recur throughout his life and shape his temperament, philosophy, and career. While the chapter's scenes of confinement and introspection are dramatized, they are rooted in this very real event and the emotional, intellectual, and physical aftermath that followed.

**Historical Basis vs. Imagined Content**

The chapter's premise is grounded in historical fact: Camus collapsed with tuberculosis at the age of 17 and was sent to recover at the apartment of his Uncle Gustave Acault, who lived in a modest flat in Algiers. The real Gustave was a butcher and amateur philosopher — a working-class autodidact with a passion for discussion — and he had a strong influence on Camus during this period. Camus's convalescence forced him to drop out of school temporarily and abandon his promising athletic pursuits. While the novel depicts long, quiet hours of reflection, the reality was indeed one of profound isolation, especially as Camus had to separate from his family for fear of contagion.

What is imagined are the detailed personal conversations, dreamlike reveries, and emotional pacing of Camus's illness. The novel characterizes this time as an early confrontation with mortality — a lens that aligns thematically with Camus's later understanding of the absurd but is not drawn from documented introspection at that moment. Similarly, while Camus likely wrestled with despair and uncertainty, much of his later articulation of the absurd — his belief in a universe without inherent meaning and the necessity of human courage and clarity — emerged more fully in his twenties. In short, this chapter captures not Camus's philosophical maturity, but the crucible in which it began to form.

**Themes: Mortality, Lucidity, and Early Philosophy**

Tuberculosis had an enduring impact on Camus's sense of time and purpose. The illness made it impossible for him to plan for a conventional life, and he once wrote that it "condemned him to live in the present." The themes of fragility, awareness, and lucidity introduced in this chapter are echoed decades later in his fiction and essays. In *The Plague* (1947), Camus's depiction of a community grappling with an epidemic is shaped by his firsthand understanding of how illness separates and isolates — a literary metaphor drawn from his youth. In both works, the human response to suffering — whether despair or dignity — is foregrounded.

Another key thread is the influence of Jean Grenier, Camus's lycée philosophy teacher. Although Grenier is not named in this chapter, his presence is implicit in the portrayal of a young Camus beginning to look beyond physical affliction to intellectual vistas. During this period of recovery, Camus read Grenier's 1933 essay collection *Les Îles*, a meditative work on exile, detachment, and spiritual introspection. Camus later credited *Les Îles* as the book that changed his life. The chapter hints at this evolution: a young man forced into stillness begins to engage with ideas that will become the core of his philosophical identity — aesthetic clarity, quiet revolt, and the refusal to seek false consolations.

The central motif of this chapter is lucid suffering. In Camus's own words, "suffering is individual; but lucidity joins us together." His first major encounter with pain — when stripped of physical strength, social connection, and certainty — becomes, in retrospect, the event that awakened him to the meaninglessness of fate and the responsibility of response. He could not control his illness, but he could choose how to face it.

### Suggestions for Further Reading

- Grenier, Jean. *Les Îles*. Paris: Gallimard, 1933. – A philosophical essay collection by Camus' lycée teacher and mentor. Camus discovered *Les Îles* while convalescing from tuberculosis in 1930; its meditative prose on travel and spiritual life deeply influenced him. The work's impact is reflected in this chapter's portrayal of a young Camus grappling with illness, mortality, and new intellectual horizons.

- Camus, Albert. *The Plague*. Translated by Stuart Gilbert. New York: Alfred A. Knopf, 1948. – Camus' famous novel of a town beset by plague, written in the 1940s, draws partly on his own experience with tuberculosis. Its insight into facing death and isolation with courage and solidarity parallels the themes of Chapter 2, as Camus confronts a "sudden chill" and the fragility of life.

- Camus, Albert. Betwixt and Between (L'Envers et l'Endroit, 1937) – Camus's first published work, written just a few years after recovering from tuberculosis. These essays reflect his early explorations of consciousness, poverty, and the limits of happiness. The preface (added later) openly acknowledges the formative role of suffering and solitude in shaping his sense of truth. Particularly relevant to this chapter's emotional and existential register.

- Camus, Albert. Nuptials (Noces, 1938) – While already included in Chapter 1's list, it's worth reinforcing here. "Nuptials at Tipasa" contrasts sharply with the enforced stillness of illness, offering Camus's clearest counter-image: a life affirmed in bodily joy and sunlight. When read alongside this chapter, Nuptials shows how Camus's experience of illness did not deaden his love for life, but intensified it'

- Camus, Albert. Notebooks 1935–1942. Translated by Philip Thody. – Though covering years slightly after the events of this chapter, the early notebooks contain candid reflections on solitude, illness, and the value of intellectual work amid fragility. The entries capture

Camus's transition from convalescent youth to serious writer.

- Zaretsky, Robert. A Life Worth Living: Albert Camus and the Quest for Meaning. Harvard University Press, 2013. – Offers a lucid, concise examination of key turning points in Camus's thought, including his tuberculosis diagnosis and its impact on his rejection of despair. Chapter 1, in particular, focuses on Camus's early years and his shift toward lucidity and revolt. Excellent for readers wanting a short bridge between life and thought.

- Todd, Olivier. *Albert Camus: A Life.* Translated by Benjamin Ivry. New York: Alfred A. Knopf, 1997. – Todd recounts the pivotal year 1930 when Camus, at 17, collapsed with TB. This biography richly describes Camus' recovery at his Uncle Gustave's flat and the mentorship of philosopher Jean Grenier during that period. It sheds light on how illness became a turning point that redirected Camus' ambitions toward writing and reflection.

## Chapter 3: Flames on the Waterfront

Chapter 3 portrays a pivotal moment in Camus's early adulthood, capturing the emergence of his political conscience and his commitment to speaking on behalf of the marginalized. Set in mid-1930s Algiers, this chapter dramatizes Camus's brief but intense engagement with political theater, leftist activism, and the growing tensions between justice and ideology. It aligns closely with the real Camus's involvement in founding the *Théâtre du Travail* (Workers' Theatre) and reflects the broader social unrest of colonial Algeria under French rule.

## Historical Basis vs. Imagined Content

The fictional setting — a workers' theater group staging a play in the industrial quarter near the Algiers docks — closely echoes historical fact. In 1935, Camus co-founded a theater troupe called the *Théâtre du Travail,* whose aim was to produce socially conscious plays for working-class audiences. He worked with other young activists to stage plays addressing issues like labor exploitation and inequality, including *Révolte dans les Asturies* ("Revolt in the Asturias"), which focused on a violent miners' strike in Spain and was soon banned by French authorities. The troupe used borrowed rehearsal spaces in Algiers and performed for small, often skeptical audiences.

Camus also joined the Algerian Communist Party briefly in 1935, believing it was a necessary platform for social justice. However, he broke with the party by 1937 over its unwillingness to address the plight of indigenous Muslim Algerians and its tightening ideological control over artistic freedom. The fictional dialogues in this chapter — confronting party orthodoxy or debating the moral boundaries of revolutionary art — are imagined, but they are consistent with the tensions Camus faced during this period. His personal notebooks from the time show increasing discomfort with political dogma and a desire to remain intellectually and morally independent.

What the chapter imagines — the camaraderie among actors, the heated rehearsals, and the inner conflict of a young man discovering the cost of rebellion — is based on the documented environment in which Camus operated, even if the characters and specific scenes are novelistic composites.

## Themes: Rebellion, Integrity, and the Ethics of Expression

This chapter marks the first explicit portrayal of Camus's lifelong tension between *solidarity with the oppressed* and *skepticism of ideological conformity*. His decision to form a workers' theater company reflects his early belief in the transformative power of art as a vehicle for justice. Theater, for Camus, was not a political tool but a way to provoke conscience. "The stage," he later wrote, "is the place where we are judged and where we judge ourselves."

Camus's experience during these years led to what he called his "first break" with political illusion. The *Théâtre du Travail* was shut down after a single season. Camus began to realize that any revolutionary movement willing to sacrifice art or truth in service of doctrine was not one he could follow. His later disavowal of both fascism and Stalinism began here, with the realization that means matter as much as ends, and that *freedom of expression* is a moral value, not a tactical luxury.

The chapter also underscores Camus's early sensitivity to colonial injustice. Although born into the French settler population, he was acutely aware of the poverty and disenfranchisement of Muslim Algerians. His brief membership in the Communist Party stemmed in part from its professed commitment to racial equality, but his disillusionment came when it failed to act on that promise. This disillusionment became a recurring theme in his later works: rebellion not grounded in ethics leads to betrayal.

### Character Note:

While "Yves" shares a name with Yves Bourgeois, one of Camus's actual co-authors on *Révolte dans les Asturies*, the character in this chapter is a composite figure. He represents the range of ideological tensions Camus experienced within the Théâtre du Travail and the broader Communist milieu. No specific political positions are being ascribed to the real Bourgeois, whose documented views remain more limited. This fictional dialogue serves to dramatize Camus's emerging ethical stance during this pivotal year.

## Suggestions for Further Reading

- Camus, Albert. *Algerian Chronicles*. Translated by Arthur Goldhammer. Harvard University Press, 2013. – This volume collects Camus's early journalism on social justice, including his 1939 exposé *"The Misery of Kabylia."* It illuminates the same commitment to justice for the oppressed depicted in Chapter 3, particularly his concern for Algerian workers and rural poverty.

- Camus, Albert. *Notebooks 1935–1942*. Translated by Philip Thody. New York: Alfred A. Knopf, 1963. – Camus's notebooks from this formative decade offer raw insights into his shifting views on politics, art, and integrity. These entries document his frustration with party dogma and his growing emphasis on individual moral responsibility.

- Todd, Olivier. *Albert Camus: A Life*. Translated by Benjamin Ivry. New York: Alfred A. Knopf, 1997. – Todd gives a rich narrative of Camus's early activism, including the founding and suppression of the *Théâtre du Travail*, his break with the Communist Party, and the ideological crossroads he faced in the late 1930s.

- Camus, Albert. *Resistance, Rebellion, and Death*. Translated by Justin O'Brien. Vintage International, 1995. – Though published much later, these essays reflect Camus's matured stance on the ethics of rebellion and the cost of violence in the name of justice — ideas whose roots appear in this chapter's formative experiences.

# Chapter 4: The Schoolhouse

This chapter offers a quiet but meaningful window into Camus's early adulthood in the late 1930s, when he briefly worked as a schoolteacher in Algiers while continuing to shape his literary and political identity. It captures the spirit of a young man balancing idealism and modesty, eager to teach not just grammar and history, but a way of seeing the world — lucidly, gratefully, and with an underlying sense of justice. The fictional setting — a sunlit classroom where Camus engages with his students and reflects on his own path — is rooted in a real, though short-lived, chapter of his life.

**Historical Basis vs. Imagined Content**

This chapter imagines a reunion in 1937 between Albert Camus and his beloved elementary school teacher, Louis Germain — whom Camus credited with changing the course of his life. While there is no historical record of a specific meeting in this year, the emotional and intellectual foundation of the scene is deeply rooted in fact. Germain was a decisive figure in Camus's early life, encouraging the young boy to apply for a scholarship to continue his education beyond primary school. In 1957, upon receiving the Nobel Prize, Camus famously wrote Germain a moving letter of gratitude, crediting him for opening "the door to everything I love in this world."

At this time (1937), Camus had recently completed his *diplômes* in philosophy and was attempting to enter the teaching profession. He had published *L'Envers et l'endroit* (Betwixt and Between) and was beginning to distance himself from Communist Party dogma. Though his hopes of becoming a teacher were curtailed by recurring tuberculosis, Camus's view of teaching as a moral vocation was already firmly established. According to Olivier Todd and other biographers, Camus regarded the classroom not just as a place to impart knowledge, but as a sacred space for cultivating independent thought and human dignity.

The conversation with Germain is imagined, but the themes of gratitude, illness, clarity, and vocation reflect Camus's real situation and values at the time. The reference to *L'Envers et l'endroit* as a "booklet" Camus offers Germain is speculative — but plausible. He had just completed and privately printed the work that year, and it is entirely in keeping with his character to offer an early copy to the mentor who helped make that intellectual journey possible.

## Themes: Simplicity, Moral Presence, and the Pedagogy of Clarity

Chapter 4 explores themes that recur throughout Camus's philosophy: the dignity of simple lives, the moral authority of honest work, and the importance of clarity — a quality Camus admired in both thought and speech. As a teacher, Camus did not aspire to grand theory but to grounded instruction. This outlook reflects his broader resistance to abstraction and ideological jargon. In his own words, "I have always loved those who do their job well, and simply" (*Notebooks*, 1935–42). The schoolhouse thus becomes a metaphor: a small space in which honesty, effort, and connection are practiced daily.

The chapter also gestures toward Camus's belief in rebellion as education. Though the word "revolt" would later define his philosophy, its seeds are already visible here: encouraging young people to ask questions, to look directly at injustice, and to carry themselves with humility and pride. That ethic came from Camus's own mentors, including Louis Germain and later

Jean Grenier. By portraying Camus attempting to "pass it forward" through teaching, the novel echoes the foundational experience that once lifted him from poverty. It is a portrait of Camus not as a public intellectual or literary figure, but as a young man trying to live the values he would later write about — truthfulness, modesty, and resistance to cruelty.

**Suggestions for Further Reading**

- Camus, Albert. *Nuptials (Noces)*. In *Lyrical and Critical Essays*, edited by Philip Thody, translated by Ellen Conroy Kennedy. New York: Alfred A. Knopf, 1968. – Published in 1938, *Nuptials* is a suite of early essays in which Camus celebrates the sensual beauty of Algeria and the urgency of living. It reflects the youthful humanist philosophy that Camus brings into the schoolroom of Chapter 4 – a worldview imbued with sunlight, sea, and a rejection of despair.

- Camus, Albert. *Notebooks 1935–1942*. Translated by Philip Thody. New York: Alfred A. Knopf, 1963. – Camus' first notebook volume spans his stint as a young schoolteacher in the late 1930s. His jottings from this period show him balancing lesson plans with literary projects and political thoughts. They inform Chapter 4's picture of Camus "the teacher," revealing how he sought to impart not just facts to students but a spirit of curiosity and rebellion.

- Camus, Albert. *The Wrong Side and the Right Side* (*L'Envers et l'endroit*, 1937). – Camus's first published book of essays, composed during this same period. These personal reflections combine a schoolteacher's eye for real-world suffering with lyrical honesty. It's especially relevant to this chapter's themes of simplicity, integrity, and personal dignity.

- Grenier, Jean. *Les Îles*. Paris: Gallimard, 1933. – This quiet, meditative work by Camus's lycée teacher and lifelong mentor helped shape Camus's early worldview. Though more closely aligned with Chapter 2, its influence on Camus's teaching style and humanistic outlook extends into this period.

- Todd, Olivier. *Albert Camus: A Life*. Translated by Benjamin Ivry. New York: Alfred A. Knopf, 1997. – Todd's biography chronicles Camus' brief career teaching in a lycée (interrupted by his health and World War II), and his first marriage and early publications. This context enriches Chapter 4's exploration of Camus' integrity and idealism as a young teacher determined to live by his principles even in a humble schoolhouse setting.

- Zaretsky, Robert. *A Life Worth Living: Albert Camus and the Quest for Meaning*. Cambridge, MA: Harvard University Press, 2013. – Offers an accessible treatment of Camus's intellectual development and moral commitments, including his views on education and clarity. Could appeal to general readers seeking a bridge between the teacher and the thinker.

# Part II: La Résistance

If Part I revealed the fire of Camus's awakening, Part II shows how that fire was tempered in the crucible of war and moral commitment. These chapters follow Camus as he emerges from youthful introspection into public resistance. The historical core of this section is Camus's real-life involvement with the French Resistance during the German occupation of France. After returning to mainland France from Algeria, Camus became editor of *Combat*, an underground newspaper that published anonymous editorials denouncing tyranny and urging civic courage. These writings earned him the moniker "the conscience of a generation," though the title always sat uneasily with him.

The novel uses composite scenes and imagined dialogues to evoke the clandestine world of *Combat* and the moral clarity Camus sought to uphold during the Occupation. Events such as harboring fugitives, sparring over editorial policy, and confronting the cost of defiance are dramatized, but all reflect real dilemmas Camus faced. The fictionalized settings — train compartments, empty offices, darkened pressrooms — are historically accurate in tone, echoing the isolation and danger that characterized Resistance life. The characters who challenge Camus — idealists, pragmatists, radicals — stand in for the many factions within the Resistance itself, and the conflicting visions of justice they represented.

At its core, Part II explores Camus's emerging philosophy of measured rebellion. Drawing on his later essays, especially "Letters to a German Friend" and *The Rebel* (1951), these chapters capture his insistence that even rebellion must be bounded by ethics. Camus opposed both the fascist machinery of death and the seductive violence of revolutionary purism. His rejection of absolute power, from either side, is portrayed not as neutrality, but as fidelity to human dignity. Readers can consult *Camus at Combat: Writing 1944–1947* for a window into Camus's real voice during this period. In this section, the novel carefully distinguishes between historical actors and dramatic composites, ensuring that while dialogue is imagined, the ethical stakes are entirely real. In sum, "La Résistance" shows Camus not only as a man of letters, but a man of action — and, just as importantly, a man of limits.

# Chapter 5: The Knock at the Door

This chapter marks Camus's entrance into the clandestine world of the French Resistance. Set in an occupied apartment under curfew, it captures the fear, tension, and moral weight of wartime Paris. The scene's fictional structure — a quiet knock disrupting a hushed room — serves as both literal and symbolic: in the moment someone seeks refuge, Camus must decide how far his commitment to justice will carry him. While the dialogue and pacing are imagined, the setting and Camus's involvement in the Resistance are deeply rooted in historical reality.

## Historical Basis vs. Imagined Content

By late 1943, Albert Camus was living in Paris, suffering from tuberculosis, and working under the radar as an editorial writer for *Combat*, a major Resistance newspaper. *Combat* had begun as an underground publication in 1941, but Camus joined as editor in 1943, shortly after arriving from Algeria. His editorials, published anonymously or under pseudonyms, were written under constant threat of arrest. The situation depicted in this chapter — a secret apartment meeting, fear of a knock on the door, moral resolve under pressure — mirrors the conditions of Resistance cells operating in occupied France.

Camus's tuberculosis limited his ability to take on physical resistance roles, but his pen became his weapon. His *Combat* writings rallied citizens to moral clarity, arguing that even in a world dominated by lies and terror, truth remained the foundation of resistance. Chapter 5 fictionalizes a moment of confrontation: someone arrives seeking help, and Camus must weigh action against risk. While this scene is invented, it embodies the type of ethical crossroads Camus and his comrades faced regularly.

## Themes: Conscience, Silence, and the First Step into Resistance

The chapter explores the moment a private citizen becomes a participant in history. Camus later described the war as the time when "history broke into the lives of individuals." Chapter 5 dramatizes that intrusion. What had once been philosophical reflections about injustice and rebellion becomes real: someone is at the door, and harboring them may mean death. In this moment, Camus doesn't act from ideology, but from *conscience*.

The motif of silence versus action recurs throughout the scene. Should one remain safely quiet? Or does silence itself become complicity? This question was central to Camus's wartime philosophy and would form the backbone of his *Letters to a German Friend*, in which he wrote, "You said the world has no meaning, and thus all is permitted. But I tell you, because it has no meaning, we must give it one." These letters, written between 1943 and 1944, reflect exactly the kind of moral resolve depicted in this chapter.

The door becomes a threshold between fear and courage, safety and solidarity. Crossing it is the moment where rebellion begins, not with slogans, but with a decision to help another person despite the risk.

## Suggestions for Further Reading

- Camus, Albert. "Letters to a German Friend." In *Resistance, Rebellion, and Death*, translated by Justin O'Brien. New York: Alfred A. Knopf, 1961. – These four letters, written during the Occupation and published after the war, form the moral backbone of Camus's Resistance philosophy. They address a fictional German interlocutor and justify rebellion as an act of conscience, not hatred. This source pairs directly with

Chapter 5's thematic crux: the necessity of acting justly, even in an unjust world.

- Camus, Albert. *Camus at Combat: Writing 1944–1947.* Edited by Jacqueline Lévi-Valensi, translated by Arthur Goldhammer. Princeton, NJ: Princeton University Press, 2006. – A collection of Camus's wartime journalism, including key editorials calling for resistance, unity, and postwar justice. Written anonymously for the underground paper *Combat*, these pieces reveal the tone, urgency, and danger behind the fictional tension in Chapter 5.

- Todd, Olivier. *Albert Camus: A Life.* Translated by Benjamin Ivry. New York: Alfred A. Knopf, 1997. – Todd's biography covers the exact moment depicted here: Camus's arrival in Paris in 1943, his clandestine work with *Combat*, and the very real dangers of Gestapo raids and betrayals. This chapter in Todd's book confirms that the scene's atmosphere — tight quarters, coded language, constant threat — is historically grounded.

- Aronson, Ronald. *Camus and Sartre: The Story of a Friendship and the Quarrel that Ended It.* Chicago: University of Chicago Press, 2004. – While focused on the broader arc of their relationship, Aronson's study offers insight into how Camus's Resistance philosophy differed from Sartre's. For Chapter 5, it highlights Camus's early emphasis on moral restraint over revolutionary fervor.

- Kaplan, Alice. *The Collaborator: The Trial and Execution of Robert Brasillach.* Chicago: University of Chicago Press, 2000. – A focused case study on a real French collaborator executed after the war, this work helps contextualize the moral gravity of Camus's position during the Resistance — and how he viewed the lines between guilt, silence, and action.

- Camus, Albert. *Notebooks 1935–1942*. Translated by Philip Thody. New York: Alfred A. Knopf, 1963. – While begun before his Resistance years, this notebook volume shows Camus grappling with personal responsibility and the role of writing in a violent world. These reflections directly inform the moral stakes of Chapter 5's "threshold moment."

## Chapter 6: The Press Underground

This chapter immerses the reader in the world of clandestine journalism during the German occupation of France. It portrays the Resistance press not as a romantic abstraction, but as a lived and dangerous reality — typeset in basements, smuggled past patrols, and read by lamplight at personal risk. Camus's role in this effort was not fictional. By 1943, he was a central figure in the underground newspaper *Combat*, which would become one of the most important organs of intellectual and moral resistance in occupied France.

### Historical Basis vs. Imagined Content

The characters, pacing, and specific pressroom details in this chapter are dramatized, but the larger setting — the secret press, the process of editing under threat, the debates about truth versus morale — is historically grounded. Camus wrote editorials for *Combat* under severe restrictions, often using false names or no byline at all. The chapter's depiction of oil-stained fingers, hand-cranked printers, and philosophical debates around what news to print mirrors the real-world tensions Camus and his colleagues faced.

Historically, *Combat* began as a small Resistance publication around 1941 and gained national influence by 1944. Camus joined the editorial board in 1943 and soon became one of its leading voices. His contributions, many collected in *Camus at Combat*, urged readers not just to oppose the Nazis but to reject hatred, avoid dehumanization, and prepare for a postwar society based on moral rebuilding. The fictional discussions in this chapter — about whether hope is propaganda, whether truth is a luxury — are grounded in the real philosophical dilemmas that Resistance journalists faced, and that Camus later reflected on in both his essays and fiction.

## Themes: Truth, Responsibility, and Moral Clarity

Chapter 6 centers on a theme that would define Camus's public life: the obligation to speak truthfully, even when truth is dangerous, and especially when lies are useful. In this, Camus rejected the utilitarian logic that justified falsehoods "for the greater good." He believed that once the Resistance adopted the tactics of its oppressors — disinformation, cynicism, calculated cruelty — it would lose its moral legitimacy.

This principle is dramatized in the chapter's editorial meeting, where characters argue over tone, fact-checking, and the purpose of their work. Camus faced precisely these issues. Should *Combat* report on atrocities in ways that inspired rebellion, even if details were uncertain? Should they boost morale with embellishment? Camus's answer was always: speak the truth, as clearly and simply as possible. In this, he laid the groundwork for the ethics of journalism in a time of crisis — one that refused to conflate outrage with righteousness or information with ideology.

The pressroom also becomes a metaphor for collective effort. No one character owns the truth. Instead, the act of resisting tyranny becomes a communal labor: one person writes, another edits, another runs the press, another distributes the papers. This reflects Camus's broader theme of solidarity. As in *The Plague*, no single hero defeats the scourge. It is endurance, cooperation, and the refusal to surrender to despair that matter.

## Suggestions for Further Reading

- Camus, Albert. *The Plague*. Translated by Stuart Gilbert. New York: Alfred A. Knopf, 1948. – This novel, set in a quarantined Algerian town, is a powerful allegory for the Nazi occupation. The underground press run by Dr. Rieux and his colleagues mirrors *Combat* and the work dramatized in Chapter 6. Camus's message is clear: heroism is not grand gestures, but persistence in the name of truth.

- Camus, Albert. *Camus at Combat: Writing 1944–1947*. Edited by Jacqueline Lévi-Valensi, translated by Arthur Goldhammer. Princeton, NJ: Princeton University Press, 2006. – This indispensable volume compiles Camus's actual wartime editorials. Readers will find many of the issues dramatized in this chapter directly addressed: how to rebuild France morally after liberation, how to denounce injustice without becoming unjust, and how to write honestly amid confusion and fear.

- Lottman, Herbert R. *Albert Camus: A Biography*. Garden City, NY: Doubleday, 1979. – Lottman's account of Camus's Resistance years captures the day-to-day logistics of the underground press: hidden printshops, couriers, censors, and the eventual emergence of *Combat* as a public newspaper. This background gives concrete historical depth to the risks and resolve portrayed in the chapter.

- Kaplan, Alice. *The Collaborator: The Trial and Execution of Robert Brasillach.* Chicago: University of Chicago Press, 2000. – This account of a pro-Nazi journalist's postwar trial and execution provides a stark contrast to Camus's principles. Kaplan's book shows what was at stake in resisting, or surrendering to, propaganda — and why Camus's commitment to a just, honest press mattered so deeply.

- Camus, Albert. *Resistance, Rebellion, and Death.* Translated by Justin O'Brien. New York: Alfred A. Knopf, 1961. – Several essays in this postwar collection reflect on Camus's wartime convictions and the ethics of rebellion. Especially relevant are "Letters to a German Friend" and "The Century of Fear," which articulate the same moral imperatives explored in this chapter.

- Zaretsky, Robert. *A Life Worth Living: Albert Camus and the Quest for Meaning.* Harvard University Press, 2013. – Offers a concise synthesis of Camus's wartime work, including the *Combat* years. A good resource for readers looking to connect the Resistance journalism in this chapter to Camus's larger philosophical outlook

## Chapter 7: Letters to the Unforgiven

Set in the smoldering moral aftermath of World War II, this chapter finds Camus reflecting on guilt, justice, and the boundaries of forgiveness. It draws directly from the ethical and political conflicts that occupied his postwar life: how to pursue justice without succumbing to vengeance, and how to respond to atrocity without becoming an executioner in turn. The scene — an intimate, imagined conversation between Camus and a fellow resistant — serves as a quiet crucible for these questions. While the chapter is fictional in form, its emotional and philosophical core is drawn closely from Camus's writings, actions, and public stance during France's postwar period of reckoning.

## Historical Basis vs. Imagined Content

In the wake of liberation in 1944, France underwent the épuration légale — a legal and extralegal purge of Nazi collaborators. Tens of thousands were arrested, and many were executed or publicly shamed. Camus, as editor of the now-legal *Combat*, played a central role in shaping the national conversation about justice and accountability. Unlike many of his contemporaries, Camus refused to endorse retribution for its own sake. He called for punishment to be governed by due process and clemency to be considered even in cases of betrayal.

The idea of "letters to the unforgiven," while a fictional device here, echoes Camus's real-life open letters and essays published between 1945 and 1946, most notably in *Neither Victims nor Executioners*. In that essay series, Camus argued that society must reject both passive submission and violent retaliation, instead choosing a third path based on reason, restraint, and shared humanity. Chapter 7's imagined act of writing to someone "unforgivable" directly parallels Camus's attempts to communicate across the moral abyss of wartime guilt — a gesture not of absolution, but of moral clarity.

## Themes: Mercy, Memory, and the Refusal to Hate

At the heart of this chapter is the theme of mercy in a time of moral fracture. Camus was haunted by the ease with which wartime hatred could outlive the war itself. In his writings and personal correspondence, he stressed the importance of restoring dialogue even with those who had fallen into error.

He understood that forgiveness is not always possible — but neither is endless condemnation a sustainable path forward.

The chapter's intimate tone — Camus reflecting on the nature of guilt, imagining what he might say to a former friend turned collaborator — mirrors the reflective posture of his postwar essays. It also speaks to his enduring belief in the value of moral honesty over ideological purity. Camus insisted that to build a just society, one must resist the temptation to adopt the very cruelty one had fought against. As he wrote in 1946: *"We must mend what can still be mended."*

This insistence on measured justice often left Camus isolated. Many on the political left saw his moderation as weakness or naïveté, while others accused him of insufficient outrage. But for Camus, moral clarity did not mean moral absolutism. It meant refusing to kill in the name of righteousness and refusing to abandon dialogue in the face of betrayal.

**Suggestions for Further Reading**

- Camus, Albert. *Resistance, Rebellion, and Death.* Translated by Justin O'Brien. New York: Alfred A. Knopf, 1961. – This collection includes "Neither Victims nor Executioners," Camus's most sustained reflection on justice after war. Written in 1946, it directly addresses the moral challenge of how a society rebuilds without perpetuating violence. Essential context for Chapter 7's themes.

- Lottman, Herbert R. *Albert Camus: A Biography.* Garden City, NY: Doubleday, 1979. – Lottman provides a detailed account of the *épuration* and Camus's efforts to resist its excesses. His chapters on the liberation of France and its aftermath show how Camus navigated the volatile line between justice and mercy at real personal and political cost.

- Todd, Olivier. *Albert Camus: A Life.* Translated by Benjamin Ivry. New York: Alfred A. Knopf, 1997. – Todd's biography sheds light on Camus's alienation from former allies who embraced purges or revolutionary violence. He also covers Camus's public interventions and the emotional solitude that came with his call for clemency and reconciliation — paralleling the inner conflict explored in this chapter.

- Judt, Tony. *Past Imperfect: French Intellectuals, 1944–1956.* Berkeley: University of California Press, 1992. – A broader account of the postwar French intellectual climate, highlighting the pressures that shaped debates on justice, punishment, and ideological purity. Useful for understanding how Camus's stance contrasted with that of Sartre and others during the purge era.

- Kaplan, Alice. *The Collaborator: The Trial and Execution of Robert Brasillach.* Chicago: University of Chicago Press, 2000. – Focuses on the highly publicized trial of a French fascist writer. Camus opposed Brasillach's execution, advocating clemency — a position that earned him harsh criticism. This case directly reflects the moral tensions dramatized in Chapter 7.

- Camus, Albert. *Notebooks 1942–1951.* Translated by Justin O'Brien. New York: Alfred A. Knopf, 1965. – In this volume, Camus's wartime reflections transition into postwar themes. His notes show how he struggled with judgment, betrayal, and the proper scope of punishment — issues at the core of this chapter's meditative tone.

# Chapter 8: The Shadow of the Guillotine

This chapter addresses one of Albert Camus's most enduring moral positions: his categorical opposition to the death penalty. Through the quiet, reasoned resistance voiced in this fictional dialogue, the novel explores not only a political stance but a deeply personal and philosophical conviction — one that Camus would maintain across his life and articulate most forcefully in his 1957 essay *Reflections on the Guillotine.* The chapter's title evokes both historical France and the broader metaphor that preoccupied Camus: the guillotine as a symbol of a society that kills in the name of justice, thus betraying its own ethical foundations.

## Historical Basis vs. Imagined Content

While the chapter's conversation — perhaps staged between Camus and a colleague debating the execution of a convicted collaborator — is dramatized, the issues it tackles are drawn directly from Camus's lived experience and writing. He was haunted from an early age by capital punishment: his father had witnessed an execution and returned home physically ill from the trauma. This family memory, referenced in *Reflections on the Guillotine,* left a lasting impression on Camus, who would later argue that the death penalty degrades not only its victim but the society that condones it.

Camus first wrote about these ideas in his postwar journalism, but he returned to them with greater urgency in the 1950s, particularly in response to executions carried out during the Algerian War. In 1957 — the same year he received the Nobel Prize — Camus published *Reflections on the Guillotine,* a searing critique of state-sanctioned killing. In it, he argued that the death penalty is irrevocable, ineffective, and morally corrosive. The fictional debate in Chapter 8 gives voice to this real-world argument: that even the most heinous crimes do not justify mirroring them with legal murder.

## Themes: Justice, Measure, and the Ethics of Punishment

At the core of this chapter is the concept of measure — Camus's philosophical term for moral restraint, proportion, and clarity in action. His objection to capital punishment was not rooted in sympathy for the guilty, but in the belief that a just society cannot maintain its integrity by institutionalizing irreversible violence. For Camus, true justice must remain distinguishable from revenge.

The chapter's conversation underscores the absurdity of punishment as spectacle — a theme Camus first introduced in *The Stranger*, where the protagonist, Meursault, faces the guillotine with grim lucidity. In that novel, the state's rituals surrounding death are shown to be hollow, mechanical, and inhuman. The echo of that experience reverberates through Chapter 8, as Camus contemplates the dispassionate apparatus of execution and its clash with the ideals of a humane society.

This chapter also emphasizes the moral solitude of those who argue for clemency in a climate of fear and vengeance. Camus knew that opposing the death penalty in postwar France — and later, in the midst of the Algerian conflict — risked alienating allies and inviting political backlash. But for him, rebellion must be bounded by limits; to fight injustice without adopting unjust means was the highest ethical calling. Chapter 8 embodies this stance in its quiet refusal to condone even legal forms of killing.

## Suggestions for Further Reading

- Camus, Albert. "Reflections on the Guillotine." In *Resistance, Rebellion, and Death*, translated by Justin O'Brien. New York: Alfred A. Knopf, 1961. – Camus's definitive essay against capital punishment, written in response to executions in France and Algeria. Drawing on personal experience, it lays out a measured, humane argument against the death penalty. This essay is the direct philosophical source behind Chapter 8.

- Camus, Albert. *The Stranger.* Translated by Matthew Ward. New York: Vintage Books, 1989. – In this early novel, the condemned Meursault confronts execution with existential clarity. The scenes of awaiting the guillotine dramatize, from the inside, the psychological and moral terrain that Camus later critiques more abstractly in *Reflections on the Guillotine.*

- Todd, Olivier. *Albert Camus: A Life.* Translated by Benjamin Ivry. New York: Alfred A. Knopf, 1997. – Todd's biography explains how Camus's opposition to the death penalty was shaped by family history and wartime experience. He details Camus's efforts to prevent executions during the Algerian War, and how *Reflections on the Guillotine* came to be written after the execution of a high-profile murderer in 1957.

- Lottman, Herbert R. *Albert Camus: A Biography.* Garden City, NY: Doubleday, 1979. – A comprehensive source for Camus's moral and political positions, including his behind-the-scenes activism against capital punishment and his increasingly solitary stance during France's postwar justice debates.

- Améry, Jean. *At the Mind's Limits: Contemplations by a Survivor on Auschwitz and its Realities.* Translated by Sidney Rosenfeld and Stella P. Rosenfeld. Bloomington: Indiana University Press, 1980. – While not directly about Camus, this book explores the moral crisis of judgment and retribution after war and atrocity. Améry's reflections offer a poignant counterpoint to

Camus's call for measure, illuminating the depth of trauma that made forgiveness and clemency so difficult in postwar Europe.

- Zaretsky, Robert. *A Life Worth Living: Albert Camus and the Quest for Meaning*. Harvard University Press, 2013. – A concise, accessible resource on Camus's ethical worldview. Zaretsky's chapter on *Reflections on the Guillotine* is especially helpful for contextualizing Camus's refusal to allow even justice to override human dignity.

# Chapter 9: Return to Light

This chapter brings the Resistance arc of the novel to a close with a tone of reflection, resolve, and cautious hope. Set in the immediate aftermath of the Liberation of Paris, it captures the mood that Camus both lived and helped to shape: a desire to rebuild society with dignity after years of occupation, violence, and moral ambiguity. In this period, Camus emerged not only as a public intellectual but as a moral voice for postwar France — a figure urging restraint, clarity, and a renewed humanism. The chapter's title, *Return to Light*, alludes directly to Camus's own postwar speeches and editorials, in which he framed the end of the war as a moment not for vengeance but for reconstruction of values.

## Historical Basis vs. Imagined Content

The events surrounding the Liberation are grounded in historical fact. Camus was in Paris during the summer of 1944, working as editor of *Combat*, which had just transitioned from an underground newspaper to a public, legal publication. His editorials from that period — often unsigned or pseudonymous — expressed joy at liberation, but warned against the intoxicating ease of revenge and ideological excess. Camus called for a France that would be freer and more just not only in name, but in its institutions and moral priorities.

The chapter's imagined scenes — perhaps a post-liberation gathering of friends, or a nighttime walk through newly unoccupied streets — are fictional. But the sentiments expressed are entirely consonant with Camus's real-life writings and public addresses during this time. The tension between exultation and restraint, celebration and concern, was a dominant tone in Camus's postwar discourse. The chapter dramatizes this mood through private reflection and public appeal, capturing Camus's instinct to turn victory into responsibility.

## Themes: Renewal, Restraint, and the Ethical Meaning of Victory

The primary theme of this chapter is measured renewal. Camus believed that the end of the war presented not only an opportunity to rebuild society physically and politically, but also morally. "We must stop just talking about man," he said in his 1946 address at Columbia University, "and actually think of him." That speech, titled *The Human Crisis*, frames much of Chapter 9's vision: Camus calls for a return to clarity and truth, grounded not in ideology but in shared humanity.

In this chapter, Camus also confronts the burden of memory. He does not urge forgetting, but rather remembering without bitterness. The Resistance is not romanticized; it was a necessity, born of pain. What matters now, Camus implies, is to build a world where resistance of that kind will no longer be necessary. This outlook echoes the spirit of his essay *Neither Victims nor Executioners*, written shortly after the war, in which he warned that punishing too harshly or forgetting too easily would both undermine justice. His message: to heal, a society must temper justice with mercy, and rebuild not through hate, but through decency.

The chapter also marks a personal turning point. For Camus, the war had clarified a lifelong conviction — that truth, dignity, and human solidarity are the only trustworthy foundations of political life. Now, with the war behind him, he commits to continuing that moral struggle through writing and public engagement. The "light" to which he returns is not only the literal sunlight of a liberated Paris, but a symbolic return to the values of reason and honesty, which he believed had been eclipsed by the nihilism of fascism and the compromises of survival.

### Suggestions for Further Reading

- Camus, Albert. "The Human Crisis." Speech delivered at Columbia University, New York, March 28, 1946. – In this luminous and sober address, Camus called for a new humanism after the war. He urged the rejection of totalitarian ideologies and warned that the future must be built not on "murder or lies," but on the recognition of human dignity. This speech provides a philosophical and emotional lens for understanding Chapter 9's vision of renewal.

- Camus, Albert. "Neither Victims nor Executioners." In *Resistance, Rebellion, and Death*, translated by Justin O'Brien. New York: Alfred A. Knopf, 1961. – Originally published in *Combat*, this postwar essay series captures Camus's resistance to both passivity and revenge. His insistence on justice with restraint and truth without cruelty directly mirrors the thematic resolution of this chapter.

- Todd, Olivier. *Albert Camus: A Life.* Translated by Benjamin Ivry. New York: Alfred A. Knopf, 1997. – Todd's chapters on the liberation of Paris and its aftermath portray Camus as a complex figure: joyful at freedom's return, yet wary of triumphalism. His biographical account helps contextualize Camus's transition from Résistant to public intellectual.

- Camus, Albert. *Camus at Combat: Writing 1944–1947.* Edited by Jacqueline Lévi-Valensi, translated by Arthur Goldhammer. Princeton, NJ: Princeton University Press, 2006. – This collection of Camus's actual editorials shows the moral tone he brought to France's moment of reckoning. Many of the ideas dramatized in Chapter 9 — freedom tempered by ethics, victory without cruelty — are first expressed here.

- Judt, Tony. *The Burden of Responsibility: Blum, Camus, Aron, and the French Twentieth Century.* University of Chicago Press, 1998. – Judt examines Camus's role in shaping postwar liberalism in France. This short, elegant book situates Camus's calls for moderation and moral rigor in a broader political and intellectual context.

- Zaretsky, Robert. *A Life Worth Living: Albert Camus and the Quest for Meaning.* Harvard University Press, 2013. – Zaretsky's accessible study includes a moving treatment of Camus's postwar speeches and how they carried forward the spirit of *Combat.* A helpful companion for readers interested in the moral architecture of Chapter 9.

# Part III: Recognition & Division

This section traces the arc from acclaim to alienation. The war is over, and Camus has become a global literary figure — lauded for *The Plague* (1947), awarded the Nobel Prize in 1957, and hailed as a voice of postwar conscience. But with public recognition comes philosophical estrangement, especially from former allies on the French Left. Part III dramatizes the widening gap between Camus's insistence on moral restraint and the ideological fervor of postwar intellectuals, particularly those who saw revolutionary violence as justifiable in the pursuit of justice.

Historically, Camus's break with Jean-Paul Sartre and his circle was catalyzed by *The Rebel*, in which he argued that revolutions often betray their original values when they resort to terror. Sartre's camp viewed Camus's stance as politically naive, even reactionary. Camus, in turn, felt betrayed by those who excused the purges of Stalinism or colonial atrocities in the name of dialectical necessity. The chapters in this section fictionalize key confrontations — some public, some intimate — while drawing heavily from real events. The emotional and moral cost of Camus's increasing isolation is portrayed not as a fall from relevance, but as a principled retreat.

Part III also includes more reflective chapters — introspective moments aboard trains, in cafes, and on cold city streets — where Camus wrestles with his identity not as a writer, but as a man under scrutiny. The emotional register here is not one of bitterness, but of quiet reckoning. Readers interested in the historical background of this schism will find valuable context in Ronald Aronson's *Camus and Sartre*, as well as Tony Judt's *Past Imperfect: French Intellectuals, 1944–1956*. The student and comrade characters who appear here are composites drawn from Camus's own orbit, shaped by letters, memoirs, and journals. "Recognition & Division" captures the tension of a man lauded by the world, but alone among his peers — a writer who refused to trade truth for popularity, even when it cost him dearly.

## Chapter 10: The Acclaim and the Ache

This chapter captures a paradox that defined Albert Camus's postwar life: the convergence of worldly success and inner suffering. By the late 1940s, Camus had become an internationally celebrated writer, following the critical and commercial success of *The Stranger* (1942) and *The Plague* (1947). He traveled, lectured, and socialized in the salons of Paris and abroad. Yet behind this acclaim lay a persistent "ache" — of illness, estrangement, and an existential fatigue that notoriety could not soothe. Chapter 10 mirrors this tension by placing Camus at the height of recognition even as he privately questions his place in the world and struggles with recurring illness and personal dislocation.

### Historical Basis vs. Imagined Content

Camus's rise to literary fame is well-documented. After *The Plague* was published in 1947, he became a global figure. Invitations poured in from Europe and America; he was praised not only as a novelist but as a philosopher of the human condition. The chapter's imagined events — perhaps Camus giving a reading in a crowded Paris salon or receiving applause at a foreign lecture — draw from real milestones in his life. What is fictionalized is the emotional layering: scenes of solitude in hotel rooms, inner conflict before speeches, or quiet reflection during moments of public celebration. Yet these imagined elements are consistent with Camus's personal writings and recollections.

Camus's Notebooks (1942–1951) offer the most candid glimpse into his private reality during this period. Despite outward success, he often expressed a sense of alienation. His tuberculosis flared up again in 1948, forcing him to spend long periods convalescing in the French Alps. He wrote of fatigue, disconnection, and self-doubt. Chapter 10's introspective tone is supported by these authentic entries, which reveal a man increasingly uncomfortable with the role of celebrity, even as he fulfilled it with grace and modesty.

## Themes: Fame, Illness, and the Burden of Recognition

At its core, this chapter is about the dissonance between public identity and private self. Camus had always resisted labels — existentialist, philosopher, prophet — but now, with his fame rising, he was being cast in roles that did not fit. He once remarked that he did not want to be a "system builder" or "moralist," only a writer who remained faithful to truth and clarity. Yet, the more celebrated he became, the more his image was consumed by others' expectations.

The chapter also foregrounds Camus's physical vulnerability. Tuberculosis, which first struck him at age 17, returned with intensity during these years. At times he could not walk more than a few steps without exhaustion. The juxtaposition of Camus delivering lectures by day and collapsing into fevered rest by night is not fictional melodrama — it reflects the lived rhythm of his life in this era. Illness reminded him of the fragility beneath his intellectual stature, and perhaps sharpened his sense that clarity and simplicity were the only worthwhile pursuits.

There is also a philosophical irony at play. Camus became famous for *The Plague*, a novel about endurance and communal responsibility in the face of suffering. Yet the man behind the novel was struggling with grief (having lost close Resistance friends like René Leynaud), a failing marriage, and a love affair with actress María Casarès that both enlivened and unsettled him. This contradiction — between writing about resilience and struggling to sustain it — forms the emotional undercurrent of the chapter.

## Suggestions for Further Reading

- Camus, Albert. *Notebooks 1942–1951*. Translated by Justin O'Brien. New York: Alfred A. Knopf, 1965. – This volume provides a rare window into Camus's inner life during the postwar years. It records his reflections on fame, writing, illness, and the demands of public life. Particularly valuable for understanding the emotional complexity that Chapter 10 evokes.

- Camus, Albert. *The Plague*. Translated by Stuart Gilbert. New York: Alfred A. Knopf, 1948. – The novel that brought Camus international acclaim. While a parable about resistance to tyranny, it is also a meditation on human endurance, grief, and moral choice. Reading it alongside Chapter 10 reveals the deep connection between Camus's fictional preoccupations and his personal trials.

- Todd, Olivier. *Albert Camus: A Life*. Translated by Benjamin Ivry. New York: Alfred A. Knopf, 1997. – Todd chronicles the years of acclaim in rich biographical detail: the public lectures, the resurgence of illness, the complexity of Camus's marriage and his relationship with Casarès. This biography provides the factual scaffolding for the emotional truths explored in this chapter.

- Zaretsky, Robert. *A Life Worth Living: Albert Camus and the Quest for Meaning*. Harvard University Press, 2013. –

> Zaretsky's accessible overview includes an insightful chapter on Camus's rise to fame, tracing how he struggled to balance recognition with personal integrity. Offers helpful perspective on the "ache" behind the accolades.

- Lottman, Herbert R. *Albert Camus: A Biography*. Garden City, NY: Doubleday, 1979. – A detailed chronicle of Camus's engagements in the literary world, including his lectures in the U.S. and his encounters with political expectations. Lottman offers additional context for Camus's simultaneous attraction to and alienation from the spotlight.

## Chapter 11: Jasmine and Silence

This chapter offers a pause in the novel's forward political motion and turns instead toward memory, place, and maternal love. Set during one of Camus's postwar returns to Algeria, it explores the enduring connection between Camus and his mother — one rooted not in conversation, but in gestures, habits, and shared silence. The scents of jasmine and sea air, the unspoken understanding between a son and his mother, and the shifting but familiar streets of Algiers all evoke a world that for Camus was both *home* and *loss*. In tone and substance, this chapter closely mirrors the themes and images of Camus's unfinished autobiographical novel *The First Man* and his lyrical early essays.

### Historical Basis vs. Imagined Content

Camus returned to Algeria several times after the war, including in 1945 and again in the early 1950s. He was reunited with his mother, Catherine Camus, who continued to live in the family's modest Belcourt apartment. Catherine was nearly deaf, illiterate, and spoke rarely — facts Camus openly addressed in his letters and fictionalized depictions. His posthumously published novel *The First Man* devotes many pages to this mother-son relationship, showing how her quiet presence grounded him. The bond between them was not defined by dialogue, but by routine, loyalty, and shared resilience.

In this chapter, Camus is portrayed walking the familiar streets of Algiers, inhaling jasmine-scented air, and sitting in simple domestic scenes with his mother. These moments are fictional, but drawn directly from Camus's reflections. In 1945, after years away in occupied France, Camus wrote about how the city had changed — and yet how his mother remained the same. Biographer Herbert Lottman describes how Camus felt comforted by this enduring relationship even as he grappled with postwar fatigue, illness, and mounting political tensions.

The chapter's intimate moments — washing dishes together, exchanging silent glances — are imagined composites. But they are fully consistent with Camus's real experience of maternal love as something nonverbal yet indelible, and of Algeria as a place where beauty and hardship coexisted in every detail.

## Themes: Memory, Belonging, and the Language of Silence

The central theme of this chapter is belonging through silence. Camus grew up in a home with little sound — his mother and uncle were nearly deaf, and conversation was rare. Yet this silence was not a void; it was a space of emotional resonance, in which gestures and routines conveyed love. In *The First Man*, Camus wrote of his mother: *"She had nothing, she said nothing, but she was there."* That enduring presence — quiet, strong, undemanding — sustained him through the chaos of his public life.

"Jasmine" in the chapter serves as a sensory link to childhood and homeland. In his 1938 essay *Summer in Algiers*, Camus celebrated the scent of jasmine as part of Algeria's overwhelming sensual richness — sunlight, heat, salt air, flowers. But this beauty, he noted, existed alongside poverty and pain. The *joy of living* (la joie de vivre) he described was not naive happiness, but a kind of acceptance of the world as it is, without illusions or bitterness. That balance — between loss and presence, struggle and delight — defines the emotional tone of this chapter.

The silence Camus shares with his mother is not a sign of estrangement, but of closeness beyond language. For Camus, who spent his public life wielding words to dissect injustice, there remained something sacred in the unsaid — especially in the private realm. His mother, in many ways, symbolized his moral center: someone who suffered without complaint, lived without cruelty, and embodied a kind of pre-verbal dignity. Returning to her after the war was not only a return to family, but a return to a truth untainted by ideology.

## Suggestions for Further Reading

- Camus, Albert. *The First Man*. Translated by David Hapgood. New York: Alfred A. Knopf, 1995. – This unfinished novel is Camus's most personal work. In it, he depicts the character of his mother (as Catherine Cormery) with tenderness and restraint. The novel's quiet scenes between mother and son— set in Algiers and steeped in silence — are the direct emotional source for Chapter 11.

- Camus, Albert. "Summer in Algiers." In *Lyrical and Critical Essays*, edited by Philip Thody, translated by Ellen Conroy Kennedy. New York: Knopf, 1968. – Camus's early essay on Algiers is a celebration of sensual life and wordless joy. It evokes jasmine, sun, and sea — and recognizes that beauty and hardship are interwoven. Its atmosphere and philosophy pervade this chapter.

- Lottman, Herbert R. *Albert Camus: A Biography*. Garden City, NY: Doubleday, 1979. – Lottman's account of Camus's return to Algeria in 1945 describes his reunion with his mother and the ways his visits to Belcourt reminded him of where he came from. The biographical details here provide the emotional and factual backdrop for Chapter 11.

- Todd, Olivier. *Albert Camus: A Life*. Translated by Benjamin Ivry. New York: Alfred A. Knopf, 1997. – Todd also covers Camus's postwar return to Algeria, including his reflections on silence, memory, and his relationship with his mother. These sections echo the emotional core of this chapter.

- Zaretsky, Robert. *A Life Worth Living: Albert Camus and the Quest for Meaning*. Harvard University Press, 2013. – Zaretsky's discussion of Camus's personal life emphasizes how his mother shaped his sense of limits, endurance, and moral clarity — key undercurrents in this chapter's portrayal of domestic stillness and emotional anchoring.

## Chapter 12: The Threshold

This chapter captures Camus on the precipice of one of the most defining — and divisive — moments of his career. Set in the early 1950s, it dramatizes the intellectual and emotional solitude he experienced as he prepared to publish *The Rebel* (*L'Homme révolté*, 1951), a sweeping critique of political violence and totalitarian ideologies, including Communism. The scene unfolds not in a political debate, but in an internal one: Camus stands at a personal and philosophical "threshold," aware that by questioning the moral legitimacy of revolutionary violence, he is about to sever long-standing alliances and become a heretic to the Left. The mood of the chapter — meditative, weighty, restrained — is drawn directly from Camus's own life during this charged period.

## Historical Basis vs. Imagined Content

The setting of this chapter — likely a solitary night, a cluttered desk, a half-finished manuscript — is fictionalized, but based on documented truth. After leaving the editorship of *Combat* in 1947, Camus withdrew from public life and focused on his philosophical work. By 1950, he had relocated to a quiet home in the south of France to work on *The Rebel.* He reportedly spent long days writing, pacing, and revising in an almost fevered state, fully aware that the book would be controversial.

*The Rebel*, published in 1951, was Camus's most ambitious philosophical undertaking. It examined the origins of rebellion and how legitimate protest can become corrupted into tyranny. Camus criticized both fascist and communist regimes, condemning the rationalizations used to justify mass murder "in the name of history." The chapter's mood — tense, inwardly resolved — reflects Camus's knowledge that the publication of *The Rebel* would cost him dearly in terms of intellectual alliances, particularly with Jean-Paul Sartre and the Parisian left.

The conversation that may unfold in this chapter — perhaps an imagined discussion with a confidant or an internal debate — is fictional. But it's historically accurate in tone and philosophical content. Camus's Notebooks (1942–1951), especially the final entries before *The Rebel*, reveal a man grappling with enormous stakes: not merely the reception of a book, but the very legitimacy of moral rebellion in an age of ideological absolutes.

## Themes: Moral Boundaries, Revolt, and the Solitude of Conscience

The heart of this chapter is Camus's belief in limits — the idea that even rebellion must be constrained by respect for human life. In *The Rebel*, he argued that the 20th century's revolutionary movements had betrayed their founding values by embracing execution, terror, and historical determinism. The result was not liberation, but a new form of enslavement.

This stance put Camus at odds with much of the intellectual left, particularly those who defended Soviet Communism as a necessary evil. Camus's refusal to bend to the prevailing orthodoxy earned him charges of naivete and betrayal. Yet for Camus, to remain silent — or worse, to justify injustice in the name of utopia — was to become complicit.

The "threshold" in this chapter is not only political, but personal. Camus understood that stepping through it would isolate him. His tone in *The Rebel* is not polemical, but sorrowful — he wanted to rescue rebellion from violence, not destroy it. The chapter captures this tension: the cost of speaking uncomfortable truths, the weight of moral clarity, and the solitude that follows from fidelity to conscience. Camus's ideal of *la pensée de midi* — a "midday thought" of balance, lucidity, and ethical restraint — is quietly echoed here.

## Suggestions for Further Reading

- Camus, Albert. *The Rebel.* Translated by Anthony Bower. New York: Alfred A. Knopf, 1954. – Camus's major philosophical essay, this work explores the origins and limits of rebellion, condemning both right-wing fascism and left-wing totalitarianism. Essential for understanding the intellectual substance behind Chapter 12 and the controversy it anticipated.

- Camus, Albert. *Notebooks 1942–1951*. Translated by Justin O'Brien. New York: Alfred A. Knopf, 1965. — These entries offer insight into Camus's thoughts during the gestation of *The Rebel*. They reveal his doubts, his anger at the "justification of murder," and his desire to formulate a rebellion that preserved human dignity. The personal dimension of Chapter 12 is deeply grounded in these notes.

- Todd, Olivier. *Albert Camus: A Life*. Translated by Benjamin Ivry. New York: Alfred A. Knopf, 1997. — Todd's narrative of Camus's life in the early 1950s captures the physical intensity and moral seriousness with which he wrote *The Rebel*. He describes Camus's isolation, his awareness of the backlash to come, and the emotional consequences of crossing the ideological threshold.

- Judt, Tony. *Past Imperfect: French Intellectuals, 1944–1956*. Berkeley: University of California Press, 1992. — Judt offers essential context for understanding why *The Rebel* provoked such strong reactions. He explains the broader climate of postwar French intellectual life and how Camus's refusal to support Communist orthodoxy made him a target among his peers.

- Aronson, Ronald. *Camus and Sartre: The Story of a Friendship and the Quarrel that Ended It*. Chicago: University of Chicago Press, 2004. — This study details the breakdown of Camus's relationship with Sartre, largely over the publication of *The Rebel*. It provides insight into the personal cost of Camus's moral stance and the bitterness of the rupture that followed.

- Zaretsky, Robert. *A Life Worth Living: Albert Camus and the Quest for Meaning.* Harvard University Press, 2013. – Zaretsky's treatment of *The Rebel* contextualizes it within Camus's lifelong project to articulate a moral worldview free from nihilism. His analysis helps readers see the deeper stakes of Camus's "threshold moment."

## Chapter 13: In Transit

This chapter unfolds aboard a moving train, but the journey it depicts is just as much interior as geographic. Camus, traveling across postwar America, is portrayed as a man both exhilarated and unsettled by the world rushing past him. The chapter captures a reflective pause in his life: a period when he was no longer bound to the Resistance and not yet fully immersed in the philosophical firestorms of *The Rebel*. In this liminal space — between continents, cultures, and convictions — Camus reflects on freedom, injustice, alienation, and the fragile hope of shared humanity. The "split" in the title refers not just to geography or culture, but to the divide opening within Camus himself as he questions the ideals of the West while yearning for something universal.

**Historical Basis vs. Imagined Content**

The framework of the chapter is rooted in historical fact. In 1946, Camus undertook a celebrated and grueling lecture tour of the United States. He traveled from New York to Boston, then across the country by train, giving talks on literature, resistance, and moral responsibility. His diary from this period, later published as *American Journals*, records vivid impressions of American cities, racial segregation, jazz clubs, and long, lonely train rides through vast landscapes. In one entry, he marvels at New York skyscrapers; in another, he confesses to profound homesickness and unease. These real moments form the emotional and sensory scaffolding for the fictional train journey depicted in Chapter 13.

The scene itself — an introspective conversation with a fellow traveler or perhaps a silent meditation on passing towns and people — is imagined. But Camus's Notebooks (1942–1951) and *American Journals* provide ample evidence that such thoughts and interactions were typical of his travel experiences. He often noted the psychological and philosophical insights that emerged during movement — between stations, languages, and cultural expectations. His travels exposed him to American optimism and technological progress, but also to its racial injustice and spiritual emptiness. The tension between those poles echoes throughout this chapter.

## Themes: Transit, Exile, and the Fracture of Identity

The central theme of this chapter is dislocation — the physical dislocation of a traveler in a foreign land, and the existential dislocation of a thinker who no longer fully belongs to any ideological camp. In America, Camus found both admiration and alienation. He was celebrated for his Resistance credentials and for *The Stranger*, but he struggled with the language barrier, the mechanized pace of American life, and the racial inequalities he observed firsthand in the segregated South.

Travel became a way for Camus to revisit the core of his philosophy: the *absurd* tension between a longing for meaning and the indifferent world. In motion, Camus found clarity. Hotels and train compartments allowed him to think more freely, less bound by the intellectual cliques of Paris. Chapter 13 captures this sensation — the temporary lucidity of a man looking at the world sideways, seeing both its beauty and its contradictions.

The "split" is also emotional. Camus is torn between the desire to connect with others — whether Americans, fellow travelers, or estranged European friends — and the awareness that such connection is always incomplete. In this, the chapter echoes themes from *The Fall* and *The Plague*, where communication is stymied, but not abandoned.

## Suggestions for Further Reading

- Camus, Albert. *American Journals.* Translated by Hugh Levick. New York: Paragon House, 1987. – Camus's personal diary from his 1946 U.S. trip. It includes observations of American life, candid reflections on loneliness and difference, and moments of quiet awe. This book forms the immediate inspiration for Chapter 13's mood and setting.

- Camus, Albert. *Notebooks 1942–1951.* Translated by Justin O'Brien. New York: Alfred A. Knopf, 1965. – These notebooks include entries from Camus's travels in Europe and South America, where he records philosophical insights triggered by motion, distance, and disorientation. A vital source for understanding the deeper internal "split" this chapter dramatizes.

- Todd, Olivier. *Albert Camus: A Life.* Translated by Benjamin Ivry. New York: Alfred A. Knopf, 1997. – Todd details Camus's American lecture tour, describing his public success and private discomfort. He also recounts Camus's 1949 trip to South America, where physical illness intensified his spiritual questioning. These travel episodes inform the broader sense of alienation and wonder explored in Chapter 13.

- Camus, Albert. *The Fall.* Translated by Justin O'Brien. New York: Vintage International, 1991. – Though published later, *The Fall* reflects many of the existential themes present in this chapter: estrangement, confession, and the difficulty of moral clarity in modern life. Its introspective tone parallels the voice of Camus "in transit."

- Zaretsky, Robert. *Albert Camus: Elements of a Life*. Ithaca: Cornell University Press, 2010. – Zaretsky's work includes an exploration of Camus's American visit and how it reshaped his views of justice, freedom, and cultural hubris. A concise supplement to the emotional and philosophical weight of this chapter.

- Arendt, Hannah. *We Refugees*. In *The Jewish Writings*, edited by Jerome Kohn and Ron Feldman. New York: Schocken Books, 2007. – Though not about Camus, this essay's reflections on exile, statelessness, and displacement offer philosophical kinship with Camus's experiences abroad. It deepens the themes of fractured identity and moral observation.

## Chapter 14: The Unforgiven

This chapter dramatizes one of the most emotionally charged and historically grounded turning points in Albert Camus's life: his confrontation with the growing radicalization of the political left, particularly regarding **revolutionary violence and colonial struggle**. Set in a lecture hall in 1952, shortly after the publication of *The Rebel*, the scene captures the moment when Camus's principled refusal to endorse terror — even in the name of justice — made him **a pariah to former allies**. In this confrontation, he becomes *the unforgiven*: too moral for the revolutionaries, too radical for the establishment, too moderate for the zealots of ideology. The dialogue reflects a historical and philosophical breach from which Camus would never return.

## Historical Basis vs. Imagined Content

While the confrontation in this chapter is fictionalized, it synthesizes **very real arguments and public reactions**. Following the release of *The Rebel* in 1951, Camus was denounced by many on the Marxist left — including in Sartre's journal *Les Temps Modernes* — for condemning revolutionary violence. In his book, Camus insisted that the end does not justify the means, and that even noble revolutions are corrupted when they permit murder in the name of history. This stance outraged supporters of Communist-aligned anti-colonial movements, who saw violence as a tragic but necessary tool for liberation.

The fictional young man in this chapter gives voice to exactly those arguments: colonial injustice, revolutionary urgency, and the perceived impotence of Camus's humanism. His criticisms are taken almost word for word from **real political discourse of the time,** including Jean-Paul Sartre's controversial claim that "violence, like Achilles' spear, can heal the wounds it inflicts."

Camus's **Notebooks (1951–1959)** document his growing sense of isolation, his refusal to recant, and his sorrow at being vilified for advocating moderation. His oft-misunderstood comment — *"I would rather be wrong with my mother than right with the executioners"* — is reinterpreted here with care, showing Camus's deep resistance to all abstractions that demanded innocent blood.

## Themes: Integrity, Moral Solitude, and the Limits of Revolution

The title *The Unforgiven* carries a double meaning: Camus is not only **unforgiven by others**, but perhaps also **unforgiving** of ideologies that demand blood as the price of change. The chapter's emotional core is not anger but sorrow — a grief that moral clarity has left him estranged from the very causes he once supported.

The chapter's powerful exchange mirrors the key theme of *The Rebel*: that **rebellion must remain humane**, and that revolutions lose their moral legitimacy when they adopt the tools of oppression. Camus argues not for passivity, but for **ethical resistance**, even if it's less effective in the short term. His appeal is not only political but spiritual — a defense of the soul in an age willing to barter it for tactical gain.

The young man in this scene, embodying the revolutionary fervor of a generation, challenges Camus with raw sincerity. Camus answers not with rhetoric, but with grave, personal conviction. The chapter culminates in a haunting depiction of **exile in the moral sense**: Camus walks into the night alone, his conscience intact, knowing that he has chosen **truth over belonging**.

**Suggestions for Further Reading**

- **Camus, Albert. *The Rebel*. Translated by Anthony Bower. New York: Alfred A. Knopf, 1954.** – This philosophical essay explores the origins and limitations of revolt. Camus's refusal to justify murder in the name of revolution is the intellectual bedrock of this chapter. Essential to understanding the confrontation at its heart.

- **Aronson, Ronald. *Camus and Sartre: The Story of a Friendship and the Quarrel that Ended It*. Chicago: University of Chicago Press, 2004.** – This detailed history of the Camus–Sartre split explains the philosophical and political differences that made reconciliation impossible. Aronson provides direct quotes from letters, reviews, and polemics that mirror the arguments in Chapter 14.

- **Camus, Albert. *Notebooks 1951–1959*. Translated by Ryan Bloom. Chicago: Ivan R. Dee, 2008.** – These journals record Camus's reaction to *The Rebel*'s reception, his reflections on being politically orphaned, and his unwavering commitment to human dignity and moral restraint.

- **Todd, Olivier. *Albert Camus: A Life*. Translated by Benjamin Ivry. New York: Alfred A. Knopf, 1997.** – Todd recounts the fallout from *The Rebel* with dramatic detail, including Camus's alienation from intellectual Paris, his deteriorating health, and his painful awareness of his status as a man without a party.

- **Judt, Tony. *Past Imperfect: French Intellectuals, 1944–1956*. Berkeley: University of California Press, 1992.** – A rigorous contextualization of Camus's political choices. Judt explains why Camus's moral stance felt so threatening to the postwar left and how his isolation was both tragic and principled.

- **Camus, Albert. *The Fall*. Translated by Justin O'Brien. New York: Vintage International, 1991.** – Though written a few years later, *The Fall* carries the tone of *The Unforgiven* — an intimate exploration of guilt, confession, and failed solidarity. It is Camus's most introspective novel, written during his deepest public solitude.

# Part IV: Isolation & Integrity

This section traces a quieter but no less consequential transformation in Camus's final years: the movement away from political argument and toward ethical presence. The title refers not only to his growing estrangement from public life but also to his deepening personal clarity. In these chapters, Camus seeks refuge not in withdrawal, but in quieter forms of solidarity — through conversations with widows, priests, old comrades, and even his own darker reflection. The tension now is not ideological but internal: how does one continue to live with conviction when words fail, when revolutions disappoint, and when old friendships fall away?

The novel draws here on Camus's real attempts to re-anchor himself — not through manifestos, but through his family, friendships, and artistic work. This is the Camus of *The Fall* (1956), whose voice is weary, self-critical, and keenly aware of the compromises he has made. It is also the Camus of *The First Man*, slowly excavating the buried emotional terrain of his childhood and seeking reconciliation with a past that never let him go.

In this part, Camus is not portrayed as saint or martyr. He is flawed — mourning mistakes, caught in ethical paradoxes, and occasionally succumbing to fatigue or pride. Yet his persistence in small acts of goodness, his refusal to give in to either cynicism or fanaticism, marks the truest form of integrity the novel seeks to highlight. "Isolation & Integrity" does not celebrate triumph. Instead, it shows a man choosing to live with coherence, even when doing so means standing alone.

Readers will find echoes of this quiet resolve in Camus's *Notebooks*, as well as in Catherine Camus's recollections of her father's late domestic life. The novel's tone here draws on the subdued clarity of Camus's later interviews and letters — words no longer seeking argument, but communion. This part affirms that solitude need not mean defeat. In Camus's case, it becomes a new form of resistance: one measured not by volume, but by consistency.

## Chapter 15: Graveside Argument

This chapter finds Camus in a cemetery at dawn, locked not in ideological debate, but in a deeply human exchange — one that probes the cost of resistance and the burden of survival. As he speaks with the widow of a fallen comrade, the conversation turns to grief, guilt, memory, and doubt. The atmosphere is subdued, yet emotionally raw: there is no philosophy without pain here, no abstraction without cost. This chapter is one of the most personal in tone, embodying Camus's belief that intellectual honesty requires confronting loss not with platitudes, but with empathy, humility, and sorrow.

### Historical Basis vs. Imagined Content

The dialogue is fictional, but it draws directly from Camus's life after the war. He lost several close friends in the Resistance, including René Leynaud, a poet and fighter who was captured and executed by the Nazis in 1944. Camus never stopped mourning Leynaud's death; in *Combat* and private letters, he memorialized his friend with profound affection and guilt. The dynamic in this chapter — a survivor meeting a grieving widow — is not based on a specific known encounter, but the emotions it explores are fully authentic. Camus's Notebooks (1942–1951) are filled with references to comrades lost, and the ache of wondering whether he had done enough.

The tone also echoes Camus's postwar journalism and essays, where he grappled not only with justice but with the emotional wreckage of moral action. In his 1946 lecture *The Human Crisis,*

Camus said: *"We must mend what can still be mended."* That
sensibility — of mourning what is broken while insisting on
restoring what remains — pervades this chapter's quiet grief.

## Themes: Grief, Conscience, and the Moral Cost of Survival

At its heart, this chapter asks: *What becomes of ideals after the war is
over?* Camus speaks not as a laureled intellectual, but as a
mourning friend and a man burdened by survivor's guilt. His
defense of Louis's death is not triumphalist. He offers no easy
meaning, only the idea that love — expressed in resistance and
sacrifice — may lend dignity to loss, even if it cannot justify it.

This is where Camus's moral philosophy reaches its most
vulnerable point. He refuses to grant purpose to suffering, yet
he also refuses to let suffering render life absurd. He holds to a
fragile belief that *what we choose to do in response to pain matters.* The
conversation with the widow reflects this: she confronts him
with the limits of ideals, and he responds not with arguments,
but with shared sorrow and honesty.

The chapter also explores the tension between personal love
and political ideals. The widow loved her husband not as a
symbol, but as a man. Her anger is not political — it is raw,
personal grief. Camus, too, resists letting Louis become a
symbol. Instead, he insists that love and conscience are not
abstractions but lived realities — and that clinging to them in
the aftermath is the only way to keep hope from becoming
hollow.

## Suggestions for Further Reading

- Camus, Albert. *Notebooks 1942–1951*. Translated by
  Justin O'Brien. New York: Alfred A. Knopf, 1965. –
  These personal entries capture Camus's lingering grief
  over the deaths of Resistance friends. They include

reflections on memory, guilt, and the impossibility of reconciling idealism with loss. A key source for the emotional realism of this chapter.

- Camus, Albert. "The Human Crisis." Speech delivered at Columbia University, 1946. – In this lecture, Camus reflects on the moral and emotional aftermath of war, arguing that rebuilding must begin with respect for life and conscience. Its call for modest, compassionate action rather than utopian rhetoric echoes the tone of this graveside conversation.

- Todd, Olivier. *Albert Camus: A Life*. Translated by Benjamin Ivry. New York: Alfred A. Knopf, 1997. – Todd's biography chronicles Camus's mourning for René Leynaud and his continued connection to the Resistance dead. Todd confirms that Camus remained haunted by their absence, and this chapter reflects the quiet burden of that memory.

- Camus, Albert. *Resistance, Rebellion, and Death*. Translated by Justin O'Brien. New York: Alfred A. Knopf, 1961. – Several essays in this collection explore postwar justice, mourning, and the meaning of sacrifice. The tone of pieces like "Letters to a German Friend" and "The Century of Fear" aligns with the spiritual questioning in this chapter.

- Camus, Albert. *The First Man*. Translated by David Hapgood. New York: Alfred A. Knopf, 1995. – Though largely about Camus's childhood, this unfinished novel shows the same reverence for silence, loss, and memory that permeates *Graveside Argument*. Camus's prose here is similarly restrained, intimate, and elegiac.

- Zaretsky, Robert. *A Life Worth Living: Albert Camus and the Quest for Meaning.* Harvard University Press, 2013. – Zaretsky addresses how Camus's concept of revolt matured into something quieter and more personal in the postwar years. His reading of Camus as a man mourning loss while defending moral clarity enriches this chapter's emotional landscape.

## Chapter 16: The Empty Cathedral

This chapter stages a quiet, introspective dialogue between Albert Camus and a Catholic priest in an empty Paris church — a meeting not of faith and unbelief in conflict, but in parallel integrity and shared humanity. Through their conversation, Camus confronts his alienation not only from political movements but from the metaphysical certainties many around him cling to. And yet, here in the silence of the cathedral, he finds a surprising kind of resonance with the very institution he is often seen as opposing. The scene is one of recognition — not theological conversion, but mutual affirmation of compassion, limits, and moral presence in a world thick with suffering and abstraction.

### Historical Basis vs. Imagined Content

There is no documented conversation between Camus and a priest exactly like this one, but the emotional and philosophical content is closely grounded in real events and writings. Throughout his life, Camus maintained a respectful distance from Christianity, while frequently engaging with its ideas in essays and personal letters. He admired the teachings of mercy, humility, and nonviolence — while rejecting the metaphysical claims of God's justice, citing the world's silence in the face of atrocity.

Camus's postwar writings — especially his *Notebooks (1951–1959)* — record his deepening interest in moral questions often associated with religion: guilt, responsibility, consolation, and presence in suffering. And during this period, his work was increasingly read and debated in religious circles, including among Catholic theologians who found in his secular conscience a profound ethical kinship. The image of Camus seeking solitude in a church is a fitting literary construct: not for prayer, but for reflection — drawn by silence, structure, and the yearning for moral clarity in a noisy, disoriented age.

## Themes: Sacred Silence, Moral Kinship, and the Secular Conscience

The cathedral here functions as more than a physical setting. It is a symbol of the interior life, of quiet defiance against the clamor of ideologies and easy answers. In this sacred space, Camus acknowledges his moral solitude — his status as a secular heretic cast out from the leftist consensus — while also discovering a common language with the priest. Both men are guardians of a flame, whether named divine or humanist. Both see compassion and restraint as sacred, and both mourn a world increasingly dismissive of them.

One of the most striking aspects of this chapter is its tone: neither polemical nor sentimental, but deeply human. The priest does not try to convert Camus. Instead, he listens, shares his own doubts, and affirms the ethical power of Camus's conscience. Camus, in turn, does not debate theology, but shares his longing — for peace, for moral clarity, for the preservation of the sacred amid the profane. This conversation mirrors Camus's view of religious faith: not something he could accept metaphysically, but something he could respect morally.

The chapter's conclusion — a mutual recognition of small lights in the darkness — speaks to Camus's lifelong philosophy of measured rebellion and quiet hope. It does not propose salvation, but solidarity. In this way, the cathedral is not a place of conversion, but a shelter for shared truthfulness and consolation without illusion.

## Suggestions for Further Reading

- Camus, Albert. *The Rebel*. Translated by Anthony Bower. New York: Alfred A. Knopf, 1954. – Camus's philosophical critique of political and metaphysical absolutism. His defense of human dignity and rejection of totalitarianism contains moral logic that resonates with Christian ethics — particularly in his insistence on limits and the defense of the innocent.

- Camus, Albert. *Notebooks 1951–1959*. Translated by Ryan Bloom. Chicago: Ivan R. Dee, 2008. – These entries include Camus's meditations on solitude, exile, and the absence of divine answers in the wake of injustice. They reflect the same spiritual honesty and longing for integrity that permeate this chapter's quiet conversation.

- Camus, Albert. *Lyrical and Critical Essays*. Edited by Philip Thody, translated by Ellen Conroy Kennedy. New York: Knopf, 1968. – Especially his early essay "Summer in Algiers," which speaks of silence, sensuality, and the sacred without invoking religion. These essays help frame the emotional resonance of the cathedral as a space of inward lucidity.

- Todd, Olivier. *Albert Camus: A Life*. Translated by Benjamin Ivry. New York: Alfred A. Knopf, 1997. – Todd explores how Camus, though secular, was often engaged with Catholic thinkers. His chapter on *The Rebel* and its reception documents how Camus became, paradoxically, closer in spirit to the Christian ethic of mercy than to the revolutionary ethic of force.

- Aronson, Ronald. *Camus and Sartre: The Story of a Friendship and the Quarrel that Ended It.* Chicago: University of Chicago Press, 2004. – Aronson examines how Camus's rejection of revolutionary violence left him estranged from the left, but drew admiration from some Christian thinkers. This context adds weight to the priest's moral sympathy in this chapter.

- Pope Francis. *Fratelli Tutti* (2020). – Though decades later, this papal encyclical echoes many of the same themes in Chapter 16: universal fraternity, dignity without dogma, and standing in solidarity with the suffering. It shows that Camus's secular ethic remains profoundly relevant even within modern religious discourse.

## Chapter 17: Under the Streetlamp

This chapter captures Camus at his most embattled: no longer merely isolated by public controversy, but now confronting the personal cost of ideological estrangement. The setting is intimate and raw — a rain-slicked alley, a cigarette's glow, two former comrades wrestling not just with each other, but with the betrayal of shared ideals. "Henri" is a fictional composite, drawn from the many friends, allies, and fellow travelers who turned against Camus following the publication of *The Rebel* and his increasingly unpopular moral stance during the Algerian War and Hungarian Uprising. The argument here is not rhetorical — it is elegiac, a farewell not only to a friendship, but to an age of unity that war once forged and ideology has now fractured.

## Historical Basis vs. Imagined Content

While the dialogue is fictional, the emotional and philosophical tensions it embodies are historically grounded. Camus had a number of friendships with fellow Résistants and intellectuals that deteriorated in the 1950s over his public opposition to revolutionary violence — especially that condoned by Marxist factions. His refusal to endorse the FLN's armed struggle for Algerian independence without equally condemning atrocities on all sides earned him ferocious criticism, particularly after his 1957 Nobel Prize acceptance, when he made the now-famous remark that he could not prefer justice over his mother's life.

This chapter's emotional climax — Camus accused of cowardice, of bourgeois hypocrisy, of betraying the oppressed — is a distillation of real debates, especially those with Sartre's circle and other radical thinkers. In *Notebooks 1951–1959*, Camus reveals the toll this backlash took on him: sleepless nights, feelings of abandonment, and a growing sense that the price of refusing to endorse murder was solitude.

Henri is thus an amalgam of those who once fought beside Camus but came to see him as a traitor to the revolution. Their confrontation here functions not as a tidy debate, but as a tragic rift, where two men who once believed in the same justice can no longer agree on what it requires.

## Themes: Loyalty, Betrayal, and the Cost of Refusing Extremes

This chapter revolves around a core tension in Camus's ethical worldview: that true justice cannot be built on the blood of innocents, and that moral clarity often means refusing both sides. Henri accuses Camus of betrayal — of failing to take sides in Algeria, of choosing purity over solidarity. Camus replies with anguish: *he has chosen humanity over ideology*, but at a cost that now feels unbearable.

The emotional power of this scene lies not in who "wins" the argument, but in the pain of parting. Henri believes Camus's reluctance to endorse revolutionary violence makes him complicit in oppression. Camus believes Henri's acceptance of bloodshed in the name of the oppressed risks becoming the very cruelty they resist.

This is Camus's defining moral position in the 1950s: the lonely road between extremes, insisting that *how* one fights matters as much as *why*. The chapter's streetlamp serves as a quiet metaphor: a pale, flickering light amid darkness and storm — like Camus's own voice during these years, refusing to go out, even as the world seemed to move on without him.

## Suggestions for Further Reading

- Camus, Albert. *The Rebel.* Translated by Anthony Bower. New York: Alfred A. Knopf, 1954. – Camus's pivotal critique of revolution, this book denounces the idea that noble ends can justify murderous means. It is the intellectual foundation for this chapter's ethical stance.

- Camus, Albert. *Notebooks 1951–1959.* Translated by Ryan Bloom. Chicago: Ivan R. Dee, 2008. – These entries document Camus's inner turmoil following the public fallout over *The Rebel* and his Nobel speech. His reflections on Algeria, violence, friendship, and betrayal offer essential background for this chapter's emotional stakes.

- Aronson, Ronald. *Camus and Sartre: The Story of a Friendship and the Quarrel that Ended It.* Chicago: University of Chicago Press, 2004. – Explores how philosophical differences over Marxism and violence led to Camus's estrangement from Sartre and others. Henri's arguments closely echo real critiques from this intellectual rift.

- Todd, Olivier. *Albert Camus: A Life*. Translated by Benjamin Ivry. New York: Alfred A. Knopf, 1997. – Todd chronicles the post-*Rebel* years with great empathy, showing Camus as both resolute and wounded by the rejection of former comrades. This chapter mirrors that personal toll.

- Zaretsky, Robert. *A Life Worth Living: Albert Camus and the Quest for Meaning*. Harvard University Press, 2013. – Zaretsky frames Camus's rejection of revolutionary extremism as part of a consistent moral path. His chapter on the Algerian War offers especially strong context for the personal and political divide dramatized here.

- Judt, Tony. *Past Imperfect: French Intellectuals, 1944–1956*. Berkeley: University of California Press, 1992. – A panoramic look at French intellectuals' postwar ideological commitments, including Camus's role as the outsider who dared dissent from dominant narratives. Judt contextualizes why Camus became "yesterday's hero" to many.

# Chapter 18: The Mirror in the Mist

This chapter serves as a thematic and psychological echo chamber — a hall of mirrors where Camus confronts the shadow-self that haunts his deepest doubts. Set in a fog-shrouded bar on Amsterdam's edge, *The Mirror in the Mist* draws direct inspiration from Camus's 1956 novel *The Fall*, whose confessional monologue and canal-side setting it closely parallels. But while *The Fall* featured a fictional narrator, Jean-Baptiste Clamence, here Camus faces a voice that may well be his own reflected back — ironic, corrosive, unflinchingly honest, and seductive in its nihilism.

The chapter dramatizes the internal reckoning Camus could never fully stage in public, especially after years of being misrepresented as either a naïve humanist or a closet reactionary. Here, in intimate dialogue, he explores the failures of his ideals, the hypocrisies of survival, and the line between moral witness and self-delusion. The mist and dim light are no accident: this is a spiritual reckoning conducted in half-light, where certainty cannot survive — but clarity might emerge nonetheless.

### Historical Basis vs. Imagined Content

While this specific encounter never occurred, the chapter's tone, setting, and central dialogue mirror Camus's own literary meditation in *The Fall*. That novel — written just four years before Camus's death — is widely seen as his most self-critical work. In it, Clamence, a former Parisian lawyer, recounts his fall from grace and his belief that *all men are guilty*, particularly those who see themselves as righteous. The Stranger in Chapter 18 is unmistakably modeled on Clamence: sardonic, broken, and eerily articulate. His accusations against Camus — hypocrisy, moral pride, selective conscience — are all critiques that had been leveled at Camus by others, and that he leveled at himself in private.

Camus's *Notebooks (1951–1959)* confirm his intense self-scrutiny during this period. They reveal guilt over personal failures (including affairs), a growing pessimism about political change, and despair at being misunderstood. But they also show his refusal to surrender to cynicism, and his enduring belief in love, presence, and the sanctity of individual life.

This chapter is fictional in form but entirely faithful to Camus's philosophical and emotional truth. It completes the arc begun in *The Rebel* and *The Fall*: the confrontation with oneself as both accuser and accused.

## Themes: Judgment, Hypocrisy, and the Persistence of Hope

The primary conflict in this chapter is not between Camus and another man — it is between Camus and the disillusioned version of himself. The Stranger's voice mocks moral striving as hypocrisy, portrays virtue as performance, and insists that all resistance is vanity. This nihilism is seductive because it is rooted in truth: Camus *has* failed his own ideals. He *has* hurt people. He *has* benefited from structures he critiques. The Stranger offers an easy escape: abandon the struggle, and you abandon the shame.

Camus resists — not with denial, but with humility. He concedes his flaws, admits complicity, and affirms that *even in failure, one must keep trying*. This is the difference between despair and revolt. Camus does not argue that he is better than others — only that honesty and effort remain worthwhile, even if they fall short.

The chapter culminates in Camus reaffirming his core conviction: that life is worth loving even when it cannot be redeemed. His invocation of "the invincible summer" is not naïve optimism, but *lucid fidelity* to what once gave him joy and meaning. His hope is fragile, unpretentious, and painfully hard-won.

## Suggestions for Further Reading

- Camus, Albert. *The Fall*. Translated by Justin O'Brien. New York: Vintage International, 1991. – This novel is the clearest precursor to Chapter 18. Its narrator,

Clamence, embodies the cynical voice that tempts Camus in this imagined scene. Essential for understanding the philosophical and emotional texture of the Stranger's monologue.

- Camus, Albert. *Notebooks 1951–1959*. Translated by Ryan Bloom. Chicago: Ivan R. Dee, 2008. – These entries expose Camus's private thoughts about guilt, fidelity, aging, and doubt. They provide a direct bridge to the confession-like honesty seen in this chapter.

- Camus, Albert. *Lyrical and Critical Essays*. Edited by Philip Thody, translated by Ellen Conroy Kennedy. New York: Knopf, 1968. – Particularly relevant are his early reflections on love of life, nature, and the body. They contrast with the Stranger's despair and help explain why Camus continues to resist nihilism.

- Zaretsky, Robert. *A Life Worth Living: Albert Camus and the Quest for Meaning*. Harvard University Press, 2013. – Zaretsky's chapter on *The Fall* and Camus's philosophical solitude illuminates the existential and moral tensions this chapter so richly dramatizes.

- Todd, Olivier. *Albert Camus: A Life*. Translated by Benjamin Ivry. New York: Alfred A. Knopf, 1997. – Todd's treatment of the late 1950s captures Camus at a crossroads: politically alienated, emotionally fatigued, but still striving for clarity. This context adds weight to the chapter's internal reckoning.

- Koelb, Clayton. *Camus and the Crisis of the Self: From Absurdism to Confession*. Boston: Twayne Publishers, 1980. – A lesser-known but astute study of Camus's late style, including *The Fall*. Useful for exploring how confession became Camus's final rhetorical form — not for absolution, but for honest reckoning.

- Camus, Albert. *Exile and the Kingdom.* Translated by Justin O'Brien. New York: Alfred A. Knopf, 1958. – This collection of six short stories (Camus' last published fiction) explores characters in moments of spiritual or moral crisis – effectively confronting their own reflections. For example, "The Silent Men" and "The Adulterous Woman" depict individuals facing solitude and existential doubt. These stories provide a creative analogue to Chapter 18's themes. They place Camus' philosophical preoccupations (exile, truth, loyalty) in narrative form, much as the chapter does through dialogue. *Exile and the Kingdom* enriches our understanding of how Camus grappled with the "mist" of isolation and the yearning for clarity and integrity, especially in his later years.

- Lottman, Herbert R. *Albert Camus: A Biography.* Garden City, NY: Doubleday, 1979. – Lottman's portrayal of Camus in the mid- to late-1950s shows a man increasingly isolated from political factions and turning inward. He notes Camus' withdrawal from Parisian intellectual life to focus on personal writing and his family, as well as bouts of depression and introspection. Lottman's research supports the background of Chapter 18: Camus alone with his thoughts, critically measuring his life's meaning and choices. The biography acts as a clear mirror held up to the historical Camus – one which confirms the psychological realism of the fictional mirror Camus faces in this penultimate scene.

## Chapter 19: Return to Tipasa

In this luminous chapter, Camus returns to Tipasa, a seaside ruin in Algeria that long symbolized, for him, a radiant reconciliation between nature and the human spirit. *Return to Tipasa* is not only a physical journey, but a spiritual homecoming — a reclaiming of the clarity and joy that war, politics, and philosophical strife had long obscured. Here, at last, Camus steps out of the dialectic of argument and into a deeper silence, where peace is not an idea but a presence, and truth arrives not as a proclamation but as sunlight on old stone.

This chapter brings full circle the affirmation Camus sought all his life: that even in the face of absurdity and pain, the simple fact of being alive under the sun can be sufficient. There is no need for revolution or metaphysical salvation. To love the world honestly and without illusion is, in itself, an act of fidelity.

### Historical Basis vs. Imagined Content

The real Camus returned to Tipasa several times in his life, most notably after the war and again in the mid-1950s. His essay *Return to Tipasa* (1952), written after one such pilgrimage, echoes almost word for word many of the reflections found in this chapter. There, he wrote: *"In the midst of winter, I finally learned that there was in me an invincible summer."* That sentence encapsulates the tone of this chapter — a moment of serenity in a life marked by unrest.

The fictional old caretaker may not have existed, but he channels the voice of the land and its people — those who live close to the rhythms of sun, wind, and sea, and who remind Camus of a simpler, enduring wisdom. His presence bridges Camus's French and Algerian identities, reflecting both the geographic unity and political division of a land Camus loved and mourned in equal measure.

The chapter's setting — the Roman ruins of Tipasa — is historically accurate and central to Camus's early and late work. It is in Tipasa that Camus first experienced a sense of sacred joy in the world itself, unadorned by dogma. Revisiting it near the end of his journey becomes not an escape but a final affirmation of that original insight.

## Themes: Harmony, Healing, and the Invincible Summer

This chapter embodies the culmination of Camus's lifelong themes — the healing power of nature, the value of lived presence, and the refusal to let political despair eclipse the joy of existence. After confronting revolution, judgment, guilt, and estrangement, Camus finds in Tipasa a place where no side needs defending, no ideology needs refuting. Here, being precedes argument.

The dialogue between Camus and the old man reflects a cultural and existential synthesis. The man's simplicity is not simplistic — it is distilled wisdom, rooted in cycles of sun, soil, and memory. For Camus, this return affirms that what survives beyond political noise is tenderness, clarity, and attention to life's immediate beauty.

Importantly, this is not a denial of suffering. Camus is scarred and sobered, still grieved by the war in Algeria, still haunted by personal flaws. But Tipasa helps him remember that sorrow and beauty can coexist, and that the act of noticing beauty in a wounded world is itself a moral stance. He rediscovers not a solution, but a kind of centeredness — a life lived in fidelity to both the tragic and the luminous.

**Suggestions for Further Reading**

- Camus, Albert. "Return to Tipasa." In *Lyrical and Critical Essays*, edited by Philip Thody, translated by Ellen Conroy Kennedy. New York: Alfred A. Knopf, 1968. – Camus' 1954 essay recounts his journey back to the Roman ruins of Tipasa in Algeria after years of war and illness. Amid winter sunlight and sea air, he rediscovers an "invincible summer" within himself. This essay is the direct inspiration and namesake for Chapter 19. It captures the rejuvenation and hope that Camus experiences in the dialogue. Reading "Return to Tipasa" reveals many lines and images reflected in the chapter – the ruins, the senses of youth reborn, and Camus' affirmation that even "in the middle of winter" one can feel the immortal summer of joy and harmony with the world.

- Camus, Albert. "Nuptials at Tipasa." In *Lyrical and Critical Essays*, edited by Philip Thody, translated by Ellen Conroy Kennedy. New York: Knopf, 1968. – This exuberant 1938 essay (from *Noces*) describes Camus' first visit to Tipasa as a young man. He bathes in the perfume of warm stone, jasmine, and ocean – a lyrical union (*"nuptials"*) with nature. In Chapter 19, the older Camus' return is imbued with the memory of that youthful ecstasy. "Nuptials at Tipasa" provides the reader with the baseline experience that Camus is returning *to*. It heightens the emotional punch of the chapter: we understand exactly what spiritual fullness Camus seeks to reclaim, because we have Camus' own rapturous account of that fullness from his youth.

- Camus, Albert. *Algerian Chronicles*. Translated by Arthur Goldhammer. Cambridge, MA: Harvard University

Press, 2013. – *Chronicles* collects Camus' reportage and speeches on Algeria through 1958, including his anguished pleas for peace during the Algerian War. This context of Algeria's turmoil sets the stage for why Camus *needed* a "return to Tipasa." By the mid-1950s, as shown in *Algerian Chronicles*, Camus was heartbroken at his homeland's violence and estrangement. Chapter 19's idyllic, restorative homecoming to Tipasa can be appreciated as Camus' answer to that heartbreak – a personal quest to reconnect with the unspoiled beauty and harmony of Algeria beyond politics. The *Chronicles* highlight how extraordinary Camus' brief moment of joy at Tipasa was, against the backdrop of a country in crisis.

- Camus, Albert. *Notebooks 1951–1959*. Translated by Ryan Bloom. Chicago: Ivan R. Dee, 2008. – These personal reflections show Camus returning again and again to the sunlit clarity of his Algerian roots as a way to combat the encroaching gloom of politics and mortality.

- Todd, Olivier. *Albert Camus: A Life*. Translated by Benjamin Ivry. New York: Alfred A. Knopf, 1997. – Todd traces Camus's conflicted return to Algeria in the final years of his life, when his efforts to call for peace between Arabs and French made him a target of both camps. This biography gives important context for the chapter's emotional weight.

- Zaretsky, Robert. *A Life Worth Living: Albert Camus and the Quest for Meaning*. Harvard University Press, 2013. – Zaretsky's interpretation of *Return to Tipasa* captures its significance as Camus's final metaphysical resting place:

a world without transcendence, yet filled with the sacredness of presence and memory.

- Durell, Laurence. *Reflections on a Marine Venus* (1953). – Though not about Camus, Durell's Mediterranean prose carries a kindred spirit — celebrating the sensual and philosophical power of sun, sea, and ruin. A literary sibling to Tipasa's setting.

# Part V: The Final Dialogue

The final section of the novel is framed by a quiet farewell: not a death scene, but a series of conversations that, taken together, reflect a life brought into gentle coherence. The chapters that comprise "The Final Dialogue" unfold like a mosaic of summations — Camus in dialogue with his mentors, his children, his readers, and finally, with fate itself. These are not dramatic confrontations; they are subtle reckonings, where philosophy gives way to presence, and polemic yields to poetry.

Historically, these final weeks were spent partly in Lourmarin and partly in Paris, where Camus continued work on *The First Man*, drafted notes for a possible adaptation of *Othello*, and reflected — often with weariness — on the long arc of his career. He was re-engaging with themes of origin, forgiveness, and personal clarity. What emerges in this section is not a public intellectual but a father, friend, and son, seeking understanding more than admiration.

Each chapter in this part is centered around an intimate exchange. With Grenier, he returns to the roots of his thought. With Catherine, he reaffirms the love that outlasts ideology. With a stranger on a train, he finds kinship in the quiet rhythm of human solidarity. In these scenes, Camus is no longer asking life to make sense. He is simply choosing to live fully within its ambiguity.

The final epilogue draws from Camus's actual death on January 4, 1960, in a car crash near Villeblevin. It is rendered with the quiet tragedy appropriate to a man who had always feared an unfinished life more than death itself. The recovery of *The First Man* manuscript — found intact in his briefcase — becomes the symbolic capstone to the novel: the unwritten chapters that still speak, the conversation with the world that remains open.

Readers interested in this stage of Camus's life will find *The First Man, Lyrical and Critical Essays*, and Todd's biography indispensable. But above all, what this part offers is not scholarly reference — it offers resolution. "The Final Dialogue" is not a conclusion, but a deep breath — a recognition that even an unfinished life can be complete when lived with fidelity.

## Chapter 20: The Door to Everything I Love

This chapter presents a reunion between Albert Camus and Jean Grenier, his former philosophy teacher and lifelong mentor. Set in the golden stillness of a Provençal afternoon in 1957, not long after Camus was awarded the Nobel Prize, it captures a profound moment of reflection between two men who shaped one another across decades. The tone is gentle, elegiac, and richly personal. In their conversation, Camus affirms that beneath all his public controversies and intellectual conflicts lies a simpler truth: that much of what he has become began in a humble classroom in Algiers, when a teacher chose to see a poor child not as an obstacle, but as a mind and heart worth nurturing.

Here, Camus expresses what he often could not say aloud in public: that he is not a prophet, not a guide, but a man still learning how to live — and how to be faithful to the light that once opened to him.

## Historical Basis vs. Imagined Content

While there is no documented record of this exact meeting in Provence, Camus did remain in close contact with Jean Grenier throughout his life. Grenier, a soft-spoken and mystical thinker, introduced Camus to writers like Nietzsche and Gide, and encouraged his early exploration of simplicity, Greek thought, and nature. Camus later credited Grenier with shaping his entire philosophical temperament. The emotional truth of this chapter draws directly from Camus's 1957 letter to Louis Germain, another teacher, in which he wrote: *"Without you, without the loving hand you extended to the poor little child that I was, without your teaching and your example, none of all this would have happened."*

Grenier also wrote warmly of Camus in his memoirs, and they corresponded well into Camus's final years. The theme of intellectual legacy, the transmission of values across generations, is deeply authentic to their relationship.

The chapter's references to *Le Premier Homme*, Camus's unfinished autobiographical novel, are also grounded in fact. He had begun drafting it in the late 1950s, and it was found in the wreckage of the car crash that killed him. In *The First Man*, Camus intended to finally tell his own story — not as an intellectual, but as a son, a student, and a child of Algeria.

## Themes: Gratitude, Legacy, and the Quiet Reconciliation of a Life

Camus's dialogue with Grenier reveals a man nearing emotional clarity — not through argument, but through affection and memory. After years of ideological warfare, public misunderstanding, and private disappointment, Camus finds solace in intimate connection: the hand of a mentor, the presence of a shared afternoon, and the reminder that even the most complicated life can be rooted in something as simple as a teacher's care.

This chapter's title is drawn from Camus's real words to Germain — that his teacher had opened for him "the door to everything I love in the world." It encapsulates the humility with which Camus approached his fame. Even at the height of recognition, he did not forget that his origins were working-class, silent, sun-drenched, and shaped by acts of kindness and quiet guidance. That enduring loyalty to one's roots, to the people who gave without seeking credit, is the moral center of this scene.

It also serves as a philosophical culmination. Camus now sees value not in being right, but in being present. In relinquishing the need to lead, he becomes more fully human. His emphasis shifts from rebellion to reverence, from theory to touch, from victory to coherence.

## Suggestions for Further Reading

- Camus, Albert. "Letter to Monsieur Germain, November 1957." In *More Letters of Note*, edited by Shaun Usher. San Francisco: Chronicle Books, 2015. – The real-life inspiration for the emotional core of this chapter. Camus's letter of gratitude to his first teacher reveals his humility, loyalty, and awareness of the personal debt behind public success.

- Camus, Albert. *The First Man*. Translated by David Hapgood. New York: Alfred A. Knopf, 1995. – Camus's posthumous autobiographical novel, found in the wreckage of his fatal car crash, revisits his childhood, his mother, and his teachers. It represents

the "return to origins" he hoped would be his final
work.

- Grenier, Jean. *Les Îles*. Paris: Gallimard, 1933. – The
  book that deeply influenced the young Camus during
  his tuberculosis convalescence. Its blend of spiritual
  reflection and aesthetic clarity helped form the ethical
  mood of Camus's early writing.

- Camus, Albert. *Notebooks 1951–1959*. Translated by
  Ryan Bloom. Chicago: Ivan R. Dee, 2008. – These
  notebooks show Camus in his most vulnerable and
  introspective state. They trace his emotional withdrawal
  from public life and his growing desire to write *The First
  Man* — a book he saw as his most necessary.

- Todd, Olivier. *Albert Camus: A Life*. Translated by
  Benjamin Ivry. New York: Alfred A. Knopf, 1997. –
  Todd's biography includes moving descriptions of
  Camus's relationship with Grenier, his increasing
  disillusionment with public roles, and his yearning to
  reconnect with his childhood landscape and values.

- Zaretsky, Robert. *A Life Worth Living: Albert Camus and
  the Quest for Meaning*. Harvard University Press, 2013. –
  Zaretsky explores Camus's search for coherence
  between his public convictions and private self,
  focusing especially on his final years and the inward
  turn represented in this chapter.

## Chapter 21: Invincible Summer

Set by the hearth in his quiet Lourmarin home, this chapter
offers a rare and tender glimpse into Albert Camus's private
world, away from the debates and intellectual upheavals of
postwar France. In the soft flicker of firelight and the closeness

of his daughter Catherine, we witness not the Nobel laureate or political dissident, but the father — intimate, flawed, gentle, and fully human.

The chapter title draws from one of Camus's most quoted lines: *"In the depths of winter, I finally learned that there was in me an invincible summer."* This scene brings that idea to life — not as a philosophical metaphor, but as a lived truth: that in love, in simple companionship, there exists a warmth capable of sustaining one through doubt, loss, and solitude. The flame that endures through the absurd, Camus suggests, is often found not in ideology, but in relationships.

### Historical Basis vs. Imagined Content

This scene is imagined, but its tone and setting are grounded in Camus's later years. By the mid-1950s, Camus had purchased a small house in Lourmarin in the Luberon countryside. There he spent time with his children, Catherine and Jean, retreating from the noise of Paris and the public eye. His correspondence and notes from this period reflect a deep yearning for peace, as well as intensifying emotional focus on his role as a father.

Catherine Camus has spoken only sparingly about her father, but when she has, it is with affection and protectiveness. She has described him as warm, playful, and deeply committed to his family. This fictionalized conversation draws from Camus's real-life values: his respect for children, his wish to preserve their innocence, and his belief in the moral power of love and tenderness, especially in a world so often defined by cruelty and abstraction.

Camus's journals and late essays also confirm that he was working on *Le Premier Homme*, a novel about his childhood and his father, during this time. The themes he discusses here with Catherine — the ache of paternal absence, the struggle to love well, and the conflict between public duty and personal responsibility — are central to that unfinished work.

## Themes: Fatherhood, Forgiveness, and the Quiet Rebellion of Love

At the heart of this chapter is a double reconciliation: Camus reconciling with himself through his daughter's love, and reconciling with the imperfection of life through its moments of grace. The tenderness between Catherine and Albert cuts through every political label that had been affixed to him — existentialist, moralist, reactionary — and returns him to the simple, luminous identity of a man trying to be present for his child.

The conversation also reframes Camus's moral clarity not as self-righteousness, but as the fragile integrity of a person who knows his faults and tries, every day, to live slightly better. The Stranger in the previous chapter sought to dismantle meaning by exposing contradiction. Catherine, by contrast, affirms that contradiction can coexist with love, and that being known and still being loved is a kind of redemption.

Here, the invincible summer is no longer an abstract force of resistance — it is the lived joy of holding one's daughter close, of speaking honestly, of being forgiven, and of witnessing the persistence of care across generations.

### Suggestions for Further Reading

- Camus, Albert. "Nobel Prize Acceptance Speech." Stockholm, December 10, 1957. – In his brief Nobel acceptance remarks, Camus speaks of the artist's duty to pursue truth and serve those who suffer. He humbly dedicates the award to his teacher and acknowledges the "invincible summer" of human warmth that sustained him. This speech's earnest, hopeful tone is reflected in Chapter 21, which finds Camus (now a Nobel laureate) reaffirming faith in human values despite the "winter" of his era. The famous line, "in the depths of winter, I found within me an invincible summer," actually comes from Camus' *Return to Tipasa* essay, but its sentiment is very much alive in his Nobel speech and in this chapter's dialogue – a testament to Camus' undying optimism in the face of despair.

- Camus, Albert. *The First Man.* Translated by David Hapgood. New York: Alfred A. Knopf, 1995. – Camus's posthumous novel, discovered in the car crash that ended his life, is an unfinished meditation on fatherhood, memory, and childhood. Its emotional tone and confessional depth mirror the father-daughter intimacy portrayed in this chapter.

- Camus, Albert. *Notebooks 1951–1959.* Translated by Ryan Bloom. Chicago: Ivan R. Dee, 2008. – Camus' notebooks surrounding the Nobel Prize (late 1957) reveal a mix of gratitude, discomfort, and resolve. He notes feeling isolated by fame, yet determined to use his voice responsibly. These private thoughts enhance Chapter 21, which dramatizes Camus' internal state after receiving the world's highest literary honor. In his notes, Camus essentially recommits to the ideals that had guided him – his "invincible summer" of integrity and compassion – even as political critics tried to claim or shame him. The notebooks thus provide the psychological realism behind Camus' steadfast demeanor in the chapter, showing how he steeled himself to remain *no one's idol but a human among humans*, grateful and resolved.

- Catherine Camus, interviews and commentaries. –
  Though rare and reserved, Catherine has spoken about
  her father with clarity and affection. Her reflections on
  his gentleness, humor, and integrity provide a real-
  world foundation for the fictionalized voice we hear in
  this chapter.

- Camus, Albert. *Lyrical and Critical Essays.* Edited by
  Philip Thody, translated by Ellen Conroy Kennedy.
  New York: Knopf, 1968. – Especially the essays
  *Nuptials at Tipasa* and *Summer in Algiers,* which express
  Camus's belief in the sensual, grounded joys of life and
  his reverence for beauty, simplicity, and familial love.

- Todd, Olivier. *Albert Camus: A Life.* Translated by
  Benjamin Ivry. New York: Alfred A. Knopf, 1997. –
  Todd recounts Camus's domestic life in Lourmarin and
  his deep emotional bond with Catherine. His portrayal
  of Camus's late years confirms the shift from public
  debate to private anchoring.

- Zaretsky, Robert. *A Life Worth Living: Albert Camus and
  the Quest for Meaning.* Harvard University Press, 2013. –
  Zaretsky frames Camus's final years as a turn toward
  inwardness and relational truth. His reflections on
  Camus as a father and moral presence underscore the
  quiet heroism this chapter celebrates.

## Chapter 22: Shared Journey

This chapter unfolds on a train bound for Paris, as Camus
shares a quiet conversation with an older woman whose
warmth and presence gently invite him into a space of
reflection and humility. The movement of the train becomes
more than physical — it becomes a metaphor for transition,

carrying Camus between solitude and communion, between the burdens of the past and the unknowns of tomorrow.

In the brief space of a shared compartment, Camus encounters not an ideological challenge, but something more intimate: the simple dignity of another person's story. The woman is unnamed, unexceptional by worldly standards, yet her capacity to listen and her gentle memory of loss mirror Camus's own emotional arc. The setting allows for a moment of quiet mutuality — a temporary fellowship of travelers, both literal and existential.

## Historical Basis vs. Imagined Content

There is no known record of such an encounter in Camus's final weeks, though he did take a train north in early January 1960 before his untimely death in a car crash a few days later. He spent the New Year with Michel Gallimard, and originally planned to return by train to Paris with his wife and children. At the last moment, Gallimard offered a car ride instead.

This chapter imagines what such a solitary train journey might have meant to him — a pause between chapters, a suspended moment in which the philosopher sheds public armor and engages quietly with a stranger. The scene captures a very real emotional and philosophical truth: that Camus found meaning not in abstract systems, but in the presence and dignity of ordinary human beings. As he wrote in *The Plague*, *"What's true of all the evils in the world is true of plague as well. It helps men to rise above themselves."*

The character of the woman may also be read as a composite figure, echoing Camus's own mother — silent, enduring — and the many anonymous lives for whom he always claimed to speak.

## Themes: Human Solidarity, Transitional Grace, and the Sacredness of the Ordinary

The title, *Shared Journey*, suggests both a literal train ride and the broader journey of life, made meaningful by those we travel alongside. Here, solidarity is not about revolution or political doctrine — it is about the ethical attention we offer one another, even fleetingly. In this exchange, Camus finds reassurance that decency, compassion, and humility still matter — even in a world that often rewards their opposites.

The older woman's grief, her quiet love of trains and rhythm, her modest serenity — all speak to the dignity of the unspectacular, the beauty of people who endure without fanfare. Camus's response is not theoretical; it is personal. He lowers his guard, not in defeat, but in grace. As he closes his eyes to the rhythm of the tracks, he affirms the belief that has always lived beneath his defiance: that what connects us is stronger than what divides us.

His final whispered line — *"We are all fellow travelers... and it is enough"* — serves as both an epilogue to this encounter and a eulogy for the man himself. Camus, who refused transcendence and rebelled against meaninglessness, found peace not in answers, but in companionship along the way.

### Suggestions for Further Reading

- Camus, Albert, and Jean Grenier. *Correspondence 1932–1960*. Translated by Jan F. Rigaud. Lincoln, NE: University of Nebraska Press, 2003. – This collection of letters between Camus and his beloved mentor Jean Grenier spans Camus' entire adult life. Reading their correspondence is like witnessing a *shared journey* of two philosophical minds: from the teenage Camus seeking advice in the 1930s, to the famous author still confiding in Grenier in the 1950s. The warmth, candor, and intellectual camaraderie in these letters shed light on Chapter 25's theme of companionship. As the novel's journey nears its end, the inclusion of Grenier (or a figure like him) in dialogue would echo this real friendship. The letters also highlight Camus' growth and the continuity of his values – a fitting capstone for the arc completed in the final chapter.

- Camus, Albert. *The Plague.* Translated by Stuart Gilbert. New York: Alfred A. Knopf, 1948. – This novel is Camus's clearest expression of human solidarity in the face of suffering. Like the older woman in this chapter, its characters endure quietly, choosing decency over despair. The novel's final pages mirror this chapter's tone: *"There are more things to admire in men than to despise."*

- Camus, Albert. *Notebooks 1951–1959.* Translated by Ryan Bloom. Chicago: Ivan R. Dee, 2008. – These entries reveal Camus's growing disillusionment with ideological struggle and his increasing appreciation for small, humane acts. The slow train, the warm stranger, and the muted reflection in this chapter come straight from his later worldview.

- Camus, Albert. *The First Man.* Translated by David Hapgood. New York: Alfred A. Knopf, 1995. – In this unfinished novel, Camus reclaims the beauty of small gestures, of memory, and of parental love. The themes of origin, identity, and quiet human connection resonate throughout Chapter 22.

- Zaretsky, Robert. *A Life Worth Living: Albert Camus and the Quest for Meaning.* Harvard University Press, 2013. – Zaretsky highlights Camus's lifelong attention to the everyday as sacred. His reading of Camus's ethics —

particularly in connection to *The Plague* and *The Fall* —
reinforces the moral resonance of this chapter's quiet
solidarity.

- Todd, Olivier. *Albert Camus: A Life*. Translated by
  Benjamin Ivry. New York: Alfred A. Knopf, 1997. –
  Todd's biography discusses Camus's final days and his
  longing to step away from the public fray. The journey
  portrayed here reflects the man Todd describes: *tired of
  conflict, longing for coherence*, and increasingly drawn to the
  companionship of the ordinary.

- Steiner, George. "The Lost World of Albert Camus."
  *New York Review of Books*, Oct. 1994. – Steiner's
  reflection on Camus's final interview and legacy adds
  interpretive depth to the themes of this chapter. He
  captures the poignancy of Camus stepping back from
  public life and seeking meaning in more personal
  terrain.

## Chapter 23: No One's Guide

This imagined conversation between Camus and a young
admirer distills the emotional and philosophical tone of
Camus's final months: reflective, modest, and increasingly
turned inward. At a quiet café table on the Left Bank, Camus
speaks not from a podium but as a man nearing the end of his
public journey — less a guide, more a companion walking
alongside. He does not renounce his ideas, but he sheds the
role of prophet. His guidance now takes the form of
encouraging others to guide themselves.

This chapter's title echoes Camus's famous 1959 interview
remark: *"I am no one's guide. I speak for no one; I have enough difficulty
speaking for myself."* That declaration shocked many at the time,
coming from the writer who had been hailed as the moral

conscience of postwar France. But it was not an abandonment of principle — it was, rather, a reaffirmation of honest limits. Camus's refusal to accept ideological certainty or assume moral superiority became itself a kind of ethical stance.

### Historical Basis vs. Imagined Content

This scene is fictional, but entirely plausible. Camus continued to meet with young writers and students well into his final year. His correspondence, interviews, and notebooks from 1958–59 show a man trying to reconcile the dissonance between public expectation and private reality. He had not ceased working — *The First Man* was underway, and he was drafting notes on adapting *Othello* for the stage — but he had withdrawn from public debates on Algeria and Cold War politics. The vitriol he received for refusing to support either side in the Algerian conflict left him disillusioned with intellectual partisanship.

The student in this chapter, "Julien," represents a generation coming of age in the long shadow of the Resistance and searching for ethical clarity amid the Cold War's moral gray zones. Camus's counsel is clear: take what speaks to your conscience, then walk your own path. His humility, compassion, and care in this conversation reflect his own belief that freedom is only real when paired with responsibility, and that truth is better whispered than shouted.

### Themes: Quiet Influence, Self-Awareness, and the Ethics of Humility

In contrast to earlier chapters filled with ideological argument, *No One's Guide* offers something rarer: a portrait of a thinker no longer trying to change the world, but trying to live truthfully within it. Camus accepts his past positions — on the Absurd, on rebellion — but allows that they are incomplete. As he tells Julien, it is not that he was wrong to write what he did, but that wisdom grows, and in that growth, one finds a softer, steadier clarity.

This chapter dramatizes Camus's final evolution: from rebel to father, from public figure to private citizen, from writer of treatises to writer of memory. It does not mean he lost courage — it means he refined it. His courage now lies in letting go of control, in trusting others to carry the light forward, in encouraging them not to idolize him, but to look inward.

## Suggestions for Further Reading

- Camus, Albert. "I Am No One's Guide." Interview in *Les Nouvelles Littéraires*, October 1959. – In this late interview, Camus famously declared his withdrawal from the role of public conscience. The full text reveals his exhaustion with polemics and his yearning for more personal, meaningful engagement with writing.

- Camus, Albert. *The Myth of Sisyphus.* Translated by Justin O'Brien. New York: Alfred A. Knopf, 1942. – Camus's foundational work on the Absurd provides the intellectual background for much of the conversation in this chapter. His later reflections, as shown here, do not negate this early work but offer a richer emotional response to it.

- Camus, Albert. *The Rebel.* Translated by Anthony Bower. New York: Alfred A. Knopf, 1954. – Camus's exploration of rebellion, ethics, and the limits of revolution. The backlash to this work — especially from Sartre and the Left — formed the backdrop for his eventual retreat from public ideological disputes.

- Camus, Albert. *Notebooks 1951–1959.* Translated by Ryan Bloom. Chicago: Ivan R. Dee, 2008. – These final notebooks record Camus's personal disappointments, intellectual fatigue, and increasing turn toward personal integrity over polemical engagement. His notes on *The First Man* and *Othello* adaptation plans also appear here.

- Zaretsky, Robert. *A Life Worth Living: Albert Camus and the Quest for Meaning*. Harvard University Press, 2013. – Zaretsky articulates how Camus's late-life humility is not resignation but a deepening of his ethical vision. His chapter on Camus's post-Rebel years captures the spirit of *No One's Guide* with insight and grace.

- Todd, Olivier. *Albert Camus: A Life*. Translated by Benjamin Ivry. New York: Alfred A. Knopf, 1997. – Todd's biography chronicles Camus's tension between public expectation and personal need. His retelling of the 1959 interviews, including the backlash and misunderstandings, gives valuable context for Camus's evolving self-definition.

- Sartre, Jean-Paul. "Reply to Albert Camus." In *Les Temps Modernes*, 1952. – While not sympathetic to Camus's position, Sartre's criticism of *The Rebel* helps explain the public fallout and the personal rupture that shaped the background to this chapter's quiet tone.

## Chapter 24: Unfinished Manuscript

This final chapter before the Epilogue unfolds with a haunting irony: it captures a moment of peace, renewal, and intimacy between Albert Camus and Michel Gallimard — mere days before the tragic car crash that would claim both their lives. In tone and substance, the dialogue carries a deep awareness of mortality, but also a profound sense of contentment. Camus, who had spent much of his public life grappling with the Absurd, here expresses a quieter, more grounded perspective.

He is no longer rebelling against death — but accepting its place within a life fully lived.

This imagined scene is tightly tethered to historical fact. Camus did spend New Year's 1960 with the Gallimards at their estate. He was due to return to Paris by train, but at the last minute, Michel convinced him to join them by car — a journey that would end in tragedy on January 4th. The manuscript of *The First Man* was indeed in Camus's briefcase when the car crashed; it was recovered, edited, and published posthumously in 1994 by his daughter Catherine.

## Historical Basis vs. Imagined Content

The conversation with Gallimard is fictional but deeply plausible. Camus and Michel Gallimard were close friends as well as collaborators, and Camus had expressed anxiety — both in writing and in letters — about the pressure to finish *The First Man*. In a 1959 letter to Catherine Sellers, he wrote: *"To work, one must deprive oneself and die without help. So let's die, because I don't want to live without working..."*. In that phrase, Camus equated work and life as twin necessities — an idea reflected poignantly in this scene.

Camus also wrote about finding peace with the cemetery in Lourmarin: *"What pleases me is that I have finally found the cemetery where I will be buried. I will be fine there."* That moment of calm resignation is echoed here, not as a foreshadowing of doom, but as a mark of acceptance. His fears about dying before finishing his novel were real. The chapter draws on that fear, but also on his desire to express something new — a novel that would carry his true legacy forward: the story of his father, his mother, and the Algeria of his childhood.

## Themes: Mortality, Legacy, and the Quiet Heroism of Continuance

The tension in this chapter is not dramatic but existential: the fear of unfinished work, of time running out. Camus had reached a place in life where he no longer feared death as much as he feared incompletion. The First Man was to be his *grand livre* — not in scale alone, but in emotional depth. It was an act of love and recovery, of trying to reunite his own fragmented past with the voice of a father he never knew and a mother who had never spoken much.

This chapter also shows Camus as softer, less defiant. Where earlier in his life he may have fought against limitations, here he speaks of learning from failure, of becoming gentler. There is no trace of public performance in this scene — only friendship, vulnerability, and a deeply humane wisdom.

The conversation with Michel Gallimard gives voice to a man who knows he may not control the end, but who has lived — truly lived — and made peace with whatever follows. And when Gallimard insists that the novel will be published in Camus's lifetime, the reader, with hindsight, feels the full weight of tragedy.

## Suggestions for Further Reading

- Camus, Albert. *The First Man*. Translated by David Hapgood. New York: Alfred A. Knopf, 1995. – Camus's unfinished autobiographical novel was found in his briefcase after the crash that took his life. It tells the story of Jacques Cormery (a stand-in for Camus), his silent mother, and his working-class upbringing. The tone is warmer and more grounded than his earlier novels, revealing Camus's late-life desire to reconnect with his roots. Catherine Camus edited the manuscript from his handwritten pages.

- Camus, Albert. "Letter to Catherine Sellers, December 1959." – In this letter, Camus writes candidly about his creative block and his fear that he might die before finishing his work: *"To work, one must deprive oneself, and die without aid..."*. It underscores the emotional weight of the novel-in-progress portrayed in this chapter.

- Camus, Albert. *Notebooks 1951–1959*. Translated by Ryan Bloom. Chicago: Ivan R. Dee, 2008. – These entries reflect Camus's psychological fatigue following *The Rebel* controversy, his estrangement from Sartre, and his desire to turn inward. His entries about Lourmarin and his shifting priorities illuminate the emotional context of Chapter 24.

- Todd, Olivier. *Albert Camus: A Life*. Translated by Benjamin Ivry. New York: Alfred A. Knopf, 1997. – Todd describes the New Year's gathering with the Gallimards and Camus's decision to ride back with Michel by car. The biography chronicles Camus's final projects and lingering fears. Todd also includes poignant observations about *The First Man* manuscript being recovered intact in Camus's briefcase.

- Gallimard Publishing Archives – The correspondence between Camus and Michel Gallimard, while limited, underscores the mutual trust and affection behind their professional relationship. The Gallimard family would later ensure that *The First Man* reached publication.

- Zaretsky, Robert. *A Life Worth Living: Albert Camus and the Quest for Meaning*. Harvard University Press, 2013. – Zaretsky reflects on *The First Man* as Camus's attempt to integrate his early lyrical voice with his mature ethical sensibility. He sees the unfinished manuscript as a final reconciliation between philosophy and feeling, memory and meaning.

# Epilogue: The Last Drive

The epilogue brings this imagined journey to a somber, poetic close with an account grounded in historical reality: Albert Camus's sudden death on January 4, 1960, in a car crash near Villeblevin, France, at the age of 46. This final scene intertwines factual detail with quiet literary grace, capturing Camus not as a mythic philosopher but as a man on a country drive — tired, reflective, and hopeful — his manuscript in a case by his feet, his life both full and incomplete.

**Historical Accuracy and Narrative Framing**

Almost everything in this scene is verifiable. Camus had indeed spent New Year's with Michel Gallimard and his family in the south of France. Though his train ticket was purchased, Gallimard offered him a seat in his Facel Vega, and Camus accepted at the last minute. The crash occurred just before reaching Sens, with Camus dying instantly and Gallimard fatally injured, dying days later. Camus's manuscript of *The First Man* was found intact in his briefcase and later posthumously edited by his daughter Catherine and published in 1994.

The epilogue's central image — Camus seated peacefully, manuscript beside him, moments before the end — is drawn from contemporary eyewitness accounts and aligns with the poetic sensibility that permeated his later work. It is not a dramatized death scene, but one that echoes his lifelong interest in moments of sudden rupture, the absurdity of fate, and the search for meaning in a fragile, luminous world.

## Themes: The Ordinary, the Absurd, and What Remains

Camus famously wrote that the Absurd arises from the tension between our longing for clarity and the world's refusal to provide it. In this final scene, that contradiction becomes almost tactile: a man who had won the Nobel Prize, who was composing his most intimate and human book, dies not as a symbol, but in an ordinary accident on an ordinary road. There is no final epigram, no grand farewell. Only the sound of wind in the trees, the chime of a village clock, and a scattered manuscript awaiting rediscovery.

The closing image of the manuscript, resting closed but whole, evokes the idea that though Camus' life ended abruptly, his work did not. His influence would continue in what had already been published, and what had yet to be revealed. There is comfort in that survival — not immortality, but endurance.

### Suggestions for Further Reading

- Todd, Olivier. *Albert Camus: A Life*. Translated by Benjamin Ivry. New York: Alfred A. Knopf, 1997. – The most thorough biography of Camus in English, including a vivid account of the final days leading up to the crash, the decision to ride with Gallimard, and the emotional impact of Camus's death on his family and contemporaries.

- Camus, Albert. *The First Man*. Translated by David Hapgood. New York: Alfred A. Knopf, 1995. – The posthumously published autobiographical novel found in Camus's briefcase after the crash. Incomplete yet deeply affecting, it explores Camus's childhood in Algiers and his longing to understand the father he never knew. It is widely considered his most personal and tender work.

- Gallimard Publishing Archives – The original publisher of Camus's works and the custodian of *The First Man* manuscript. Their stewardship ensured the preservation of the pages recovered from the crash site.

- The Guardian, January 4, 2010. "The Death of Albert Camus." – A commemorative article exploring the details of the crash and reflecting on Camus's influence 50 years after his death. It includes photographs of the accident scene and quotes from family and friends. [theguardian.com]

- Flashbak.com, "The Road to Villeblevin." – A photographic account of the Route Nationale and the tree-lined stretch where the crash occurred. This imagery inspired the epilogue's stark visual rhythm of trees, silence, and finality.

- Robert Zaretsky. *A Life Worth Living: Albert Camus and the Quest for Meaning.* Harvard University Press, 2013. – Zaretsky reflects on Camus's final writings and the poignancy of his death just as he was turning toward a more grounded, reconciliatory vision of life.

- Scribd.com, "Letters of Albert Camus" – Includes the quote to Catherine Sellers where Camus equates the inability to work with a kind of spiritual death: *"To work, one must deprive oneself, and die without aid. So let's die, because I don't want to live without working…"*

www.ingramcontent.com/pod-product-compliance
Lightning Source LLC
Chambersburg PA
CBHW031944260626
47157CB00017B/2304